WOMEN IN ANCIENT ROME

Paul Chrystal

AMBERLEY

For my teachers:
John Hogg, Dick Jenkinson, Tim Ryder, Stan Ireland, David Rankin

First published 2013
This edition first published 2014

Amberley Publishing
The Hill, Stroud
Gloucestershire, GL5 4EP

www.amberley-books.com

British Library Cataloguing in Publication Data.
A catalogue record for this book is available from the British Library.

ISBN 978 1 4456 4376 2 (paperback)
ISBN 978 1 4456 3532 3 (ebook)

Typeset in 10pt on 12.5pt Celeste.
Typesetting and Origination by Amberley Publishing.
Printed in the UK.

CONTENTS

PREFACE

Another book on Roman women? The unremitting flood of books
and journal articles on every conceivable aspect of the lives
of Roman women justifies this question. Since the mid-1970s
women in the ancient world have more than made up for
centuries of neglect by historians of the ancient world – so why
this book now? The answer is simple: most of the work published
caters, quite rightly, either for the academic, the researcher or the
student of classics and classical civilisation. The aim of this book
is to satisfy and inspire these audiences, but also to provide an
accessible yet rigorous survey of the subject for the burgeoning
lay market. Never has interest in the classical world been more
intense. *Women in Ancient Rome* meets the need for a clear and
exciting account of aspects of the lives of women in Rome; it
will be of use and value to teachers and students of Roman
social history, while at the same time providing an intriguing
and informative account of women in Rome for the general
reader.

The book has only been possible thanks to the patience and
persistence of the teachers, as dedicated above, who taught me
at school and at university – my thanks go out to them and I am
grateful for the opportunity to show them at last the fruits of
their labours – they of course will judge if it was all worth their
while. I would also like to thank Nicola Gale at Amberley, for
commissioning the book and for providing invaluable support
and encouragement whenever needed; my wife, Anne, who has
rarely seen me of late, ensconced as I have been in other women,
the women of Rome; Dr Inga Mantle for permission to use
her photographs (figures 5 and 6); and Dr Caroline Vout, who

published them in *Omnibus*; and Andante Travels, Salisbury, for the use of a number of their photographs (figures 3 and 19). With the illustrations I have tried to be original and refreshing; most books published on the subject feature instructive and interesting photographs – familiar faces gaze out to us through the centuries and we now feel almost as if we know them. I have illustrated this book with less well-known images, using pictures taken from postcards, trade cards and from books published in the late nineteenth and early twentieth centuries. These, I hope, will provide an original take on Roman women while still being useful and stimulating. Unless stated otherwise, the translations are mine.

Paul Chrystal, York, 2013

INTRODUCTION

The history of women in ancient Rome is fascinating and exhilarating. It gives an insight into one of the most dynamic, successful super-power civilisations the world has seen and, at the same time, illuminates any number of admirable, exciting, evil, slatternly and dangerous women fighting to be heard and seen against insurmountable odds in a world run by men, for men.

However, intriguing as it is, any study of women in ancient Rome is beset by a problem of evidence, or rather, the lack of it. Women, in common with slaves and children, were second-class, marginalised citizens, and they were subordinate to men – be it a father or a husband or a guardian. They were excluded from public office and the military, were politically insignificant because they had no vote, and they had little or no voice or stake in most areas of state religion or in political, historical or philosophical writing, which was largely written by men; women's education was delimited by early marriage and the rigours and tedium of domesticity and serial childbirth. Livy puts it well in the debate on the repeal of the Oppian Law in 195 BC: 'Women cannot hold magistracies, priesthoods, celebrate triumphs, wear badges of office, enjoy gifts, or booty; elegance, finery, and beautiful clothes are women's emblems, this is what they love and are proud of, this is what our ancestors called women's decoration.'[1]

Much of what we know about Roman women we derive through the prism of middle-class, educated or powerful men; and many of the women we do hear about populate the elite classes, the lower and servile orders being largely absent. We must also remember that for around the first 500 years of Rome's history there was little or no historiography. It was only with

Quintus Fabius Pictor around 200 BC, writing in Greek, and
the Latin *Origines* of Marcus Porcius Cato (the Censor) some
forty years later, that historical events began to be recorded; the
exhaustive work only really began with Livy and Dionysius of
Halicarnassus at the dawn of the Empire. In the absence of actual
verifiable facts, then, much of the early history of Rome, including
descriptions of notable women and male attitudes towards them,
consisted of ideals and stereotypes based on legends and stories.
Moreover, some of these legends will have been manipulated and
re-interpreted to fit the historian's agenda, or to reinforce the
messages about the present or the past he or his patron wanted to
publish. It is as well to remember, too, that historians, scientists,
love poets, letter writers, satirists and epigrammists often tend
towards the unusual, outrageous and the salacious; historians and
letter writers mainly describe women and their actions refracted
through men's actions and achievements and from the margins
of a male world.

'Silent' is a word that is sometimes used to describe Roman
women, because of the paucity of first-hand, direct evidence for
the their lives; 'silent' can also be used to describe how the typical
Roman male liked his women, rather like stereotypical Edwardian
children, silent and unobtrusive.[2] The silence is deepened because
the woman's *familia* was a very private institution: she was
encouraged as wife and mother to be discreet; what she said and
did in the home tended to stay in the home; only writers and poets
extolled, or vilified, exceptional high-profile women. For us, then,
they say little themselves. However, down the years, Roman men
describe a large number of exceptions to the rule of silence: in
politics, law, business, religion, the fine and the dark arts we meet
extraordinary, notorious and remarkable women who excelled
and won the admiration, or otherwise, of their male counterparts.
These women might be paradigms of the Roman *matrona* – the
good wife, bearing and then raising the children, making and
keeping the home – or else they might have shaken off their
traditional restrictions and forged an identity of their own in a
largely suspicious, paranoid, patronising and critical world. Most
women were somewhere in between.

Occasionally, though, Roman women do speak to us through art, graffiti and through funerary inscriptions; thankfully, these are not always the impersonal and formulaic eulogies they are often made out to be. Even more occasionally, we hear women speaking through literature; sometimes we get an oblique eloquence, for example, through the recipients of letters or in the writings of gynaecologists where we can assume a patient interview, a physical examination or some direct history taking has occurred.

All of this, qualified as it is, is the very seedcorn of our knowledge and the foundation on which we base our research and conclusions. But are the women we·hear about the exception rather than the rule, or do they represent the tip of the iceberg? There lies the unanswerable question; we simply do not know how far these outstanding women represent Roman women in general. It seems sensible and prudent, then, to assume that the answer lies somewhere between the exception and the iceberg – not to take what little evidence there is as typical, but to see it as a mould being broken – examples of out-of-the-ordinary women who acted against type and tradition: obtrusively, impetuously, valiantly, capriciously or notoriously.

The Roman woman is also something of a moving target, her position and role in society down the years changing, almost imperceptibly, but changing for all that. Perceptions of women and the laws, conventions and social constraints governing women naturally shifted quite significantly over the centuries between the foundation of Rome in 753 BC and the early Empire, the focus of this book. Institutions such as *manus* marriage and the power of the *paterfamilias,* and of *tutores,* guardians, weakened – to the benefit of women. Increasing independence galvanised by the absence of husbands – away fighting foreign wars and running overseas possessions – brought with it more responsibility for managing the household, its slaves and finances; war widowhood led to independent wealth, not necessarily tied up in land. The influx of things Greek, and booty from conquered or annexed nations, spawned more affluence, bigger dowries and, for some, encouraged a culture of luxury. This, and the fact that the males in elite families suffered badly in the aftermath of the Sullan civil wars and the internecine warfare following Caesar's crossing of the Rubicon, coincided with an increase of power and influence for women in the more privileged Roman family. Women in Rome were never emancipated but, if the poetry and histories are to be even half-believed, a relatively well-off, or commercially resourceful woman of Lesbia's time could live a very different life – a more independent life – from a woman of Lucretia's ancient day. Even so, Martial probably reflected the popular male concensus when, at the end of the first century AD, he asserts that the *matrona* will never be equal to men unless she remains *inferior marito* – subject to her husband.[3]

With these challenging but inspiring caveats in mind the book covers important aspects of the lives of women in ancient Rome. It opens with the place and role of women in the *familia*, the domestic setting, as daughter and *matrona* – wife and mother – under the control of father, husband or guardian. We then look at marriage, the wedding ceremony, divorce and dowries, followed by a look at how women expressed and exerted themselves in public. This is followed by chapters on the education of girls and women, and the educated, sophisticated woman this education sometimes produced: the *docta puella*. The role and depiction of women as soothsayers and in the occult precedes a survey of aspects of state religion specific to women, and the magnetism of Eastern cults. Women's medicine and women as health professionals are then examined; a chapter on sex and sexuality which shows how women were perceived as sex objects in art, graffiti and literature, and as mistresses and prostitutes, concludes the book.

I

WOMEN IN THE *FAMILIA*

This chapter looks at Roman women in the family, the *familia*, and in the domestic setting, covering female infant exposure, girls and daughters, motherhood, the *matrona*, examples of female loyalty and fortitude and the role of guardians (*tutores*) in their lives. The evidence is seen through the eyes of male writers or in funerary inscriptions written largely by men.

The glue that held all families together was the *paterfamilias*, the father figure who exercised his authority over the *familia*, his *patria potestas*. His function was to ensure that family members helped each other to ensure the survival of their family, and to cement alliances with other *familiae* to guarantee mutual assistance when required. The function of marriage, and of women within that marriage, was to produce children – preferably male children – to ensure the survival of the family, to maintain the growing labour force, to feed the ranks of the military and the army of administrators needed to keep Rome and her overseas possessions safe and operational. Women as wives, although biologically vital, were, like children and slaves, subordinate to fathers or to husbands. As far back as the Law of Romulus, Roman legislation evolved to protect the family unit in which *patria potestas* was pivotal. This fact obviously defines the 'official' role of women within the *familia*, although it is difficult to say exactly how far it governed women's lives on a day-to-day basis.

Certainly, much of the epigraphical evidence would suggest a high degree of subservience, compliance and unobtrusiveness among the women honoured. Most of what we have is formulaic, trotting out standard qualities and typical domestic virtues; its value as evidence of a woman's actual life may be diluted as a result.

Fairly typical is 'Here lies Amymone, wife of Marcus, the best and most beautiful, wool spinner, dutiful, modest, careful with money, chaste, stay-at-home.'[1] It ticks all the boxes for the stock eulogy; Amymone's virtues reflect the ideal Roman wife, the *matrona*. Many of the qualifying epithets are here: *optima, pulcherrima, lanifica, pia, pudica, frugi, casta, domiseda*. Claudia was much the same: beautiful, loving, mother of two children (one dead, one living), clever in conversation (*sermone lepida*), good bearing (*incessu commoda*), looked after the home, and made wool (*lanam fecit*).[2] The seven most frequent 'adjectives', as assessed by Werner Riess, are *dulcissima* (sweetest), *pia* (dutiful), *bene merens* (well-deserving), *sua* (his or her), *carissima* (dearest), *optima* (best) and *sanctissima* (most chaste).[3] We could add to the list: valued a traditional lifestyle (*antiqua vita*), friendly and amusing (*comis*), modestly turned out (*ornata non conspiciendi*); a one-man woman (*univira*) and religious, but not with all that superstition stuff (*religiosa sine superstitione*). These epithets crop up with extraordinary regularity.

The evidential value of such epigraphs may be further diluted if they are seen as self-serving advertisements by the husband or son, reflecting, for all the world to see, their social and financial standing. They, unlike most, could afford to pay for a tombstone, and the eulogy proclaims the dutiful observance expected of a son or husband (*pietas*).

Indeed, at least one inscription, for the Perusian Allia Potestas, freedwoman of Allius, seems almost to be a pastiche of the form, holding back nothing: Allia is perfect in every respect, 'unblemished because she never did anything wrong'. It may well be true; but, were it not for an erotic element where Allius refers to her breasts and thighs, it might be written off, like many others, as near-meaningless complacency on behalf of the bereaved, a stock eulogy hurriedly chosen from a monumental mason's list. A degree of sexuality is evident too in the grave relief built for Ulpia Epigone, who is shown half-naked; this erotic element, however, is offset by the presence of a wool basket – one of the enduring emblems of the good Roman *matrona* – and of a small dog symbolising fidelity and affection.[4]

At the very least, then, tombstone inscriptions help us because they describe an ideal, if not the absolute reality, of wifely, feminine virtue; they tell us what men expected from a wife or a mother. They probably reflect the normal, everyday, tolerably happy marriage in which husband and wife rub along together and miss the other when one of them dies. Some wives would have been all the things the standard epigraphs tell us; others less so. Moreover, in a society where the woman's world was usually defined by the confines – physical and social – of the *familia* and the house, the *domus*, the eulogy – hackneyed as it often seems to us – may be the best a woman could wish for, or even desire: a fitting tribute to a dedicated wife or mother from a loving husband or son for a life well lived.

However, it is not all impersonal formulae. The bereaved relatives of Allia Potestas and Ulpia Epigone exhibit a degree of individuality, singling out unique characteristics of the deceased. Other eulogies and reminiscences do likewise, and because they are just too subjective, too personal, they probably reflect aspects of real-life characteristics.

Take for instance the widower who lists his wife's virtues in the standard way but then poignantly adds a footnote to explain just why he has set up the tombstone: to show people just how much he and his wife were in love.[5] Or the ever-grateful freedwoman who died aged forty and describes on her tombstone the husband who befriended her when she was seven, bought her out of slavery and married her. Eternal wifely devotion comes in an inscription on a memorial from Rome, set up by Furia Spes, a freedwoman. Furia and her husband were childhood sweethearts; she implores the spirits of the dead to look after him until she meets him again in the afterlife, soon, hopefully. A tombstone from Rome commemorates Ummidia Ge and Primigenius, buried together after they were crushed to death in a crowd on the Capitol – the detail says it all. The grief of the mother burying her son in Solenta, Dalmatia, is tangible, not least because she tells us that she, *infelix genetrix*, was still grieving for her recently deceased daughters. Again, the detail is poignant: the son was feeding their oxen when he was gored to death; the only hope is that by describing his death in this way she gained some sort of closure.[6]

The first-century BC inscription of a butcher and his wife gives both sides of the story. Lucius Aurelius Hermia says that his loving and much-loved wife, Aurelia Philematium, was devoted and dutiful. But we do not have to take his word for it; she tells us that she was chaste, modest, faithful and enjoyed a quiet life with Lucius. They had known each other since she was seven – some thirty-three years previously.[7] Naevoleia Tyche set up a tomb to herself, her husband and their slaves outside the Herculaneum Gate in Pompeii. It is her name at the top, in letters larger than her husband's: an expression of feisty single-mindedness? She did all the work organising the tombstone – so *her* name takes pride of place. Pompeius urges readers to go and bathe in the baths of Apollo when they have finished reading his tombstone – he only wishes he could, with his wife, just like they used to. At the other extreme, the personal epitaph left for Julia Maiana at Lugudunum by her brother and son is tragic: her husband killed her after a marriage that had lasted twenty-eight years.[8]

Of course it was not just men who were bereft; the *infelix uxor* is represented on the tombstone of Julius Classicianus, who died in Britain after the Boudiccan rebellion; his wife, Julia Pacata, set up the tombstone, describing herself as an 'unhappy widow'. Seneca provides a list of women who were determined to stay *univira* after the deaths of their husbands. *Univira* can be qualified by *unicuba* – married one man only, slept with one man only,[9] as is the case with Postumia Matronilla, and Veturia who gave birth to six children in her sixteen-year marriage before she died aged twenty-seven. Only one child survived her.[10]

For the most part, then, the funerary evidence speaks a standard epitaph for a standard Roman woman's life. Many wives and mothers would have been loyal, unobtrusive and would have got on with maintaining the household and raising the children. There are, nevertheless, glimpses of personal emotion and individuality left for the world to see that indicate marriages and families that obviously thrived on mutual love, respect and affection.

The literary evidence, too, must be used with caution, but, as we shall see, it reveals quite a lot all the same. We have no way of knowing, for example, how far Pliny's letters came straight from the heart, or how far they were freighted by the exigencies of official responsibility, by his social status and by the expectations of his audience. Undoubtedly, some of what we read in Pliny and indeed Cicero is experiential, inspired by personal experience, actual events and emotional reactions to those events. Equally, other work may well be window dressing: writers writing to the gallery, so to speak. Historians such as Livy, Tacitus and Appian tended only to deal with women and the family tangentially; that is, where they impinged on politics and wars or where they interceded with the actions of men. Martial may well have been posturing much of the time, just to deliver a pithy and shocking epigram, but elsewhere he may have dropped this masquerade and written honestly and sympathetically. Seneca exemplifies the dichotomy: as a philosopher he can list good reasons why a wise man should never marry, but Tacitus shatters this professional illusion when he tells us how much Seneca loved his wife.[11] What and how an author writes is often dictated and circumscribed by his or her genre: for example, there is no place for a routine happy marriage in comedy; the faithful woman never stars in the love poetry from Catullus to Ovid; there is no room for the perfect wife in satire; the woman in the street (or for that matter, on the street) has no leading role in epic; nor has the happily married *matrona* in tragedy.[12]

The social context is important too. Not only is much of what we read refracted through the eyes of middle- or upper-class Roman men, it also, in the main, reflects middle-class and upper-class women in their comfortable households with their comfortable lifestyles. Although we do get glimpses of prostitutes, slave women and freedwomen, there is comparatively little evidence relating to the daily life and routine of the servile and poorer classes, busy working in their shops, toiling in the fields, raising their families and looking after the house and complying with their husbands and fathers.

As with the epigraphical evidence, though, there are snatches of subjectivity and personal feeling in the literature. There is no reason to question Cicero's heartfelt grief over the death of Tullia, and the other expressions of sorrow for the deaths of girls who died young; we can believe that Pliny genuinely admired what Arria and Fannia stood for and that Tacitus and Quintilian really did think it important that a mother do everything she could to educate her children. Such laudable and enlightened aims may have helped to boost an author's literary reputation and public image but they do not necessarily preclude an element of genuine sympathy and feeling.

As an example, only the most cynical reading of three epigrams by Martial that mourn the death of Erotion, his delight (*deliciae*), just before her sixth birthday, would deny the poet's true grief. In the first he hopes she will not be frightened by the horrors of Tartarus and that the turf over her body will not weigh too heavily; in the second, he asks for the anniversary of her death to be celebrated by subsequent owners of the house, where she lies buried.[13]

So, the evidence from tombstones and from writers has its limitations; it does, nevertheless, occasionally reveal true feelings and attitudes which raise it above the predictable and formulaic stock. We can, therefore, derive something credible about attitudes to women and how women interacted and acted within the family as mothers, wives, sisters and daughters. Dutiful, discreet, compliant, faithful, unobtrusive, modest, but at the same time, loved, loving and badly missed.

Some girls got off to the worst possible start in life. Generally speaking, the birth of a daughter was greeted less enthusiastically than that of a son, if not by the mother then at least by the father. *Patria potestas* empowered him, by virtue of *ius patrium, ius vitae necisque*, the power of life and death, to kill or sell off unwanted or surplus members of the family. In extreme cases, baby girls were exposed, largely, it seems, for financial reasons: a girl could not always go out to work and contribute to the household income; she could also require an expensive dowry in the relatively near future.[14] According to the Twelve Tables (4,1), deformed babies of either sex should be disposed of as soon as possible after birth; Dionysius of Halicarnassus[15] alleges that Romulus (in the so-called Law of Romulus) ordered Roman citizens to raise all their boys but only the first-born girl, unless she was deformed, in which case she too might be killed, given the approval of five neighbours. Whether this was ever actually observed it is impossible to know. Nevertheless, legalised child murder had its supporters and its opponents: Philo of Alexandria (20 BC – AD 50) equated exposure of infants with infanticide and reports cases of strangulation and drowning.[16] Livy tells in 207 BC of a monstrously deformed child being cast adrift, alive in a box, to rid Rome of such a repulsive portent.[17] Suetonius describes a decree in 63 BC that all boys should be exposed; Musonius Rufus in the first century AD deplores child murder.[18] Soranus, the gynaecologist, provided a checklist for midwives to help them determine the newborn disorders which permitted exposure.[19] It was not until AD 374 that child exposure was outlawed when infanticide became the legal equivalent of murder. In a earlier bid to restrict the practice, Constantine had offered free food and clothing to new parents and legalised the sale of babies, mainly into slavery, in AD 329. However, it was still going on some years later: the skeletons of around 100 infants were excavated from the bottom of a drain in Ashkelon dating from the sixth century AD.

In an otherwise touching letter, Hilarion, away on business in Alexandria, is quite adamant that his pregnant wife, Alis, expose their baby, if it is a girl – the affection he shows Alis makes the demand all the more chilling: 'Please, please look after the child; I'll send you money if I get paid soon. If you have the baby before I get back let it live if it's a boy; if it's a girl, expose it ... how can I forget you? Please don't worry.'[20] Ovid, in the story of Iphis and Ianthe, tells a similar tale: 'Low-born Ligdus was poor but he had morals and was honourable; his pregnant wife was near her time and he wished her an easy labour and a boy: "We can't afford to raise a daughter, they're too much of a burden."' Ligdus was adamant, but happily Iphis, their baby girl, was secretly raised as a boy and was eventually changed into a boy by the gods.[21] Mythology this is but its message surely reflects real-world practice; significantly, Ovid sees Ligdus as moral and honourable.

Some women were forced to give their girls away or sell them through abject poverty; one wretched papyrus tells of a widow, Aurelia Herais, who has to surrender all claim to her nine-year-old daughter.[22] Many girls would end up in the slave markets; others would be sold as potential prostitutes. Orphans with nowhere to go were common among the lower classes.[23] From a demographic standpoint, the Law of Romulus and exposure of daughters, along with the high rate of perinatal mortality, with childbearing telescoped as it was into adolescence and early adulthood, may well have contributed to a shortage of childbearing women by the end of the Republic.

There is an argument that, due to the high rate of infant mortality, Roman parents inured themselves to the harsh fact that their baby might well die so as to minimise the grief that is normal in such a tragic situation. The employment of wet nurses, and the knowledge that some Romans 'farmed out' their infants for the first two years or so of their lives, may suggest a level of parental indifference. Cicero says as much: 'no one pays any notice if he dies in the cradle'. The tombstone of twelve-year-old Julia Pothousa from Arcadia may endorse this; her parents wish that she'd died earlier, before they had grown to love her.[24]

Some fathers exercised their *ius vitae necisque* on moralistic grounds: around 642 BC Horatia, the fiancée of one of the Curiatii, mourned his death after he was slain by one of her three brothers, two of whom died also in the fight. The surviving brother, Publius, stabbed her to death, proclaiming that 'any woman who mourns an enemy of Rome will die like this'. Her father sanctioned the sororicide, adding that he would have killed her himself had her brother not.[25] In 449 BC Appius Claudius, one of the legendary authors of the Twelve Tables, ardently pursued a young lady called Verginia; her father stabbed her in the heart to save her from the *stuprum* (debauched or lewd behaviour) that a liaison with Appius Claudius would, he believed, have inevitably brought.[26]

Of course, most baby girls were allowed to live, and were loved by mother and father alike. Cicero is distraught at the death of Tullia in childbirth in 45 BC, when she was about thirty, or Tulliola as he affectionately called her; he also addresses her as *deliciolae*, darling. He pours out his grief in two letters to Atticus in which he describes his anguish, sorrowful memories and being consumed day and night by grief; there is no solace to be found, not even in his library. In the first letter, profound depression has caused him to cut himself off from all society, living in a deep, dark forest, coming out only at night, weeping inconsolably. Affection between father and daughter seems, to Cicero, quite natural; his letters are full of recollections of his efforts to make her happy, devoid of any criticism – even on the vexed question of her marriage to Dolabella.[27]

Plutarch, in his life of Aemilius Paulus, records, after Cicero in his *De Divinatione*, the touching scene when Paulus, proclaimed general against Perseus, King of Macedon, found his young daughter, Tertia, crying; when he asked her why, she threw her arms around his neck and, kissing him, said, 'Father, do you not know that Perseus is dead?' She actually meant her little dog of that name, to which Aemilius, perhaps a little tactlessly, replied that this was indeed a good omen. Gnaeus Julius Agricola clearly loves his baby daughter; indeed, she provides some comfort when his son dies soon after she is born.

A teenager called Eucharis is remembered on a tombstone; she was fourteen at the time of her death, unmarried, educated and a celebrated dancer and actress. Her grieving, proud father has her tell us, 'I had had an education and was taught as if by the Muses ... the patrons of learning ... are silenced by my burnt corpse and by my death.'[28] A mother's grief over her daughter, Marcia Doris, celebrates the 'best and most devoted daughter', while Bitte's mother shows the cruel irony in her daughter's death when she has her poignantly say in the inscription, 'Here I lie, a marble statue, instead of a woman.'[29] Epitynchanus tells us that Philete, *filia dulcissima*, the sweetest of daughters, died on her seventh birthday.[30]

Valerius Maximus records the story of the Sabine Valesius's desperate attempts, ultimately successful, to save the lives of his dying children – two boys and a girl. To Valesius, it seems, sons and daughters were equally precious.[31] Pliny the Younger, a century and a half later in his letter to Marcellinus, bewails the premature death of the Fundanus's daughter, Minicia Marcella, soon before her thirteenth birthday. Despite her youth, she displayed considerable maturity and all the qualities befitting a grown woman, a *matrona*; she was a sweet child and modest, affectionate to her father and respectful to her nurses and teachers; she died with stoic fortitude. Significantly, Pliny, though saddened, is equally troubled by the fact that Minicia did not live long enough to see marriage – the *sine qua non* of girls around that age – although she was engaged. Tragically her dowry was transferred to pay towards the funeral arrangements. The passage is telling because it neatly reflects the situation of girls in middle-class Roman society; girls married

young, soon after puberty – marriage and child-rearing was the
expectation, a crucial, if not *the*, goal in life. Females like Minicia
went straight from being little girls to womanhood, with all the
stresses and responsibilities that brought.

The Roman world was a very dangerous place, for children as well
as adults. Ten-year-old Julia Restuta from Salonae in Dalmatia was
the victim of a fatal mugging – robbed and killed for her jewellery;
eight-year-old Revocata and her four-year-old brother both drowned
off Brattia on the Dalmatian coast; fourteen-year-old Murra died
when she was hit on the head with a toy weapon in Lugudunum.[32]

Daughters, then, if they survived childbirth and were not
exposed, were cherished by loving parents. Nevertheless, when
we look at other evidence we begin to get a more objective idea
of how daughters were regarded. For example, wills reveal the
discrimination women often faced in the relative size of their
legacies compared to their male counterparts; daughters, as we
shall see, were often used as pawns in betrothals and marriage
alliances to further the political career of a father or husband.

We deal with marriage in the next chapter; suffice to say that
marriages were pre-arranged by the father in keeping with his
position of power at the head of the family, or by a guardian or
some other male relative; girls seldom had a say in whom they
married. Catullus prescribes the very business-like protocol that
marriage not only makes the young girl dear to her husband
but also less loathsome (*invisa*) to her father; she shouldn't fight
against her father's choice, she must obey him and her mother.
After all, the girl owns only one-third of her virginity – her parents
have the other two-thirds and they have exercised their right to
pass her on to their son-in-law, along with the dowry.[33]

The essentials of Roman womanhood lie in the concept of
matrona: the Roman wife and woman of the household. The
qualities expected of a *matrona* are all there in the inscriptional
evidence, as we have seen. They include *pudicitia* (sexual propriety,
the opposite, almost, of *stuprum*), modesty, virtuousness, loyalty,
strength of character and fortitude, *pietas* towards the family,
a one-man woman (*univira*), and devotion to her children. A
girl took on these responsibilities the minute she arrived at her
husband's house during her wedding ceremony.

Two famous inscriptions provide
the ideal *matrona* and mother. Murc
without peer when it came to *virt*
and intelligence, modesty, integrity, c
of wool and loyalty; all the usual c
important because it explains why fune
often read like characterless formula
achievements was circumscribed by her duty to the ˢ̣ʰₒₗd
and the family. Most women fulfilled this adequately an̩ₜₒ the
same characteristics and virtues appear over and over aga̧ the
funerary inscriptions are often a reflection both of the restrict̩ₙₛ
on women's activities in Roman society and the dedication th̬y
were expected to show towards the *familia*.[34] Murdia, nevertheless,
stands out because the inscription also shows that she was at pains
to ensure the fair distribution of her property after her death.

The gold standard of wifely conduct can also be seen in the
second-century BC Turia inscription – the Laudatio Turiae erected
in Rome by husband Quintus Lucretius Vespillo.[35] This celebrates,
at some length, the life of a dutiful and exceptional wife and
gives another catalogue of those qualities expected of the good
matrona: *pietas*, wool-working, looking after the household goods,
modesty of dress and elegance, financial generosity, bravery and
shrewdness in the face of her husband's enemy, Lepidus, in 46
BC when he was proscribed. Turia concealed Lucretius in their
roof space and convincingly acted out the role of the bereft
wife dressing in rags, looking dishevelled and grieving over an
apparently lost husband.[36]

In the *Agricola*, published in AD 98, Tacitus ascribes matronly
qualities to Agricola's mother, Julia Procilla, *rara castitas*, 'a
paragon of feminine virtue'.[37] It was her guidance that imbued
Agricola with all the right characteristics; it was she who, 'in her
wisdom, tempered his ardent passion' and steered him away from
the enfeebling philosophising at Massilia, a city steeped in all
things Greek.

This chimes with Tacitus's general belief that 'in the good old
days the children of any respectable mother were brought up, not
in the room of a hired nurse but on their mother's knee. She was
honoured to look after the home and to do right by her children.'

quote the examples of Cornelia, mother of the
goesotta, Julius Caesar's mother; and the mother
ni; Aia Balba Caesonia, as the three role models to
Augustitilian agreed that it was a mother's duty to ensure
emulate. receive the best possible education, whatever her
her chil ment, also citing Cornelia as a fine role model.[39]
own ac
Cor i is described as the ideal *matrona* by Plutarch in his *Life
of Go Gracchus*. We know little of her life, other than that Pliny
the ier records how she was born with her vagina closed up
(la ul adhesion), an inauspicious condition presaging, it seems,
th deaths of her two revolutionary sons.[40] The daughter of Scipio
Africanus, she remained dignified when speaking of the exploits
and tragic deaths of her two boys: her company and conversation
were much enjoyed by scholars and monarchs – an example of
'how far a noble nature, an honourable ancestry and a virtuous
upbringing, can fortify [wo]men against grief'.[41] There is more
praise in Plutarch's *Life of Tiberius Gracchus* where he narrates
the story of how Tiberius Sempronius Gracchus, Cornelia's
husband, elected to die in place of her. Two snakes had ominously
appeared on the marital bed; Tiberius chooses to kill the male
snake (signifying himself) rather than the female (representing
Cornelia) – Plutarch sees his unenviable choice as a demonstration
of his love and respect for Cornelia. Tiberius duly died soon after,
leaving her with their twelve children to raise, nine of whom died,
and an estate to run. Nevertheless, she 'proved herself a woman of
such discretion and noble ideals and so devoted a mother'. Despite
a proposal of marriage from the famously ugly Ptolemy VIII
(Physkon), Cornelia remained a widow and *univira*. The surviving
daughter, Sempronia, married Scipio Africanus the Younger; the
surviving sons, Gaius and Tiberius, she 'brought up with such care
and such ambitious hopes, that ... they were considered to owe
their virtues even more to their education than to their lineage'.[42]
Cornelia provided the education.

At the end of the first century BC Propertius describes a different
Cornelia, the daughter of Scribonia and wife to Lucius Aemilius
Paullus, Augustus's step-daughter.[43] She too can boast excellent
credentials as a *matrona*: dutiful daughter, dutiful wife and dutiful
mother, the ideal role model for her children. All the fine, matronly

Two famous inscriptions provide a detailed description of the ideal *matrona* and mother. Murdia's son tells how she was without peer when it came to *virtus* (virtuousness), diligence and intelligence, modesty, integrity, chastity, obedience, working of wool and loyalty; all the usual qualities. The inscription is important because it explains why funerary inscriptions for women often read like characterless formulae: the range of a woman's achievements was circumscribed by her duty to the household and the family. Most women fulfilled this adequately and so the same characteristics and virtues appear over and over again: the funerary inscriptions are often a reflection both of the restrictions on women's activities in Roman society and the dedication they were expected to show towards the *familia*.[34] Murdia, nevertheless, stands out because the inscription also shows that she was at pains to ensure the fair distribution of her property after her death.

The gold standard of wifely conduct can also be seen in the second-century BC Turia inscription – the Laudatio Turiae erected in Rome by husband Quintus Lucretius Vespillo.[35] This celebrates, at some length, the life of a dutiful and exceptional wife and gives another catalogue of those qualities expected of the good *matrona*: *pietas*, wool-working, looking after the household goods, modesty of dress and elegance, financial generosity, bravery and shrewdness in the face of her husband's enemy, Lepidus, in 46 BC when he was proscribed. Turia concealed Lucretius in their roof space and convincingly acted out the role of the bereft wife dressing in rags, looking dishevelled and grieving over an apparently lost husband.[36]

In the *Agricola*, published in AD 98, Tacitus ascribes matronly qualities to Agricola's mother, Julia Procilla, *rara castitas*, 'a paragon of feminine virtue'.[37] It was her guidance that imbued Agricola with all the right characteristics; it was she who, 'in her wisdom, tempered his ardent passion' and steered him away from the enfeebling philosophising at Massilia, a city steeped in all things Greek.

This chimes with Tacitus's general belief that 'in the good old days the children of any respectable mother were brought up, not in the room of a hired nurse but on their mother's knee. She was honoured to look after the home and to do right by her children.'

He then goes on to quote the examples of Cornelia, mother of the Gracchi; Aurelia Cotta, Julius Caesar's mother; and the mother of Augustus, Atia Balba Caesonia, as the three role models to emulate.[38] Quintilian agreed that it was a mother's duty to ensure her children receive the best possible education, whatever her own achievement, also citing Cornelia as a fine role model.[39]

Cornelia is described as the ideal *matrona* by Plutarch in his *Life of Gaius Gracchus*. We know little of her life, other than that Pliny the Elder records how she was born with her vagina closed up (labial adhesion), an inauspicious condition presaging, it seems, the deaths of her two revolutionary sons.[40] The daughter of Scipio Africanus, she remained dignified when speaking of the exploits and tragic deaths of her two boys: her company and conversation were much enjoyed by scholars and monarchs – an example of 'how far a noble nature, an honourable ancestry and a virtuous upbringing, can fortify [wo]men against grief'.[41] There is more praise in Plutarch's *Life of Tiberius Gracchus* where he narrates the story of how Tiberius Sempronius Gracchus, Cornelia's husband, elected to die in place of her. Two snakes had ominously appeared on the marital bed; Tiberius chooses to kill the male snake (signifying himself) rather than the female (representing Cornelia) – Plutarch sees his unenviable choice as a demonstration of his love and respect for Cornelia. Tiberius duly died soon after, leaving her with their twelve children to raise, nine of whom died, and an estate to run. Nevertheless, she 'proved herself a woman of such discretion and noble ideals and so devoted a mother'. Despite a proposal of marriage from the famously ugly Ptolemy VIII (Physkon), Cornelia remained a widow and *univira*. The surviving daughter, Sempronia, married Scipio Africanus the Younger; the surviving sons, Gaius and Tiberius, she 'brought up with such care and such ambitious hopes, that ... they were considered to owe their virtues even more to their education than to their lineage'.[42] Cornelia provided the education.

At the end of the first century BC Propertius describes a different Cornelia, the daughter of Scribonia and wife to Lucius Aemilius Paullus, Augustus's step-daughter.[43] She too can boast excellent credentials as a *matrona*: dutiful daughter, dutiful wife and dutiful mother, the ideal role model for her children. All the fine, matronly qualities are here – her life was faultless from beginning to end: 'Nor did my lifestyle change; it was blameless throughout, I lived respected between both torches [marriage and funeral].' Cornelia is just the sort of woman to embody Augustus's moral legislation, the *Lex Julia de maritandis ordinibus*. She is the opposite of Cynthia, Propertius's decadent mistress: Propertius enumerates traditional *matrona* qualities to highlight, by comparison, the unconventional and outrageous behaviour of Cynthia. Cornelia, though, in the eyes of Propertius, is a somewhat empty character who lives a proper but uninteresting life, following her own *cursus honorum* to the letter: to him she is a victim of Roman tradition who, despite her obvious intelligence and attractions, lived a rather submissive, confined life.[44] We shall meet the gifted Cynthia again when dealing with women and the fine arts.

Pudicitia was clearly evident in Cornelia, Lucretia and Verginia – the three great *matronae* of Rome. It is variously translated as chastity, sexual honour or sexual propriety and is, according to Livy, equivalent to the laudable quality of *virtus* in men.[45] For Lucretia and Verginia, as we shall see, the preservation of *pudicitia* was so important that it cost them their lives. Women also exhibit *virtus*, with its connotations of manliness (*vir*) and traditional male attributes of strength and bravery, as well as of virtue. Seneca describes the *conspicuous valour* of Cornelia and Rutilia as *conspecta virtus*. In the *Ad Marciam* he spells out his belief that women are just as capable of displaying *virtutes* as men.[46] The elderly Ummidia Quadratilla shows vitality (*viridis*) and a physique unusual in an octogenarian woman.[47]

Matronly virtues, familial devotion and *pietas* were not, of course, the preserve of the middle and upper classes. These qualities were also exhibited by women of the lower classes, as a first-century BC inscription for Larcia Horaea clearly shows: she was a confident and faithful freedwoman, respected in her social circle, obedient to her master and mistress, faithful to her husband – virtues that won her her freedom and status as a *matrona* in her own right.[48] As we have seen, another freedwoman, Allia Potestas, has more than her fair share of virtues – perfect in every way, she is first up in the morning and the last to go to bed in the evening, forever weaving, faultless to the end.[49] Neither were

matronly virtues confined to women of Roman birth. Martial
describes a Claudia Rufina; she is of British stock, a barbarian,
but nevertheless is a Latin at heart and would pass any time for a
Roman or a Greek. Like all good *matronae* she is fertile, *fecunda*,
univira and looking forward to her children's marriages.[50]

Love and affection for their children is clearly evident in
matronae. In the first half of the first century AD, Seneca
concludes that fathers are extremely demanding of their children,
sometimes reducing them to tears; mothers, on the other hand,
are more sensitive and indulgent, 'sitting them on their knees,
sheltering them in the shade, protecting them from unhappiness,
tears and distress'.[51] In AD 144 Marcus Aurelius gives a rare
glimpse of a warm relationship between mother and son: a very
personal letter to his friend Fronto describes his mother sitting on
the edge of his bed chatting to him; it shows an intimacy that is
almost unique in the surviving evidence and a world apart from
the often featureless, impersonal tombstone inscriptions.[52]

Papyrus evidence describes an over-solicitous third-century
AD mother fretting over her son's minor accident at work.[53] For
Cornelia it is her two sons, the brothers Gracchi, who are her real
jewels (*ornamenta*), not the ostentatious sparklers she wears.[54]
In the third century AD Dio Cassius tells how the intelligent
and witty Julia Domna, wife of Septimius Severus (reigned
193–211), championed the cause of her younger son, Geta, in
his claim for Caracella's throne – although her motives may not
have been entirely altruistic.[55] Evidence of a mother's love for
her daughter can be found on a funerary inscription raised by
Quarta Senenia, a freedwoman, for Posilla. She achingly regrets
the absence of physical contact and intimacy between them,
poignantly remarking that while there had not been a problem
dressing her body for the funeral, she had not had the chance to
dress her when she was alive.[56]

We noted above how Pliny the Younger gives an example of a
caring grandmother; he describes Ummidia Quadratilla as being
sprightly, *viridis*, and in good physical shape until her last illness
– very unusual for a woman – *etiam ultra matronalem modum*. In
his letter Pliny is most concerned about his protégé, Ummidius
Quadratus, and the preservation of his good character. Pliny

was anxious because the recently deceased seventy-nine-year-old grandmother was something of a rich old raver, enthusiastically managing a troupe of pantomime dancers, playing draughts, being decadent, and generally living it up. However, despite her wealth and the evident luxury of her home, she reverently shielded Ummidius from it all: he lived *severissime*, she *obsequentissime*; he lived an austere life, she an indulgent one. Pliny is highly respectful of the old lady and the efforts she went to in bringing up her grandson with such *honor*, with *pietas*.[57] In the end she left one-third of her fortune to her grandson and the other third to her granddaughter.

Statius manages to combine a moving description of wifely devotion, a mother's devotion to her daughter and a stepfather's pride in his stepdaughter. It comes in a poem inspired by his unpopular desire, in his autumn years, to move the family back to Naples from Rome. His wife Claudia's loyalty (*fides*) to him has been equal to that of the heroines of Greece and Rome; her devotion to her daughter is just as great:

> Nor is your concern and devotion [*pietas*] for your daughter any the less, you love her as a mother, your daughter is never out of your heart; night and day you hold her transfixed in your innermost soul.

He praises his stepdaughter's beauty, her good attitude, her accomplishments on the lute and in singing. Her mother's concern is that she is unmarried and that Rome is the best place for her to find a husband; Statius argues that she will find a husband be she in Rome or Naples.[58]

An example of sisterly affection for a brother was found on the side of the Cheops pyramid in the fourteenth century by a traveller; it had been carved in the second century AD by Terentia and describes him as *dulcissimus*. Sadly, the inscription was subsequently lost when the facing of the pyramid was removed.[59]

Good mothers sometimes earn the devotion of their children. A second century AD fragment shows filial devotion – and a lack of it – when Sempronius rebukes his elder brother, Maximus, for not looking after their mother and for causing her heartache after their father's death. Sempronius advises Maximus to give their other brothers a good slap if they upset her. Maximus is now the father figure, assuming *patria potestas*; he should join Sempronius in worshipping her as a goddess, good and virtuous as she is.[60] Agricola was quite naturally mortified when his mother was brutally murdered by marauders from Otho's navy.[61]

The incidence of early death, divorce and re-marriage in Rome led to a great number of stepmothers and stepdaughters: Seneca, in a piece written while he was in exile for alleged adultery with Julia Livilla, the sister of Caligula, gives an account of Helvia's commendable behaviour towards her stepmother. Helvia's natural mother died in childbirth. Helvia's stepmother was happily left with no choice but to assume a birth mother's role because of the absolute obedience and loving affection Helvia had shown her. In short, their relationship was little different from a natural mother–daughter relationship:[62] Helvia displays all the characteristics of the *matrona*. Her sixteen years as wife of the governor of Egypt were entirely blameless, adopting as she did a discreet lifestyle which won her a reputation locally for being *unicum sanctatis exemplum* – a unique example of integrity. Filial and sibling affection is evident in another Helvia passage where Seneca recommends his mother takes refuge with his aunt, obviously a good listener and 'the best comfort there is, a mother to us all ... hug her tightly'.[63]

We have felt Cicero's inconsolable grief at the death of his daughter. Other writers describe emotion and empathy between husbands and wives; Martial gives us a widow's tragic double grief:

> Nigrina brought home her dear husband's ashes, holding them close to her heart and complaining that the journey home was all too brief. When she surrendered the sacred urn to the tomb (and she was jealous of that tomb), she couldn't then help feeling that she had been widowed twice over for the husband who had been snatched from her.[64]

Quintilian is distraught at his young wife's death, aged nineteen, by which time she had given birth to two sons who also predeceased their father. She exhibited every virtue a woman could have; he adds poignantly that her girlish qualities made it seem as if he had lost a daughter.[65]

There is much literary evidence of love for living wives. A letter from Pliny to Calpurnia reflects mutual affection:

> You write that you are missing me terribly and take comfort only when you hold my books, often placing them where I should be. I'm glad that you miss me and I'm glad that you are comforted in this way. As for me, I read your letters over and over again, constantly picking them up as if they had just arrived. In doing this I burn with desire all the more.[66]

The letter also hints at his appreciation of his wife's literacy and intelligence as confirmed for us in 4, 19, a letter to Corellia Hispulla, Calpurnia's aunt, spoiled rather by his smug appreciation of his own talents. She was

> very clever, very prudent, and her love for me is a mark of her chastity. You can add to these qualities her study of literature which has been developed by her devotion to me. She has all my books, reads them and even learns them by heart ... she has even set my verses to music and sings them accompanied with a lyre, taught not by a musician but by love – the best teacher.

To Pliny, Corellia Hispulla herself shows many traits worthy of a *matrona*, demonstrated not least by the role she played bringing up her niece:

> You are a paragon of dutiful conduct and you love the best and most devoted of brothers as much as he loves you; you love his daughter as if she was your own, and your affection for her is not so much as an aunt but more as the father she lost ... nothing else would be worthy of a woman educated in your hands, steeped in your ideas and who had seen nothing but purity and integrity in your company.[67]

Notably, it is to Corellia Hispulla whom Pliny writes – and not to her husband – when advising on the choice of a rhetoric teacher, a *rhetor Latinus*, for her son; it is important that he has only the best.[68]

Ovid, in his *Tristia*, composed in Black Sea exile, describes the loyal and devoted wife. She is *exemplum coniugis bonae* – the model of a good wife; she would hold first place among the sacred heroines of mythology and, somewhat disingenuously and sycophantically on Ovid's part, would be an equal to the first lady, Livia, wife of Augustus – if he is allowed to compare the great with the small.

The praise of the *matrona*, be it inscriptional or literary, to some degree follows a pattern: 'paragons of feminine virtue' are everywhere, the spinning of wool, the low profile, the devotion, the being seen and not really heard, being *univira* – they are all symbols and emblems of 'the good wife'.[69] Nevertheless, there is ample funerary and literary evidence to show that women were appreciated as individuals for their love and devotion to the family – sometimes to the death – their social skills, their education and their single-mindedness.

Matronae were recognisable in the street by the *stola* they wore – a long, ankle-length dress – or *instita*, the shoulder straps of the *stola*, and their *vittae*, hairbands. These instantly marked out the *matrona* from unmarried girls, women without Roman citizenship, adulteresses, prostitutes and other women of dubious occupation such as dancers, actresses and anyone else working in the entertainment or catering industries. The words *stola, instita* and *vittae* themselves became metonyms for respectability and chastity: Ovid uses them when he disingenuously dissuades *matronae* from reading his *Ars Amatoria*; Martial mentions the decency (*pudor*) of the *stola*; Valerius Maximus *verecundia stolae*, the modesty of the stola.[70]

Strength of character, loyalty and bravery were among other hallmarks of the *matrona*. The rape of Lucretia by Sextus Tarquinius, and her subsequent suicide, firmly implicates matronly *pudicitia* and valour in the traditional foundation of Rome. Livy tells how Tarquinius blackmails Lucretia by threatening to put it about that she had been *in flagrante delicto* with a slave; he threatened to have her and a slave killed, their corpses placed alongside each other in bed, if she did not yield to him.[71] Lucretia cannot live with the shame that such a calumny would bring and succumbs; her body is defiled but, she protests, her mind remains pure.[72] Despite the forgiveness of her father, Lucretius, and of Collatinus, her husband, Lucretia commits suicide: brave, virtuous and inextricably linked with Rome's proud early beginnings. Rome, like Lucretia, was compromised and violated by the Tarquins; the noble reaction of Lucretia and her avengers symbolises Rome's honourable struggle against regal tyranny and led to the rejection of monarchy for a Republic. Livy makes her an unimpeachable exemplar of feminine virtue in a Rome, his Rome, now beset by increasing adultery and failing marriages.[73]

The rape is all the more heinous and significant because Livy prefaces it with a story spotlighting Lucretia's virtue. During a drinking session, which included Tarquinius and Collatinus, at the siege of Ardea, the subject of wives, good or otherwise, came up; an alcohol-fuelled decision was then made to ride back to Rome and Collatia to establish whose was the most virtuous. The princes' wives were found ensconced in a sumptuous dinner party, *in convivio luxuque*. On the other hand, even though it was late at night, Lucretia was sitting surrounded by her maids in the hall working away at the wool by lamplight. This of course left no doubt as to who had won the contest. According to Ovid Lucretia was working on a cloak for Collatinus.[74]

Pliny the Younger gives an example of a *matrona*'s exceptional devotion to her husband in a letter to Maecilius Nepos. Arria, 'a shining example and comfort', does everything she possibly can to show her husband, Aulus Caecina Paetus, that his impending suicide, ordered by Claudius, will not be painful. 'Paetus, it doesn't hurt' (*Paete, non dolet*); and this after she has bravely shielded the news of their son's recent death from her husband to spare him additional grief:

Whenever he asked how the boy was doing she responded: 'He's had a good rest and is ready to eat something.' Then, when she couldn't hold her tears back any longer, she left the room and burst into tears, succumbing to her anguish. Her grief sated, she dried her eyes, composed herself and went back into the room almost as if she had left her bereavement outside. It was a glorious thing for her when she pulled out a dagger, plunged it into her breast, pulled out the dagger and offered it to her husband with the immortal, almost divine, words: 'Paetus, it doesn't hurt.' By doing what she did and saying what she said she was looking glory and immortality straight in the eye. On the other hand, it was an even greater thing when, without the reward of immortality and without the reward of glory, she hid her tears and concealed her grief and continued to play the mother when she had lost her son.[75]

Later in the letter we learn of Arria's brave determination to end her own life:

'It's no use' she said: 'you can have me die a horrible death but you can't stop me dying.' As she said this she leapt from her chair, banged her head really hard against the wall opposite and slumped to the ground. When she came round she said: 'I told you that I would find a hard way to die if you denied me the easy way out.'

Martial too honours *casta* Arria's bravery; he, perceptively, has her say that her wound *non dolet* but the one that Paetus is about to inflict on himself certainly will hurt her.[76]

Such courage ran in the family: Arria's granddaughter, Fannia, had been married to Helvidius Priscus, an agitator against Vespasian, who had him executed in AD 75. Pliny extols the virtues of Fannia, doubting very much whether the world will see the like of her again – the perfect model of a wife with the rare qualities of charm and amiability, clever enough to appreciate the value of her husband's library, which she spirited away into safekeeping in exile despite orders to burn his books. Fannia has displayed *fortitudo, sanctitas* and *castitas, gravitas* and *constantia*: bravery, purity of mind, purity of body, dignity and self-control. She followed her husband twice into exile and was herself condemned to exile for her troubles; Tacitus sees this loyalty as an example of female *virtus*.[77] Fannia later died from tuberculosis contracted from a consumptive Vestal Virgin whom she had volunteered to nurse.[78]

Arria and Fannia were not alone: Pliny the Elder describes

how a woman joined her husband in suicide by jumping, roped to him, into Lake Como after she had diagnosed his condition (variously thought to be a urogenital cancer, syphilis or urogenital tuberculosis) as incurable.[79] Porcia, the wife of Brutus, stabbed herself in the thigh to show her husband that she too could endure pain and was worthy of sharing his concerns.[80] When Brutus was killed in 43 BC she committed suicide by swallowing hot coals, an act that Valerius Maximus describes as 'her woman's spirit equal to her father's manly death'.[81]

Tacitus recounts a number of female suicides. Paxaea commits suicide with her husband Pomponius Labeo, governor of Moesia, arraigned by Tiberius in AD 34 for maladministration. Lucius Antistius Vetus was proscribed by Nero for his involvement in the Pisonian conspiracy in AD 65: his mother-in-law, Sextia, and daughter, Antistia Pollitta, joined him in opening their veins,[82] but not before Pollitta had remonstrated with Nero: 'she wailed like a woman' but she also 'screamed at him in a most unwomanly rage'.[83] Aemilia Lepida takes her life to avoid persecution, Sextia opts to die with her husband, Mamercus Aemilius Scaurus, who is under prosecution,[84] as does Paulina, the wife of Seneca,[85] although she is finally confounded by Nero and lives on 'praiseworthy in the memory of her husband'.

Wifely suicide is an extension of the *univira* ideal: not only should a woman marry only one man but she should not outlive him. Arria admonishes Vibia, wife of Scribonianus, who lived on after her husband had been murdered in her very arms;[86] Arria urges her own daughter to commit suicide should her husband die before her. She displayed other signs of character and purpose: she risked her life when Paetus

> was dragged back to Rome after Scribonianus had been killed. He was about to board the boat when Arria begged the soldiers to take her too. 'Surely a consul should be allowed a few slaves to serve his meals, dress him and put on his shoes – only I excel at all these things.' She didn't get her way, so she hired a small fishing boat to follow the big boat in her little one.[87]

Sulpicia dressed up as a slave to follow her proscribed husband,

Lentulus Cruscellio, into exile in Sicily. The wife of Rubellius Plautus accompanied him in exile and two of the wives of the Piso conspirators went with their husbands. Valerius gives us two further instances of fortitude: first, as we have seen, Turia, who in 42 BC bravely and successfully concealed her proscribed husband, Quintus Lucretius Vespillo, in the rafters of their house;[88] second Tertia Aemilia, wife of Scipio Africanus, who had full knowledge of her husband's affair with a slave girl but chose to turn a blind eye and, on Scipio's death, emancipated the girl and organised her marriage to one of her freedmen.[89]

Tertia Aemilia also illustrates the tolerance expected of Roman wives, highlighting the double standards prevalent in Roman marriage. A woman was adulterous if she had a liaison with any man, while a man was only an adulterer if his mistress was married, thus leaving the door wide open for legitimate extramarital affairs with prostitutes, concubines, slave girls and widows. Consider Augustine, converted to Christianity in AD 387, who explains how his mother never argued with his father over his sexual indiscretions.[90] It is of course impossible to conclude anything about women's attitudes to this; most women probably accepted the situation, seeing it as a relief from the often relentless cycle of sex, impregnation, childbirth and more sex. However, the very real possibility of a promiscuous man infecting his wife, or indeed his unborn child, with a sexually transmitted infection has gone unremarked.[91]

Appian records a number of brave and devoted acts by women following the proscriptions imposed after the assassination of Julius Caesar in 44 BC. The wife of Acilius used her jewellery to bribe and deflect the soldiers who had come to arrest him, and escaped with him to Sicily; Apuleius's wife threatened to turn him in if he refused to let her escape with him; Antius's wife concealed him in a blanket to effect their escape; and the wife of Rheginus hid him in a sewer and dressed him as a donkey-driving charcoal seller to make good their escape.[92] Dio Cassius describes a woman who heroically defended another woman's virtue in his record of Pythias, a slave girl who under interrogation and torture stood up for Nero's wife, Octavia, in AD 63. She defiantly spat in the face of her interrogator, Tigellinus, when he questioned Octavia's virtue, exclaiming, 'My mistress's vagina is cleaner than your mouth.'[93]

Sempronia, the Catilinarian conspirator, showed bravery too but, not surprisingly in the circumstances, hers attracted condemnation and vilification. Sallust writes that she exhibited a boldness worthy of a man; she was well married with children; she was versed in Latin and Greek, accomplished in the lyre and a good dancer, she was an excellent and convivial conversationalist: in short her social and artistic skills and abilities were highly commendable. That said, though, Sallust adds that, marriage and motherhood apart, she displayed none of the qualities expected of the conventional *matrona*: she was impulsive, louche, passionate, a perjurer, an accessory to murder, a liar and a spendthrift. Sempronia to Sallust was a kind of anti-*matrona*: while undoubtedly brave and gifted, she broke the mould and stepped far beyond the traditional boundaries laid down for Roman women. Her support for Catiline and the stigma this would have brought, her independence of mind and her ostentatious social skills would have caused outrage and anger in some quarters.[94]

Despite its apparent frequency, female bravery was thought exceptional. Seneca, in the same breath as he extolls *virtus* in women, specifically Helvia and Marcia, qualifies his remarks when he compares them with women generally. Marcia is far removed from the '*infirmitas muliebriter animi*' – womanish weakness of mind – while Helvia is advised to stay away from 'womanly weeping'. All women have their vices, *vitae*.[95]

Matronae sometimes acted bravely *en masse*. The proposal in 195 BC to repeal the *Lex Oppia* of 215 BC evoked distaste and condemnation when women came out from their homes and demonstrated in the Forum to support the repeal. The law had restricted the use of luxuries by women in the wake of the Battle of Cannae some twenty years before. It limited the amount of gold women could own and required that all the assets of wards, single women, and widows be handed over to the State; the wearing of dresses with purple trim and riding in carriages within Rome or nearby towns was also prohibited, except during religious festivals. The feeling among women was that the law had served its purpose and had run its course. Livy records the speech given by Marcus Porcius Cato and his embarrassment and disgust at what he saw as indecorous behaviour ill befitting Roman women.

To give it some context, Cato, generally no friend of women, had famously paraphrased Themistocles when he asserted, 'All men rule their wives; we rule all men; our wives rule us.'[96] He harps back to the days of the ancestors who permitted women no public activity or commercial dealings without a guardian, and who safeguarded the power of fathers and husbands. Cato is appalled by this populist action and the very public demand that they be heard.[97] The repeal, nevertheless, was approved, thanks in no small part to the reasonable arguments of Lucius Valerius:

> For a long time our matrons lived by the highest standards of behaviour without any law, what is the risk when it is repealed, that they will give in to luxury? ... Are we to forbid only women to wear purple? When you, a man, can use purple on your clothes, can you not permit the mother of your family to have a purple cloak, and will you let your horse be more finely saddled than your wife is dressed?

Around the same time Plautus joins in the paranoia and anxiety when he has Megadorus, the misogynistic neighbour of Euclio, the old miser in the *Aulularia, (The Pot of Gold)*, deliver a rant on female extravagance, with particular reference to those employed in the tailoring and clothing trades.[98] The palaver had not died down some 200 years later when Valerius Maximus reminded his readers that 'men of the period had no conception of the extravagance to which women's indomitable passion for novelty in fashion would lead or the extremes to which their brazenness would go'.[99]

Women often played an important and assertive role in some families when crises loomed. After the assassination of Julius Caesar, the family meeting (*consilium*) called by Brutus at Antium included Cato the Younger's half-sister, Servilia, their mother, and Porcia – Brutus's wife and cousin.[100] Servilia is reputed to have influenced even the rigorously conservative Cato and actually ran the *consilium*. The following year she chaired another meeting, which discussed what to do about Lepidus, her son-in-law, who had joined Mark Antony and was declared an outlaw. Casca and Cicero were also present; Servilia also represented the eyes and ears in Rome for Cassius and Brutus when they fled the city.

Cicero relies heavily on the support of his wife, Terentia, during his exile in 58 and 57 BC.[101] His letters to her reflect his isolation, homesickness and affection, both for her and for their daughter: Terentia is 'fidissima atque optima uxor ... mea lux' (most faithful and best of wives ... light of my life). Tullia and Terentia both interceded bravely on Cicero's behalf during his exile.[102] They also had to deal with his business affairs, the slaves and household, as well as the upbringing of their young son; Terentia remained the supportive wife even though their marriage was annulled because of his exile. The two women demonstrated ostentatiously by wearing their hair unkempt and donning black mourning clothes, visiting friends in Rome in order to canvas support for Cicero's return. When their house on the Palatine was torched by Clodius's mob, Terentia sought sanctuary in the house of the Vestal Virgins. According to Plutarch, in earlier days Terentia seems to have been influential in her husband's handling of the Catilinarian conspiracy. In the same piece he records how Cicero himself says that Terentia was more active in his political life than she ever was in domestic affairs.

Ovid's third and last wife is equally supportive and loyal to Ovid in his exile: nine of his *Tristia* are addressed to her. He describes his first two wives as 'useless' and 'faultless but faithless' in the same poem as he expresses his gratitude to the third.[103]

By the end of the Republic, then, women were taking on a more influential role in the family, lending support and encouragement to beleaguered husbands – another indication of the increasing independence of women and their enhanced importance within the Roman family. Given the right cause, they were not afraid to make their case in public demonstration, much to the chagrin of many men.

In the earlier days of the Republic spinning and weaving were crucial skills in Roman households at all levels of society; as we have seen, they became a badge of the good mother and wife. Augustus wore homespun clothes and promoted the traditional skill of weaving,[104] boasting that all the women in his household could spin. Livia's domestic staff comprised five patchers, two supervisors, six women in charge of clothing, one cloak maker, one tailor and two fullers. The Statilii Tauri family had eight spinners, one supervisor of the wool, four patchers, four weavers, two dyers and four fullers.[105] Ovid reminds us that the goddess Pallas Minerva not only teaches children reading and literature but also how to weave and spin.[106] By the mid-first century AD, Lucius Junius Moderatus Columella, the Spanish-born writer on agriculture (*De Re Rustica*) and husbandry complains that homespun clothes were now unfashionable and clothing was routinely bought from shops instead at extortionate prices.[107] Bread-making suffered the same fate when bakeries and bakers' shops replaced home-made bread in the second century BC. Indeed, Aelius Aristeides tells us that only in the poorest households did women do routine housework – slaves did most, if not all, of it.[108] On the catering front, if Trimalchio's Fortunata is anything to go by, the *materfamilias* was heavily involved, in a managerial capacity, in the preparation and serving of meals. Fortunata organises the slaves throughout and her evening is only finished when she has made their supper.[109]

As important as competency in spinning and weaving was in the Roman family, over time it became increasingly redundant and symbolic as Rome society became more and more urbanised. Unlike her Greek counterpart, the better-off Roman woman would spend much of her time supervising the slaves – ensuring that they performed all the mundane tasks a lower-class housewife might be expected to do. This freed her up to go out – shopping, attending festivals and spectacles, visiting friends, educating their children and going to those dinner parties Nepos tells us about.[110]

Apart from bewailing the popularity of shop-bought clothing at the expense of homespun, Columella is nostalgic for the times when women reputedly did do all the housework, when they provided a sanctuary for stressed husbands returning from work to an environment of complete respect and harmony, where even the prettiest wife complemented and complimented her husband's achievements by her own enthusiastic efforts around the house. In so doing Columella isolates an interesting comparison with the old and the new as it relates to the domestic role of women. In those days everything was jointly owned and the woman's domestic work was as important as the husband's public work, obviating the need for household managers. Nowadays, he laments, women are obsessed with luxury and laziness, the making of wool has ceased and women moan when they have to look after the farm just for a few days.

Later, he prescribes a woman's responsibilities in the rural homestead. When the weather prevents work in the fields she should busy herself with wool work, using wool she has prepared earlier. She should check that the slaves are fully occupied; anyone who is ill – or pretending to be – should be taken for treatment (an unproductive slave is no asset); she should never stand still but keep on the move: teaching wool work, learning wool work, doing wool work, checking on the slaves in the kitchen, ensuring that the kitchens, cowsheds and pens are clean; she should periodically clean the sickroom.[111] No rest, then, for the woman of the house.

Despite the exceptions we have described above, women continued to be largely constricted by fathers and by early marriages. A further restriction for women came in the form of guardians, *tutores*. As mothers or aunts, women themselves could not be guardians; as daughters they came under the guardianship of male *tutores*. The death of a father or husband meant the appointment of a guardian to look after the affairs of prepubescent (under fourteen) sons, and of daughters of any age – a privilege originally laid down in Table 5, 1 of the Twelve Tables that women, apart from Vestal Virgins, shared with lunatics and spendthrifts (5, 7).[112] *Tutela impuberis* ended at age twelve for girls and was immediately replaced by *tutela mulieris*. Cicero, and later Ulpian writing in the early third century AD, both explain that women need guardians because women are socially and intellectually inferior, and they have no knowledge of legal or commercial matters.[113] Gaius, in his *Institutiones*, confirmed that, on reaching puberty, boys relinquished their guardians, but not girls – the reason being *propter animi levitatem* – they were considered to be what today some would disparagingly call 'airheads'. Even less flatteringly, when a woman was about to marry, a new guardian would be appointed to arrange her dowry only if the existing one was deaf or insane. Ulpian explains that a guardian's approval is necessary in the following circumstances: 'if they take legal action in accordance with statute or judgment, if they undertake an obligation, if they transact any civil business, if they permit a freedwoman of theirs to cohabit with the slave of another, if they alienate saleable property'.[114]

From a financial standpoint, the best thing for a woman was to be a *vidua* – a woman with no man. This gave her a status of *sui iuris*, and was brought about by widowhood, divorce or by taking over the household after the death of parents and before marriage. Even then, though, a guardian was obligatory. *Viduae* were naturally much sought after by bounty hunters.

However, in something of a concession, the *Leges Iuliae* and the *Lex Papia-Poppaea* allowed freeborn women to be released from guardianship on the birth of their third child (*ius trium liberorum*), freedwomen on the birth of the fourth;[115] one of the benefits of this independence was that women could now make their own wills. Women had some protection, in theory at least, from rape by their guardians, who could face a sentence of deportation and confiscation of property if convicted.[116]

The power of the guardian waned over time as women became more independent and business-minded: women could appeal against guardians' decisions to the magistrates; they could also apply for a guardian to be replaced. Terentia's guardian was Philotemus, whom Cicero came to loathe.

Women were restricted in their ability to control the destinies of their children. All children fell under the control of the father, the *paterfamilias* in the *familia*, daughters as *filiafamilias*. Women had no legal control over their children: the father, in law at least, had custody of his daughter's children, determined how they were educated and whom they married, and controlled their property. In practice, the extent of this power was probably quite variable and depended on the relationship between father and daughter: we have already seen how some mothers looked after their children's education. Nevertheless, *patria potestas* prevailed and, for widows and unmarried mothers, influence over their children was further diminished by the guardian. Even after divorce, any children remained under the power of the mother's father, whatever the child's best interests.

It is difficult to assess just how far the plays of Plautus and Terence reflect actual Roman experience since the plays are coloured by Greek mores, as portrayed in Menander and other playwrights of the New Comedy. Of the men and women in Plautus's audiences, more would have had experience of a marriage than would be familiar with the plays of Menander: if, then, Plautus or Terence were to raise a laugh then they would surely have imbued their characters with traits and mannerisms that were recognisable to their audiences from their own everyday experience; their plots would reflect Roman life to some degree and their characters would be recognisable as Romans.[117] The prologue to the *Poenulus* is a case in point, with Plautus playing to a strictly Roman audience; here he admonishes the *matronae* in the audience for their irritating laughter, and then requests that the wet nurses do not bring in crying babies.[118] These comedies are particularly important because they shed light on aspects of non-elite Roman family life; unlike much of the rest of the literary evidence they describe domestic situations in the lower classes.

Anna Raia has counted the appearances of women in Plautus:

> The fifty-four women in Plautus's plays – and there are sixty-one if we count the seven women who are discussed but never appear – can be grouped into five stereotypes: the *puella* or young maiden, the *matrona* or married woman, the *meretrix* or courtesan, the *ancilla* or handmaid, and the *anus* or old woman. The comedies feature: eleven *puellae*, four of whom are invisible; thirteen *matronae*, two of whom are never seen; nineteen *meretrices*, one of whom doesn't appear; twelve *ancillae;* and five personages who fit the category of the *anus*.[119]

This compares with 154 male roles; three of the plays have no speaking female parts at all: the *Captivi, Pseudolus* and *Trinummus*. Reasons for the imbalance may be that Plautus was mirroring the restrictive social situation of women in Greece, that he was reflecting the subordinate position of women in his own society, or that it was simply easier to limit female characters from a production point of view because actors in Rome were all men. A combination of all three of these reasons may be responsible.

A number of characters are drawn in such a way that would confirm that Plautus echoes standard Roman attitudes to contemporary women, interpolating Roman elements into his

Greek originals.[120] Of the *puellae,* Persa, in the play of the same name, stands out as having all the qualities of a marriageable young girl: she is honourable and bravely defends her reputation, her *pudicitia* and *virtus,* in the face of her duplicitous father and the *leno* (pimp); she nevertheless displays *pietas* in her obedience to her father. In short, Persa has all the qualities of a potentially fine Roman *matrona.*

Of the *matronae,* in the *Casina,* Myrrhina advises her friend, Cleostrata, to be the good, traditional wife: she should be *morigera* – compliant with her husband, grateful for her home, possessions, security, her husband's success; she should ignore his infidelities. In the *Stichus* the father, Antipho, asks his daughters' advice on the *optimae matronae mores,* what makes the the best kind of wife. Panegyris and her unnamed sister, both themselves married, describe a woman who does not gossip, who chooses right over wrong, does nothing she will later regret, and who is happy and patient in good times and in bad. Again, all qualities traditionally prescribed for the good *matrona.* Incidentally, the sisters themselves refuse to remarry, staying faithful as *univirae* to their husbands, who have long been absent on business.

Other Plautine *matronae* are less well equipped for the role. Indeed, of the eleven who make an appearance, all are of maturer years: the young, novice wife presumably had no comedic role to play – the older *matrona* was a much more fertile source of laughs. This possibly reflected real life – it may have been considered gratuitous or inappropriate to make fun of a very young girl in the early years of the serious business of marriage – her situation simply was not funny. More typical of Plautus's *matronae* are Artemona in the *Asinaria,* Cleostrata in the *Casina,* Dorippa in the *Mercator,* and Matrona in the *Menaechmi.* These four women represent a Plautine *matrona* stereotype: they are all *irata,* angry women (and in no way *morigera*), and *dotata,* dowried. The angry woman nagged, spied, dominated and was conspicuous; their dowries brought with them all sorts of problems, making the wife thus endowed bossy, imperious, arrogant, self-important and expensive. While these contradict traditional *matrona* qualities, they may reflect the real world in that they chime with the criticism and satire levelled at conspicuous women by later writers such as Catullus, Martial and Juvenal. They reflect a degree of real experience that is described in poetry and satire, albeit exaggerated and honed to fit in with the requirements of the genre and the expectations of readerships.

In general, Plautus is somewhat negative, misogynistic even, in his portrayal of women.[121] In the *Truculentus*, the *meretrix* Phronesium is clearly greedy and meretricious – 'ut mos est mulierum' (that's just how women are)[122] – all women it seems, not just prostitutes; later Phronesium admits that women really are even worse than they are given credit for, and that women prefer doing bad things to doing good.[123] How women in the audience reacted to such generalisations it is impossible to know; we can assume, though, that such stereotypes were all too familiar to the men, and that this will have coloured Plautus's depiction of his female characters.

Alcmene, the wife of Amphitryo in the *Amphitryo,* is a very complex character. As Anna Reia points out, she exhibits characteristics of the *pudica puella*, the *amans amica*, the loving girlfriend, the *matrona irata*, the *angry wife* and, in her adulterous affair with Jupiter, the *meretrix.* Plautus probably draws on a New Comedy character which in turn owes something to Sophocles' Deianeira in the *Women of Trachis*, and to the ideal, *univira matrona* from Plautus's own Rome.[124] Her (unsuspected) dalliance with Jupiter is one of the few descriptions of physical love in Roman literature as articulated by a woman; her dignified protestations of fidelity to Amphitryo on his (real) return embody the essence of good matronly behaviour, indignant as she is at being thought otherwise. Alcmene is indeed a paradox: Plautus has her passionately vocalise her love in an ostentatious way that was at odds with good matronly decorum and objectionable to men; he then has her proudly list her credentials as a good *matrona.*

Plautus died in 184 BC; the plays of Terence were being performed around 170 and 160 BC. The eloquence of Alcmene may be seen as a precursor to the much freer expression found a few years later in Terence and is indicative of how quickly things were moving on in Roman society in that short time. Chremes, the *paterfamilias* in the *Andrea*, puts his daughter's happiness first when it comes to the choice of a husband; Antipho in the *Phormio* marries a young girl because he loves her, against the wishes of his father and despite the fact that she has no dowry, and is an orphan from a family of no standing. In the *Hecyra* (*The Mother in Law*), we have a play whose action is monopolised by women: two mothers-in-law, a courtesan and a pregnant daughter(-in-law)/wife. Pamphilus marries Philumena to please his father, even though he really loves Bacchis, a prostitute. His predicament prevents him from consummating the marriage and he continues to consort with the increasingly capricious Bacchis. In the end he warms towards Philumena, impressed by the dignity, reticence and modesty she shows, despite the rejection that is *her* predicament. Pamphilus is then called away, at which point Philumena, who has discovered that she is pregnant, leaves the marital home and returns to her parents: she had been raped just before her marriage. Her father, Laches, decides that his wife, Sostrata, is to blame for the rift between the two families because 'all mothers-in-law hate their daughters-in-law'. Pamphilus returns and, according to his rights, rejects Philumena and the baby. It turns out, though, that Pamphilus was the drunken rapist, as revealed by the ring he took from Philumena during the assault, and then gave to Bacchis. He is finally reunited with his wife and child.

Terence's characters are more moral and responsible to each other – reflecting perhaps the gradual breakdown of the strict, impersonal and less intimate family relationships prevalent in Rome in earlier years. Compared with Plautus there is much less caricature and more sympathy, particularly with regard to older people, fathers and women.[125]

In that they lived in the household, the concubine or *paelex* was an integral part of some Roman families. Festus records the existence of the *paelex* from around the reign of King Numa in the eighth century, where they are forbidden to touch the Temple of Juno – transgressions required a loosening of the hair and the sacrifice of a lamb. Scipio Africanus kept a concubine, famously tolerated, indeed rewarded, by his wife Tertia Aemilia;[126] conservative Cato the Censor kept one and eventually married her. At the Imperial level both Domitian and Commodus had them. For example, Plautus (Casina in the *Casina*), and Pliny the Younger (Lutulla), both mention concubinage, *contubernium*, quite casually.

So what do we learn from this survey of Roman girls and women in the domestic setting? Funerary inscriptions are often impersonal and formulaic but some are tinged with personal, real emotion. They idealise what was expected of the Roman wife but, in some instances, they show that wives loved their husbands, sons their mothers, husbands their wives and parents their children, girls and boys. As a newborn the baby girl was vulnerable to exposure or abandonment either at the whim of her father or because of poverty. The girl or woman was in the power of her father and, after marriage, was expected to take an active but discreet role in the running of the marital home. As a *matrona* she was expected to be virtuous, strong-willed but not obtrusively so, conversational, modestly dressed, loyal, compliant, and to look after her children, particularly their education. The *univira* was the ideal, the worker in wool was highly respected – both were badges of the good wife. Literature gives examples of genuine affection between spouses and the love of parents for their children. As time went by richer women acquired a greater degree of domestic authority and influence, delegating mundane and menial tasks to slaves and enjoying a social life outside the home. They nevertheless remained under the control of fathers, husbands and guardians, although increasing wealth and independence allowed them to take more of the initiative in public and in family matters. They were recognised for their determination and bravery both as legends and as real-world women – but they were never able to shrug off the traditional suspicion and discrimination vocalised by Roman men when they did exceed their matronly obligations. Women had little legal responsibility for their own children; politically, financially and, as we shall see, in religion and in education, women remained largely powerless and sidelined.

2

BETROTHAL, MARRIAGE, THE WEDDING

The Roman woman was essentially domestic and domesticated; her function as a wife was to bear children and keep the home while her husband went about his work, advancing his career or perfecting his trade. The very word for marriage, *matrimonium*, has its roots in *mater*, mother: marriage literally spelt motherhood. In the early days of the Republic the Roman woman married into a state of *manus* – dependence before the law; she had little chance of initiating divorce, no rights over property and no jurisdiction over her children. If a woman's husband died when she was pregnant, the baby became the property of her late husband's family. A woman was someone else's property throughout her life: first her father's, then her husband's and finally, depending on circumstances, her son's. She was, first and foremost, daughter, wife and mother. If a woman's father or husband died, she did not become independent: a guardian was appointed to look after her affairs. Even when *manus* marriage became obsolete, to be replaced by a freer form of marriage, and when divorce became more common, things changed little for the average woman. Livy asserts that a woman's servitude lasted so long as her male relatives were alive.[1]

Girls of the upper classes seem to have married, in general, earlier than their counterparts lower down the social scale: the former married between their early and late teens while the latter tied the knot in their late teens and early twenties. As menarche usually occurred around the ages of thirteen and fourteen it seems very likely that some marriages were prepubescent.[2] Early marriage in girls suited men; apart from the respectability and sexual gratification it brought, a man who was married could expedite his *cursus honorum* and climb the ladder of political, military or forensic success.

There were restrictions on marriage. These included the Twelve Table law banning marriage between patricians and plebeians – repealed in 445 BC by the *Lex Canuleia,* with children able to inherit the father's social status; the Augustan *Lex Julia de maritandis ordinibus* prohibiting marriage between senators and their near relatives and freedwomen; marriage to convicted adulteresses or those in a dubious profession (actors, dancers, prostitutes); serving soldiers below a certain rank (although many soldiers did marry local women) until the reign of Septimius Severus when the ban was relaxed in AD 197; provincial officials were prohibited from marrying women from the province; guardians could not marry their wards.[3] *Incestum* originally prohibited second cousins and nearer relatives from marrying but over time was relaxed to allow even first cousins to marry by the second century BC, for example Marcus Aurelius and the younger Faustina. *Incestum* was punishable by death.

The Apostle Paul gives some of the basics in his *Opinions,* from around AD 150: a couple can get engaged before or after puberty; marriage cannot take place without the consent of the father where he retains *patria potestas;* the insane cannot be married, subsequent insanity is not grounds for dissolving a valid marriage; a freedman who marries his patroness or her daughter will be sentenced to hard labour in the mines; a man cannot have both a wife and a concubine; marriage is ended either by divorce, death or captivity (by a foreign power) lasting over three years.[4]

Betrothal comprised mutual promises (*sponsiones*) – essentially an informal agreement to marry (*stipulatio*). For the future groom's family the promise was to take the bride into marriage; for the bride's family it was, until the first century BC, to deliver her into the groom's *manus* and provide a dowry. When a man proposed to a girl, however young, he immediately benefited from the financial and political privileges enjoyed by a married man; on the other hand, a woman was not allowed to betroth herself to a prepubescent male.[5] In the fourth century AD the promise to marry was underwritten by *arrha sponsalica,* an earnest payment.

The betrothal was marked with a kiss and the slipping of an iron ring (*anulus pronubus*) onto the third finger of the future bride's left hand. According to Aulus Gellius this finger is significant because it is connected by the autonomic nervous system to the heart.[6] A party – the *sponsalia* – ensued. The termination of an engagement could be initiated by either party without penalty; it simply required the doom-laden words *condicione tua non utor*, the man to return any part of the dowry that had been paid and the woman to return any gifts from her intended husband.[7] A man or woman who got engaged or married without terminating an existing betrothal was guilty of disgraceful behaviour, *infamia*. Under Severus a man could prosecute an unfaithful fiancée for *stuprum* and adultery, although there was no corresponding obligation for him to be faithful so long as his indiscretion did not involve a married woman or an unmarried Roman citizen. We shall see below how betrothals were abused in a bid to circumvent the *Lex Julia*.

Betrothal usually led to marriage, of course. Gaius, in his *Institutiones*, outlines how *manus* marriage worked. It was a state of subordination to the husband and came about in three ways: by usage (*usus*), sharing of bread (*confarreatio*) or by a kind of arranged sale (*coemptio*).

In *usus* the wife passed from *patria potestas* into her husband's family after one year of uninterrupted cohabitation – *capitis deminutio minima* – and the wife became *materfamilias*. By entering into *manus* (*conventio in manum*) the wife fell under the control (*manus*) of her husband and her property became his; however, she did enjoy intestacy rights on a par with those of his children. If the husband died and her father was deceased she was then placed under the authority of the husband's closest relative on the paternal side, guardianship (*tutela*), theoretically for life. The original objective of guardianship was to safeguard the woman's property; while she could inherit and bequeath her patrimony as she wished, the management of affairs such as the purchase of slaves or land, dowries and *manus* all came under the authority of the guardian, the *tutor*. For a woman, marrying into *manus* also meant renouncing her religion and assuming her husband's; she adopted his gods and his ancestors.

Under *manus* a wife's property was taken over by her husband, as were any gifts or bequests. From 186 BC widows could be granted the right by their husbands to choose their own guardian[8] and, if widowed or divorced, became legally independent (*sui iuris*) and able to make a will; dowries on divorce were returnable to the wife, subject to conditions. On the minus side the wife, as mother, had no legal authority over the actions of her children, who remained under the *potestas* of the father; she could neither adopt nor, before AD 390, be a guardian to her children, even if she were widowed.[9]

By the end of the second century BC *manus,* not surprisingly, had become virtually obsolete: free marriage had become the norm under the late Republic and Empire as Romans became wealthier and the richer families sought to protect the family's fortunes by ensuring that the bride's property remained with her. Apart from the ability to own property, the wife, although under her father's *potestas,*[10] was legally independent of her husband and could initiate divorce proceedings. This independence of sorts no doubt added to the growing instability of the institution of marriage. The fact that a law existed to outlaw the practice suggests that female slaves used marriage to their master as a means to achieving freedom: soon after marriage the woman would desert the master.[11]

If (according to the Twelve Tables) the wife absented herself from the marital home for three nights during a year, then *manus* was avoided. The advantage, as with widowhood and divorce, was that the women, in common with *viduae,* unmarried women, became legally independent (*sui iuris*) when her last male ascendant died, and could own property and inherit equally with any brothers;[12] women were then free from the control of a husband or father.

Confarreatio, sharing of bread, was an uncommon religious ceremony largely restricted to patrician families and to those applying to hold various priesthoods for which birth from a *confarreatio* marriage was obligatory: the rex sacrorum, the flamen dialis, the flamen martialis and the flamen quirinalis. *Confarreatio* involved sacrifices to Jupiter Farreus of a sheep, emmer bread (*farreus*), fruit and *mola salsa;*[13] ten witnesses as well as the Pontifex Maximus and the flamen dialis were present. Divorce was very difficult and could only be instigated by the husband, then later through a dissolving ceremony, *diffareatio*; in the case of flamen dialis divorce was impossible – the only time it seemed to have happened was by special dispensation from Domitian.[14]

Coemptio was a legal procedure in which the husband notionally bought his wife. With five witnesses in attendance he paid one 'penny' to the father or guardian (the weigher) and received his bride in return.[15]

Marriage itself was in some ways something of a nebulous concept; no ceremony was legally required. The trigger was the intention of both parties to cohabit and form a union together in which they would recognise each other as man and wife, *affectio maritalis*.[16] If there was any outward display of 'being married' it was simply the act of leading the bride into the groom's home, *domum deducta*, where, henceforth, she would live: in *domicilium matrimonii*. Once she was over that threshold, the bride assumed the status and responsibilities of a *matrona*. According to Modestinus, 'marriage is the union of a man and a woman and the sharing of the rest of their lives'.[17] According to Ulpian,[18] 'just having sex does not a marriage make, what does is a favourable disposition toward the idea of marriage'. A man could get married without actually going to the ceremony – *in absentia* – through a letter of intent or through a messenger slave; a woman, because of *domum deducta*, had to show up.[19] Ulpian gives us the amusing story in which Cinna said that if a man married by proxy and then fell into the Tiber on his way home from a dinner party (presumably celebrating his *in absentia* wedding), then the wife must mourn his death.

Wedding ceremonies may have been optional but they were common. Our evidence for the Roman wedding ceremony is scanty to say the least; however, it is possible to piece together some detail from various sources. Typically, among middle- and upper-class families, the bride was specially made up; her hair was done in a traditionally primitive style – separated into six locks with headbands and piled on top (*tutulus*); the parting was done using an iron spearhead (*hasta recurva*); she wore a wreath of marjoram (*amaracus*). Her dress (*tunica recta*) – for one-time use – was a plain white tunic fastened with the 'knot of Hercules' (a good luck charm) which had been spun on a vintage loom; her veil (*flammeum*) was a flame-red headscarf that matched her shoes.[20] She would give up her childhood dolls, toys and girl's dress (*toga praetexta*) to the household gods. The ceremony took place in the house of the bride's father, where the words of consent were spoken (*Ubi tu Gaius, ego Gaia*) and the matron of honour (*pronuba*) joined the couple's right hands (*dextrarum iunctio*), the high point, the defining point of the ceremony. A pig was sacrificed, the *tabulae nuptales* – the marriage contract (where there was one) – was presented by the *auspex*, signed, and the first instalment of the dowry was handed over.[21] The guests cried out, '*Feliciter*' (Good luck). Then there was the feast (*cena*) paid for by the groom (limited by Augustus to 1,000 sesterces), after which the bride was formally taken from her mother's arms and escorted to the groom's house by three boys whose parents had still to be living: one on the bride's right, one on the left and the third in front carrying a torch. The crowds would chant the *Thalassius* as they passed by.[22] On arrival at the groom's house the torch was thrown away and the bride smeared the doorway with oil, fat and sheep's wool. The groom lifted the bride over the threshold to avoid that unlucky stumble. She then touched fire and water and was led to the bedroom by *univirae*.[23]

Statius's *epithalamium* gives more detail.[24] The divinely beautiful Violentilla surpasses all the *matronae* of Latium, and is urged by the goddess Venus to make the most of her beauty and renounce her chastity for Stella, her soon-to-be husband. She is financially independent but her mind is richer still. Much of the content of the poem is conventional, but the allusion to wealth and intelligence is an interesting indication, perhaps, of what Lucius Arruntius Stella was looking for in a wife.

Sham weddings were not unknown during the early Empire: Nero 'married' a male lover, Pythagoras, in AD 64 and, according to Suetonius, in between raping a Vestal Virgin and committing incest with his mother, had a young boy, Sporus, castrated before marrying him. Around the same time Sempronius Gracchus married a boy cornet player with a dowry of 400,000 sesterces.[25] Valeria Messalina, wife of the emperor Claudius, married a common Roman citizen, allegedly with the knowledge of her husband. The senator Gaius Silius had the dubious privilege of being Messalina's target; she forced him to divorce his wife, the aristocratic Junia Silana, sister of Caligula's first wife, Junia Claudilla. It all ended in tears, though, when Claudius had both Messalina and Silius executed, not for the marriage, but for a plot to depose him. Martial describes the wedding between Callistratus and Afro, complete with dowry. In the Republic Cicero had insinuated a gay marriage when he attacked Mark Antony in the *Philippics* for marrying Gaius Scribonius Curio, 'who set you up in a steady and stable marriage as if he had given you a *stola'*, the traditional dress of a *matrona*; the slur being that Antony is weak, submissive and lacking *virtus*.[26]

Superstition, practicalities and religion played their parts; there were certain days on which marriage ceremonies were avoided because they were deemed unlucky. Kalends, Nones and Ides were out because, as Varro tells us, the days after these were 'black days';[27] *Mundus Cereris*: the three days of the year (24 August, 5 October, and 8 November) when ghosts were afoot because the doors of Hades (*mundus*) gaped open; the Lemuralia (9, 11 and 13 May) devoted to celebrating the festival of the dead: hence, *mense Maio malae nubent* (they marry ill who marry in May); 18–21 February for similar reasons: the Parentalia in honour of family ancestors; May and early June because time was better spent farming the land, or because the cleaning of the Temple of Vesta by the Vestal Virgins was not completed until 15 June; 1, 9 and 23 March were to be avoided because the dancing priests of Mars, the Salii, were moving the shields.[28] In short, a wedding should take place on a happy day, *hilaris dies*. One famous anecdote from the end of the second century BC involved Caecilia who was married to Metellus; she was anxious to find out what the future held for her betrothed niece so she and the niece took up post in a temple and waited – the gods were reticent, until the bored niece asked to sit down next to her aunt. Her aunt innocently, but prophetically, invited her to take her place – and dropped down dead; Metellus then married the niece.

Day of joy notwithstanding, so long as three main conditions were met then the marriage was permitted and legal (*iustum matrimonium*).[29] The first was *conubium* – legal right to marry;

slaves had no *conubium* and *conubium* did not exist between Roman citizens and foreigners; the second required that the couple had reached marriageable age, or puberty: twelve for girls and fourteen for boys; the third was consent between the man and his wife. Marriage and betrothal (*sponsalia*) were both consensual in Roman law; according to Paul a marriage only exists if all parties are in agreement. According to Ulpian, non-objection on the part of the girl was tantamount to consent; she could only refuse where there were questions regarding the moral integrity of the groom.[30]

Once married, the bride immediately assumed the full day-to-day responsibilities of the *matrona* as *materfamilias*. She ran the house, managing the slaves and acting as hostess to her husband's guests and to any women visitors for whom she would have organised the invitations. She would go with her husband to social events and to dinner parties; she may sometimes help with running any family business and generally assisting the husband on his journey along his *cursus honorum*. Some would find time to go to the theatre or the games. Motherhood, especially of sons, brought more respect, widowhood more still. The wife would keep her spouse apprised of the news back home when he was away in the provinces running foreign territories or fighting Rome's enemies; only from the reign of Tiberius could she accompany him on his postings overseas.[31]

On marriage the woman took the social rank of her new husband, thus providing an opportunity for upward social mobility; up until the middle of the second century AD she was able to retain this status on divorce or widowhood.

Plutarch illustrates the deference expected of a wife in his *Moralia*. Marital harmony, *concordia*, was the goal but only on the basis that the husband was clearly in charge: things may be difficult in the marriage at first but the new wife must persist, avoiding any use of potions or charms; she should worship the gods her husband worships, not her own. The wife who is miserable when he is in a jocular mood – and vice versa – is quite useless; such behaviour shows her as peevish and mean-spirited: her emotions should be dictated by the moods of her husband.[32] Arguing with him in public is to be avoided – she should acquiesce (be *morigera*); she should renounce her own friends and embrace those of her husband.

Cicero gives us an interesting insight into an unhappy marriage. Cicero's brother, Quintus, was married to Pomponia, Atticus's sister: in one letter we find him telling Atticus, during a troubled period of their troubled marriage, that a recent row was due to Pomponia's tetchiness and rudeness, while Quintus was a model of patience.[33] Partiality notwithstanding, Cicero was quite appalled by Pomponia's, admittedly unreasonable, behaviour. After their divorce, Quintus thought better of remarrying, preferring instead the sanctuary of a single bed.

Plutarch, in his *Precepts of Wedlock*, offers another insight. Criticised for divorcing Papiria when all looked well with the marriage from the outside, Aemilius Paullus gives this explanation:

> It is a mistake for a woman to rely on her wealth, her breeding and her looks; she should think more of the qualities which affect her husband's life, of those traits of character which make for harmony in domestic relationships. Instead of being impassive or irritating in everyday life, she must be sympathetic, inoffensive and affectionate ... it is a succession of small inconspicuous pin-pricks and irritations, occurring day after day between a man and his wife, which destroys the marriage.[34]

Women, married or otherwise, and drink were not a happy mix. Whatever its effect on men, alcohol was seen as a catalyst for sexual infelicities in women. Juvenal probably spoke for many men when he asked, 'Quid enim Venus ebria curat?' (What does love care when she is drunk?).[35] Servius (*ad* Virgil, *Aeneid*, 1, 37) says that in the old days women were forbidden to drink wine, except at a few religious festivals, citing as evidence Egnatius Metennius, who whipped his wife to death for drinking from a pitcher; he literally got away with murder when tried by Romulus. Gellius (10, 23, 1–2) confuses the issue, though, when he claims that women never drank *temetum* but did drink other wines. *Temetum* was associated with sacrificial wine so, by implication, this explains how women were excluded from sacrificial activity. According to Valerius Maximus, women in the old days did not drink because it led to depravity: a drunk woman was only one step away from a fornicating woman. (2, 1, 5).

Pliny the Elder leaves a number of unfortunate drink-related stories in his chapter on viticulture. He tells how, according to Fabius Pictor, a *matrona* was starved to death by her family because she broke open the box containing the keys to the wine cellar. He explains how Cato asserted the right male relatives had of kissing their women (*ius osculi*) when they met, not to show affection or courtesy, but to ascertain whether they had been drinking – an early form of breathalisation. Gnaeus Domitius once judged that a woman had drunk more than was good for her, and without her husband's knowledge; he fined her a sum equal to the value of her dowry.[36] Alcohol was implicated in the exile of Julia, Augustus's daughter, to Pandateria – not only had she to put up with the lonely isolation but her father decreed that the island would be alcohol free.

Counselling for alcohol abuse or wife battering was doubtless unavailable, but marriage guidance, nevertheless, there was. The temple of Juno Viriplaca (husband appeaser) on the Palatine Hill offered reconciliation between squabbling couples.[37]

Roman girls could be betrothed at twelve and married within the year.[38] An example of a thirteen-year-old wife can be found on an inscription found in Gaul; it remembers Blandinia Martiola, who died aged eighteen years, nine months and five days, the wife of Sequanian, a plasterer. We have already met Aurelia Philematium; her marriage when she was seven was precocious even by Roman standards.[39]

Pliny had already been married twice before when, aged around forty, he wed the much younger Calpurnia Fabata in AD 100. We have seen Quintilian's grief at the death of his nineteen-year-old wife, the mother of two deceased sons even then.[40] We have also noted Pliny's concern that the young Minicia died before she could be married off.[41] Faggura, wife of Julianus, was married and a mother by the time she was fourteen years old.[42] Tullia, Cicero's daughter, got engaged when she was twelve, married at sixteen and was widowed when she was twenty-two. Octavia, the emperor Claudius's daughter, married at thirteen while Agrippina, mother of Nero, married when she was twelve. On the other hand some elite women married later: Julia, Caesar's daughter, was twenty when she married Pompey; Agrippina Maior was about eighteen when she and Germanicus tied the knot in AD 4; and Antonia Minor was around twenty when she married Drusus.

Harkness shows that inscriptional evidence backs up the early age of female marriage, particularly in the middle- and upper-class families who were more likely to be able to afford tombstones. From the 171 inscriptions in the study, sixty-seven (39 per cent) showed women married before they were fifteen and 127 before the age of nineteen (74 per cent).[43]

Most marriages were arranged by the *paterfamilias*, or by another male relative, as a function of his *patria potestas.* Just how important a duty this was, and how vital it was to find the right match, is shown in a letter by Pliny to Junus Mauricus who had asked him to find a husband for his niece; her father, Arulenus Rusticus, had been executed by Domitian in AD 93. Pliny has just the right man – the equestrian Minicius Acilianus – who can boast all the credentials worthy, not just of the girl, but of the family as a whole.[44]

The father's consent was a legal requirement where one or both of the partners were under *patria potestas*; however, not surprisingly, some older couples took the initiative and made their own decisions – Cicero's daughter, Tullia, much to her absent father's dismay but with her mother's complicity, proceeded with her third marriage to the infamous Publius Cornelius Dolabella.[45] Tullia's previous marriages were less controversial: she was betrothed at twelve in 67 BC to her first husband, Gaius Calpurnius Piso Frugi and married him in 63 BC; in 57 BC he died and she was betrothed to Furius Crassipes when she was twenty-three; the subsequent marriage was dissolved in 51 BC.[46]

Livy tells the, probably apocryphal, story of how in 187 BC Scipio was persuaded by members of the Senate, while dining with them on the Capitol, to marry his daughter off to Tiberius Gracchus, which he duly promised to do. When he got home, he had to face a wife who was outraged that she had not been consulted, even if the intended was the famous Tiberius Gracchus.[47] The tale is replicated in the next generation when Tiberius Gracchus was betrothed to the daughter of Appius Claudius.[48] Cato the Younger blocked the marriage of two of his daughters to Pompey and to Pompey's son.[49] Couples did have recourse to appeal where the *pater* refused to sanction a betrothal.

Arranged marriages were not necessarily the emotionally arid, restrictive and restricting contracts they are often made out to be; as in various societies today, they probably involved more mutual consent, *concordia*, than we have actual evidence for. They were prudent arrangements designed to protect the family politically, economically and socially. No doubt Roman parents would have argued that the arrangement was intended to be in the daughter's best interests; how many twelve- or thirteen-year-olds would have been in a position to make an informed decision about who to marry?[50]

A 13 BC marriage contract survives from Egypt and, although it probably owes as much to Egyptian legislation as it does to Roman, it is, nevertheless, interesting. Thermion and Apollonius, and Thermion's guardian, agree to share their lives together (*affectio maritalis*) and that Thermion has delivered a dowry, including a pair of gold earrings weighing three quarters and some silver drachmas. He will now feed and clothe her; he will not abuse her verbally or physically, kick her out or marry another woman – if he does any of these things, the dowry goes back. For her part, she will fulfil her obligations; she will not sleep away from the home without his permission, she will not wreck the house or have an affair – if she does, she loses the dowry.[51] Cato the Elder was probably not altogether typical when he famously expelled Manilius from the Senate for publicly kissing his wife in front of their daughter and, even more amusingly and eccentrically, admitted that *he* only ever kissed his wife during thunderstorms.[52]

A dowry (*dos*), certainly among the wealthier classes, was an expected, though not legally required, part of the bride's baggage. By the early Empire, around 1 million sesterces payable in three annual instalments was the norm among the wealthier classes. It became the husband's property but was recoverable on divorce, or if the husband died after the death of his father-in-law. Valerius Maximus[53] records that Gnaeus Cornelius Scipio Calvus, while on active service in Spain, requested leave to go home to arrange his daughter's dowry; the Senate was reluctant to allow such a key commander to leave the field and voted a dowry out of the public purse worth 40,000 asses – a small amount compared with later dowries, but significant for the time. The precedent for such public largesse was set around 280 BC when the Senate voted a dowry for the daughter of the famously incorruptible Gaius Fabricius Luscinus Monocularis, whose family was in financial straits.

Polybius tells how Scipio Africanus generously paid the dowries of his two daughters in one-off payments to their respective husbands, Tiberius Gracchus and Scipio Nasica – 50 talents each (about £1.25 million today).[54] In 50 BC, Cicero was unable to find the money to pay the third instalment of Tullia's dowry in her marriage to Dolabella. Cicero toyed with the idea of arranging a divorce and writing off the first two instalments which had been paid.[55] Financial embarrassment came again in 47 BC when he divorced Terentia and had to find the money to repay the dowry; his scheme to remarry and win a new dowry failed when the marriage to Publilia, his well-off ward, ended after a few months.[56] Terentia, however, remarried and lived to the age of 103.[57]

Aemilius Paulus married one of his daughters, Aemilia Paulla Secunda, to a member of the illustrious, though by then not so affluent, Aelia dynasty – Q. Aelius Tubero – giving a dowry in silver of 2 lbs from the booty collected after his victory over Perseus of Macedon at the Battle of Pydna in 171 BC.[58]

We need go no further than Pliny to realise the importance of the dowry: twice he generously contributes to the dowries of young brides. Once to the daughter of Quintilianus, who needed clothes and a retinue of servants appropriate to her new husband's social standing; the other to Calvina, a relative of his who was deep in debt. As well as contributing 100,000 sesterces to her dowry he paid off her debts, making himself sole creditor, and then wrote off her debt to him.[59] Aulus Gellius records that dowry recovery had become so complicated by the end of the Republic that Sulpicius Rufus wrote a book on it.[60] On divorce a husband whose wife had been found guilty of adultery might retain one-sixth of the dowry; as he would have custody of the children he would also keep one-sixth for each child up to a maximum of three children. Repayments were made in three instalments unless the husband had been proven adulterous, in which case it was repaid in one lump sum. After Augustus's Julian laws a wife found guilty of adultery was punished by exile and a fine equal to half her dowry.

The dowry was not a gift to the husband; its purpose was to help defray the extra costs incurred in accommodating and maintaining the wife and possibly her slaves. The dowry was usually invested in land, with only the profits available to spend.

As we have seen, double standards persisted in how extramarital sex and adultery were perceived. An adulterous husband attracted no stigma; an adulterous woman did, and much worse, as Cato the Elder tells: if a man discovers his wife's adulterous behaviour he can kill her with impunity; when the boot is on the other foot, she can do absolutely nothing.[61] Under the *Lex Julia* women convicted of adultery joined the group of fallen and stigmatised women that included prostitutes, actresses, dancing girls, women with criminal records – collectively the shameful, *probrosae* – and were forbidden to marry freeborn citizens of Rome. They could not testify in a court of law, nor could they, while unmarried, inherit. Prostitution was sometimes the only escape.

The old slave woman in Plautus's *Mercator* vocalises the hypocrisy, bewailing the legal double standard and declaring that there would be more men living on their own than there were women if they were judged the same in law.[62] To Ovid, the man who worried about his wife's adultery was nothing short of provincial: 'rusticus est'.[63] At the imperial level, Scribonia was divorced by Augustus because of her intolerance to his affairs; her long-lasting successor, Livia, was tolerant. Claudius's errant wives were sensible enough to ensure that his bed was warmed by surrogates. The double standard was not lost on Plutarch: 'A husband who bars his wife from the pleasures in which he himself indulges is like a man who surrenders to the enemy and tells his wife to go on fighting.'[64]

Divorce was uncomplicated – it simply required the evaporation of *affectio maritalis* by one or both parties. And, by the end of the Republic, it became relatively common – probably much more so among the upper and middle classes than the lower classes for whom there is less information and evidence, and for whom little was to be gained apart from the prospect of further poverty. Caution is required in relation to assessments of its frequency, however, since a couple, if in *potestate*, could not initiate proceedings; they had to go through the father, a procedure which probably sometimes acted as something of a filter, if not a brake. Moreover, some of the literary evidence for rampant divorcing comes largely from Seneca, Juvenal and Martial – not the most objective of social commentators – who saw it as another sign of permissiveness among women: 'the woman who marries so frequently doesn't actually marry – she's a legal adulteress (adultera lege est)', according to Martial;[65] a whore offends him less than a serial divorcer. Rapsaet-Charlier's study of 562 women of senatorial rank and their marital activity between 10 BC and AD 200 revealed only twenty-seven definite and twenty-four possible divorces, twenty of which were in imperial families, mainly Julio-Claudians.[66] Five of the definites were claimed by one woman, Vistilla, who, Pliny the Elder tells us, had seven children by six different husbands.[67]

Naturally, divorce (along with death) was a significant factor in spawning second and third marriages. In the early days of the Republic serial marriage was, however, rare; Plutarch says that divorce was restricted to men divorcing women on certain specific grounds: where the wife poisoned the children, stole the house keys or drank (too much) wine. Where other, spurious, reasons were put forward as grounds the men were punished by confiscation of their property, half of which went to Ceres, the other half to the wife.[68] According to Dionysius of Halicarnassus these restrictions meant that were no divorces at all in the first 520 years of Rome's existence.[69] This, of course, conveniently ignores the Twelve Tables' 'res tuas tibi habeto' – take your things and go (oh, and leave the keys). However, Spurius Carvilius Ruga spoilt it all in 231 BC when he successfully sued for divorce because his wife was unable to bear children and provide an heir – to Spurius, the whole point of their marriage. Whether it is true or not, the case is interesting in itself: apart from assuming that it was his wife who was the infertile partner, Ruga was not required to pay the penalty even though his grounds were spurious; a legal precedent was thus set, allowing men to divorce their wives with virtual impunity. One of the consequences of this was the introduction of pre-marital contracts to legislate for the return and recovery of dowries (*actio rei uxoriae*).

The following settlement was made in 13 BC between a couple, Zois and Antipater, living in Egypt, who 'agree that they have separated from one another and severed their arrangement to live together' – the *affectio maritalis* is no more; the dowry (120 drachmas worth of clothing and some gold earrings) is returned and they agree that the marriage contract is null and void. Both are free to remarry.[70]

Dowry recovery was, not surprisingly, open to abuse. Valerius Maximus tells how a Caius Titinius, married to Fannia, made a claim to retain her dowry when he divorced her on the grounds of her alleged *stuprum*. The judge, Caius Marius, knew that Titinius had foreknowledge of Fannia's louche character and had only married her in order to procure the dowry. Fannia got off with a nominal fine; Titinius received a fine equal in value to the dowry. Fannia was able to return the favour to Marius when she later concealed him during his flight from Sulla.[71]

Marriage was very much a pragmatic affair: its objective, as we know, was to produce legitimate children, to maintain the birth rate, to ensure the survival of a particular family, to supply the Roman army, the bureaucracy, the land and the law with a source of recruits. Even Rome's hedonistic love poets acknowledged the importance of this. Catullus in his wedding hymn (*Carmen* 61) urges: 'produce sentries for the borders'; Propertius is much less enthusiastic: 'Why should I breed sons for Rome's triumphs? No blood of mine will ever produce a soldier.'[72]

Soranus, the Greek physician practising in Rome around AD 100, neatly sums it up when he remarks that 'women are married for the sake of bearing children and heirs, and not for pleasure and enjoyment'.[73] So vital was the ability to raise a family that, as we have seen in the case of Spurius Carvilius Ruga, infertility was valid grounds for divorce. Turia was not only prepared to divorce her husband because she was unable to bear him children but also to find him another, fertile, wife; she would then act as a sister- or mother-in-law in the new *ménage à trois*. Turia's husband was incandescent with rage at her suggestion,[74] preferring to stay married, even though it would mean the end of his family line. Sulla divorced his allegedly barren wife, Cloelia.[75]

Trimalchio, in Petronius's *Satyricon*, has no such qualms and congratulated himself on *not* divorcing Fortunata because she failed to give him children.[76] Catullus, in his wedding hymn, tells how Hymen's blessing is required if their household is to produce children (*liberos dare*) – parents cannot rely on offspring without her blessing. Junia, the bride, must take care not to deny her husband sex, in case he goes looking for it elsewhere; indeed, Catullus urges the couple to 'fool around as much as they like and have children soon (*liberos date*)'.

Among elite families marriage was used to cement political alliances and, although the women often may well have been little more than pawns in these arrangements, they did play a significant role in some highly political and prestigious families. Examples include the marriage between Scipio Africanus and Aemilia, the daughter of L. Aemilius Paullus, victor of the third Macedonian War; Julius Caesar betrothed his daughter, Julia, to Pompey although she had been promised to Servilius Caepio; to compensate, Pompey offered his daughter to Caepio although she was engaged to Sulla's son, Faustus, at the time.

At the highest level, the desire for successful political advancement was sufficient grounds for casual divorce. Plutarch tells how Quintus Hortensius Hortalus, the orator, tried to forge close links with Cato by requesting the hand of his daughter, then already married to Bibulus; Cato refused but did agree to divorcing his wife, Marcia, so that Hortensius could marry her instead. Cato gave Marcia away at the wedding. Hortensius died a few years later, there were no children from the marriage and Cato remarried Marcia, then a very rich woman.[77]

We cannot know how frequent this wife-swapping was, but it did recur. Suetonius cites a perfect example of a political merry-marriage-go-round of Byzantine complexity in his *Life of Augustus*: here Octavian is either betrothed or married and divorced in rapid succession to three women. On this path of marital carnage were strewn one fiancée, Claudia (stepdaughter of Mark Antony and barely of marriageable age), whom he divorced still a virgin after relations broke down with Fulvia, his mother-in-law; Scribonia

– married twice before to consuls – divorced when he grew tired of her nagging; and then Livia Drusilla, pregnant, already married and his eventual long-term wife. Julia, his daughter by Scribonia, is, in turn, married off three times – to Marcellus, Octavia's son – a mere boy, then to Marcus Agrippa, already married with children to one of Marcellus's sisters, and then to Tiberius whom he forced into a divorce as he was then married with children to a pregnant wife. Tiberius, of course, was Livia's son and future emperor of Rome. Virgil reflects the contemporary *mores* in the behaviour of Aeneas: he loses Creusa, his first wife, at Troy, deserts Dido in Carthage, although they were not of course married; and marries Lavinia, daughter of an Italian king. On the positive side, in the first century AD Agricola married Domitia Decidinia who was from a noble family: she brought him social prestige and helped him to progress his political ambitions; Tacitus adds that the marriage was happy, strong and loving.[78]

And it was not all one-way traffic. A chance encounter between Valeria and Sulla at a gladiator show, where the aristocratic lady deliberately made physical contact with the dictator, led to a marriage which benefited Valeria's family.[79]

Suetonius maintains that Augustus's affairs were motivated not by lust but subterfuge, using the women to expose the intrigues of their partners, his political opponents. Lust, though, was probably responsible for the occasion when, out to dinner, he led the wife of an ex-consul from the dining room to their bedroom, and later returned her to the party, her ears burning and her hair all over the place.[80] Pompey, who had five wives, was another serial divorcee; he divorced his first wife to marry Aemilia, stepdaughter of Sulla – at the time Aemilia was pregnant and settled in marriage.

In 18 BC Augustus, no doubt all the wiser from personal experience, was sufficiently concerned about the permissiveness in his Empire, particularly the growing infrequency of marriage, the increasing levels of adultery, and the falling birth-rate, to introduce the *Lex Julia de maritandis ordinibus* and other moral legislation in a bid to reduce adultery, encourage marriage and increase the population in Italy. Romans needed to be reminded what marriage was for: it was for producing children;[81] the marriage that ended in the death of one of the partners rather than in divorce had become,

it seems, something of a rarity.[82] Women, of course, were affected
by this legislation: unmarried women aged between twenty and
fifty were penalised, as were widows who had not remarried
within a year (later relaxed to two years). The main penalty was
the withholding of legacies; on marriage half of the legacy could
be paid; all of it on the birth of a child who survived; the other
was a 1 per cent tax imposed on unmarried women where they had
more than 20,000 sesterces. Roman senators and their descendants
could only marry women of the same status – no freedwomen,
slaves, actresses or prostitutes. As we have seen, the laws allowed
freeborn women to be released from guardianship on the birth of
their third child, freedwomen on the birth of the fourth.

Adultery had always been a private affair, a civil matter, often
dealt with within the family; it was now open to glaring public
scrutiny. A cuckolded husband now had to divorce his wife
within sixty days; failure to do so might result in prosecution
for complicity and possible punishment as an adulterer himself.
Where found guilty the wife and her lover were banished – to
separate islands; she lost half her dowry and one-third of her
property; he lost half his property. A man who subsequently
married an adulteress was committing a criminal offence. Under
Constantine both parties were sentenced to death.[83] We have seen
how Augustus's own adulterous daughter, Julia, was a notable
convict under this law, and was exiled to Pandateria, modern-day
Ventotene in the Tyrhennian Sea.

In order that adultery could be proven in law, divorce became
notifiable and a divorce court was established in which seven
adult males had to witness the formal declaration of divorce.
Famous cases of adultery by women leading to divorce include
Pompey v. *Mucia*, *Lucullus* v. *Claudia* and *Caesar* v. *Pompeia* after
the Bona Dea scandal, not for adultery but for being implicated in
a sacreligious incident which brought ignominy on the state and
on the sanctity of the Vestal Virgins – the High Priest's wife must
be above suspicion.

Under the new law, men lost the right to kill their wives and
fathers their daughters; they could still still slay their wives'
partners if the transgressor was a slave or freedman and if
in flagrante delicto in the marital home. In what can only

have caused a certain amount of dangerous confusion, fathers were still allowed to murder their adulterous daughters if they simultaneously killed the adulterer. Valerius Maximus provides the few recorded cases of women being put to death by their fathers: Pontius Aufidianus executed his daughter when she was seduced by her teacher, Fannius Saturninus; Fannius suffered the same fate. Atilius, an ex-prostitute himself, killed his daughter because she was tainted by *stuprum*. [84]

A man could now be prosecuted if he committed adultery with a married woman, if he condoned his wife's adulterous behaviour, or if he indulged in *stuprum* with a mistress who was not a registered prostitute. The law was amended by Tiberius to put an end to the practice where 'respectable' women registered as whores to facilitate their extramarital affairs.

Not surprisingly, Augustus's laws were generally unpopular – they amounted to what today we would term the workings of a 'nanny state'; consequently, they were diluted somewhat by the AD 9 *Lex Papia Poppaea* – named after the consuls of that year. Aulus Gellius[85] probably summed up the public, or rather male public, mood when he quotes Augustus's speech in the Senate in 17 BC:

> If we could survive without a wife, citizens of Rome, all of us would do without that nuisance, but since nature has decreed that we neither manage comfortably without them, nor live in any way without them, we must plan for our lasting preservation rather than for our temporary pleasure.

The same air of resignation comes from Varro: 'A husband must either put a stop to his wife's faults or else he must put up with them. In the first case he makes his wife a more attractive woman, in the second he makes himself a better man.'[86]

Various efforts were made to circumvent the legislation: Suetonius says that attempts by men to delay marriage and the birth of children by engagements to young, prepubescent girls were met with stricter legislation relating to subsequent divorces and the length of engagements. Fiancés had been exempt from the penalties paid by bachelors (*caelibes*); now Augustus voided betrothals unless the marriage took place within two years. Earlier in his life, Augustus himself (when Octavian) had betrothed his daughter, Julia, to fifteen-year-old L. Junius Silanus, one of Mark Antony's sons, when she was two years old. Tacitus confirms that the *Lex Julia* was unsuccessful: the benefits of childlessness were too great.[87] The attractions of the mistress – a woman of a young man's choosing, not his father's – or of a courtesan, off-limits in the marriage stakes, or of an independent woman from a lower class, were all too obvious.

We have seen that a woman's status as *univira* was one of the characteristics valued by husbands in the good Roman wife – a status which became less common as the Republic neared its end. Widowhood and subsequent remarriage, though, held none of the stigma for women or men that it was to attract under, for example, Christian belief, although there was a condition. Ovid tells that a widow allows a reasonable period of time to elapse for mourning:[88] parents and children merit twelve months while husbands get ten. No such restriction was imposed on widowers and there was no obligation for women to mourn fiancés; they could get engaged while in mourning. Women who re-married while in mourning, though, were accused of incurring *labes pudoris,* the stain of shame, or *infamia,* even if the husband had been a wastrel.[89] The new marriage, however precipitate, remained valid. Another benefit of a holding period before remarriage was that it eliminated questions of paternity – *turbatio sanguinis* – confusion of the blood. Women could remarry straight after giving birth even if it were within the ten months.[90] The ten-month rule was occasionally relaxed for religious and political expediency as, for example, after the disastrous Battle of Cannae when the shortage of *matronae* compromised the observance of the rites of Ceres.[91] Augustus's *Lex Julia* did away with any sentiment, requiring widows to remarry within twelve months.

Unsurprisingly, rich widows attracted more than their fair share of bounty hunters. Pliny the Younger writes that the perfidious and parasitical Regulus persuaded the vulnerable and dying widow Verania to add a codicil to her will in his favour. He was less successful, however, with Aurelia. She got dressed up for the signing of her will; Regulus arrived as witness and impudently asked her to leave her fine clothes to him, as if she were on her deathbed; understandably, she thought he was joking, but she signed anyway, and lived on.[92]

3

WOMEN IN THE PUBLIC EYE

This chapter looks at the public lives of elite and extraordinary women. As the Republic drew to a close, some elite and better-off women were at liberty to enjoy a more public life outside the home. They went to the theatre and they went to the games; they went with their husbands to dinner parties. Subsequent chapters will reveal how, in common with women from the lower social orders, they performed religious ceremonies and visited temples in both the state religion and in the more exotic, mystery cults. As sophisticated, educated and independent women they could consort with the *litterati*: some women were able to exasperate and captivate love poets; to irritate and outrage writers of epigrams and satire. Some women could pursue a career, for example, as midwives or doctors; many more, mainly but not exclusively from the lower classes, lived a life of prostitution or worked in the entertainment industry as dancers or musicians; others helped run businesses.

Nevertheless, despite this relative independence, Roman women were excluded from public office (*civilia officia*) of any kind. They were, therefore, not allowed to sit on juries and they could not institute an action in criminal courts except in very special cases such as parricide or filicide. They could not act on behalf of others in the civil court although they were permitted to bring actions here, subject to the approval of their guardian. To Valerius Maximus forensic activity was unladylike; he cites Gaia Afrania as an example of annoying female litigiousness, preferring to note the date of her death in 48 BC rather than her birthday; according to Ulpian the ban on litigation initiated by women was all Afrania's fault – not so much because she brought so many actions, but because of how she conducted herself in court. Juvenal, too, laments the constant recourse to the law by women, citing a lay person, Manilia, who tells the celebrated lawyer Celus how to pursue his case, both as prosecutor and council for the defence.[1] According to Diocletian, defending a client in court is man's work (*virile officium*).

In 56 BC Cicero savages Clodia, Catullus's Lesbia, in the *Pro Caelio* after she brought an action against Marcus Caelius Rufus claiming conspiracy to poison her; he had borrowed gold from her, allegedly under false pretences. He sets her up as an *accusatrix* – anathema to Romans, as women had no right to act as prosecutors in criminal courts. Cicero's allusions to the unruly house she keeps (at odds with the traditional Roman *domus* dominated by the *paterfamilias*) and the comparisons he makes with Quinta Claudia, a famously respectable ancestor of Clodia's, all serve to reduce her to no better than a whore before the jury.[2] Fulvia Flacca Bambula and her mother Sempronia Tuditani both attended the trial of Titus Annius Milo after Milo and his gangsters murdered Clodius, her husband, in 52 BC; Fulvia was called as a witness for the prosecution after strengthening her case beforehand by a very public and inflammatory show of grief: she dragged her husband's corpse through the streets of Rome into the Curia where it was burnt as if on a pyre.[3]

The case of Attia Viriola is interesting. Pliny recounts how this woman, wife of a praetorian senator, brought an action after she was disinherited by her octagenerian father less than a fortnight after he brought home his new wife, Attia's new stepmother. It illustrates how women were able to bring lawsuits in the early Empire; moreover, the public galleries were full of women, including daughters and stepmothers, anxious to hear the verdict in what was possibly something of a test case.[4]

Valerius Maximus grudgingly concedes that women, being what they are and acting immodestly, could no longer be kept silent in the late Republic. Where women do break free of their constrictions it is not because they are women, it is because they exhibit qualities more appropriate to men than to women. Valerius Maximus cites the case of Maesia Sentia who in 77 BC conducted her own defence and, through her forensic expertise, secured her own acquittal. Valerius ascribes this success to a masculine spirit which earned her the name Androgyne. As we have seen, around the same time, Sallust attributes male characteristics to Sempronia, to explain away her talents and skills.[5]

Even Lucretia, that paragon of female virtue, is defeminised by both Ovid and Valerius Maximus who, in praising her, ascribe masculine qualities to her and to her actions: to Ovid she is a *matrona* with a manly spirit: 'animi matrona virilis';[6] to Valerius Maximus she is 'dux Romanae pudicitiae' – 'a leader in Roman sexual propriety – who, by a wicked twist of fate, possesses a man's spirit in a female body'.[7] *Dux* is almost always used to describe a man; where it is used for a woman it signifies two powerful, unnerving foreign women: Dido and Boudicca.[8]

The independent and clever women who moved in the cultivated, soiree world of the neoterics and the elegiac poets represented the kind of women who shunned the docile, acquiescing lifestyle of the *matrona*. While the poets loved what they saw in their sophisticated ladies, more conservative Romans like Sallust and Cicero were less impressed: their feminine talents and influence disturbed them, their permissive ways appalled them.

Women with political influence must have caused particular anxiety. At the turn of the first century BC, Gaius Marius (157–86 BC) enlisted the help of a Syrian prophetess called Martha whom he allowed to be carried around in one of his litters and who advised him on sacrifices. Martha had been bold enough to offer her visionary services to the Senate – who were not interested – and to the senators' wives, who were. One of these was Julia, wife of Marius and aunt of Julius Caesar; Martha had impressed Julia by picking out the winner of a gladiatorial contest they were watching.[9] Another loose cannon was Chelidon, alleged mistress and client of Verres (c. 120–43 BC) who apparently ran a legal salon, and was attacked by Cicero for her troubles.[10] We have already encountered others: Servilia who was politically active on the Republican side after Caesar's assassination; Sempronia, complicit in the Catiline conspiracy, and Clodia Metelli, mocked and vilified by Cicero in his high-profile defence of Marcus Caelius Rufus.

Plutarch[11] describes a certain Praecia – a beauty and a wit

– who was instrumental in helping Lucius Licinius Lucullus win the governship of Cilicia in 74 BC and subsequently the much sought-after command against Mithridates. Praecia, though little more than a prostitute according to Plutarch, had a reputation as something of a fixer and wielded great influence and power. She began an affair with the equally influential, and dissolute, Publius Cornelius Cethegus, arch-enemy of Lucullus; she was soon dictating everything Cethegus did: 'Nothing important was done in which Cethegus was not involved, and nothing by Cethegus without Praecia.' Lucullus saw his chance and proceeded to insinuate his way successfully into Praecia's affections to the extent that Cethegus was soon backing Lucullus for the governorship.

The ambitious and assertive Fulvia Flacca Bambula (c. 83–40 BC) is famous for gleefully pricking the decapitated Cicero's tongue with a hairpin: she took exception and revenge after Cicero had insinuated that Mark Antony, her third husband, only married her for her money.[12] Cicero's head was on public display in the Forum after his proscription in 43 BC. Fulvia too is likened to a man – 'a woman in body alone' – by Velleius Paterculus[13] who evidently regarded her vengeful and gruesome act as unladylike and by implication the sort of thing only a man should do. This is Dio's account: 'Fulvia took the head into her hands before it was removed, and after abusing it spitefully and spitting upon it, set it on her knees, opened the mouth, and pulled out the tongue, which she pierced with the pins that she used for her hair, at the same time uttering many brutal jests.'[14] Pomponia, the widow of Cicero's brother, Quintus Tullius, and sister of Atticus was even more sadistic: when Philologus, the freedman who betrayed the Ciceros, was brought to her she ordered him to cut off strips of his own flesh, cook them and then eat them.[15]

Fulvia deserves to be remembered for more than just her sadism: her achievements are quite remarkable by any standards. Before Antony, she had been married to two other powerful men. The first was the notorious Publius Clodius Pulcher in 62 BC, then in 51 BC Gaius Scribonius Curio, an ally of Julius Caesar. Plutarch, in his *Life of Antony*, describes Fulvia as no wool spinner, no doer of housework, in effect no ideal *matrona*; Fulvia's ambition was to rule over a powerful man, an ambition she achieved as Mark Antony's third wife. Antony must have been impressed, and her influence must have been significant, because he struck coins bearing her image as a representation of Victory – the first time that Roman coinage had featured a woman. Another possible first was the renaming by Antony's supporters of the city of Eumenia in Phrygia to Fulviana; subsequent mintings of the coins bear this name.

Fulvia exerted considerable influence on Mark Antony before and after the assassination of Julius Caesar, harnessing the gangs of former husband Clodius to help Antony against Dolabella, taking an enthusiastically active role in the subsequent bloody proscriptions, accompanying her husband to his military headquarters in Brundisium[16] and confounding Cicero's attempts to have Antony declared an enemy of the state in his absence.[17] Antony even renounced Lycoris for Fulvia; Lycoris was the accomplished mime artist whom Cornelius Gallus celebrated in his elegies. Fulvia's daughter, Clodia Pulcher, married the young Octavian. According to Dio,[18] Fulvia was one of the most powerful people in Rome at this time and proceeded to fight Antony's corner, winning support from veterans when she toured Italy, children in tow,[19] despite the tensions caused by Antony's affair with Cleopatra; she even helped raise eight legions for Antony to fight against Octavian in the Perusine War in 41–40 BC.[20]

Velleius Paterculus[21] records that she 'was creating general confusion by armed violence' and that Octavian's troops tied obscene messages to stones and fired them directly at Fulvia. Two were aimed at her clitoris with the unmistakeable suggestion that she was a tribade, a lesbian;[22] Fulvia and Antony were invited to open their arses wide to receive the projectiles. They in turn responded by calling Octavian a cock-sucker and wide-arsed, suggesting that he too was open to penetration: the ultimate insult for a freeborn man. Martial[23] preserves for us the lascivious epigram which Octavian reputedly composed for Fulvia: 'Because Antony is shagging Glaphyra, Fulvia has decided that my punishment will be that I shag her too. Me fuck Fulvia? What if Manius begged me to bugger him? Would I? I think not, if I had any sense. Fuck or fight, she says. Doesn't she know that I love my prick more than life itself? Let the trumpets blow!' Octavian is implying that the ensuing civil war was caused because Fulvia was put out by his rebuffal.

Fulvia Flacca Bambula was not the only Fulvia who wielded power in the turbulent days of the first century BC. During the Catilinian conspiracy Gaius Cornelius and Lucius Vargunteius were deputed to assassinate Cicero on 7 November 63 BC; Quintus Curius, a senator who became one of Cicero's chief informants, warned Cicero of the threat through his mistress, Fulvia; by posting guards at his house Cicero deterred the would-be assassins.[24] Fulvia was not one of those vulnerable women whom Catiline recruited as informants and *agents provocateurs* in his battle with Cicero – former prostitutes who had fallen on hard times towards the end of their careers, and were thus open to exploitation by the conspirators. Fulvia, on the other hand, was of good birth; she had learnt of the conspiracy from her indiscrete and tactless lover, Quintus Curius. When she revealed the details to various people the plot was confounded and Cicero was voted consul.

Epicharis, a player in the Pisonian conspiracy against Nero in AD 65, excited a different kind of anxiety. An exceedingly brave freedwoman, she was informed against when trying to recruit more conspirators. Tacitus paints a picture of an insecure Nero who inflicted torture on her female body (*muliebre corpus*), and orders the beatings, burnings and verbal assault to be intensified so as not to be outdone by a woman (*ne a femina spernerentur*). Epicharis had the last word, though, when, crippled by the torture, in order not to betray her colleagues, she hanged herself. Tacitus ensures that his readers, and history, remember her courage, her illustrious behaviour – and the cowardice and treachery of her co-conspirators: freeborn equestrians and senators themselves busy shamelessly informing on each other, their families and friends.[25] A famous example is Lucan, the epic poet, selling his own mother, Acilia, to Nero's thugs.

The Twelve Tables enshrined the right of fathers to punish their children – be they boys or girls – including the administration of capital punishment, eventually made illegal around AD 370.[26] Men were always subject to the public justice of the state, but women were sometimes referred to their families for *in camera* trial. Examples are the suppression of the Bacchanalia in 186 BC[27] when women implicated in the orgiastic rites were handed over to their families for execution; the case of Publilia and Licinia, *nobiles feminae*, accused of poisoning their consular husbands and strangled by their relatives in 154 BC,[28] according to Livy and Valerius Maximus;[29] and Pomponia Græcina, a distinguished lady, *insignis femina*, wife of the Plautius who returned in triumph from conquered Britannia. She was accused of some foreign superstition, *superstitio externae*, and handed over to her husband's judicial decision. 'Following ancient precedent, he heard his wife's case in the presence of kinsfolk and found her innocent.'[30] This shows that in the eyes of the law, women were considered to be the responsibility of the family rather than of the state, even in serious cases such as murder. Augustus's *Lex Julia* put an end to the family kangaroo courts.

An interesting footnote to the Bacchanalian scandal is that both the whistle-blowers were handsomely rewarded. Hispala Faecenia, a freedwoman and former courtesan, was, like Aebutius, her male accomplice, awarded 100,000 sesterces; he received exemption from military service, she, freeborn status and its benefits. Such was the anxiety caused by the cult, such was the relief of the authorities at having suppressed it.

Not all public exposure was welcome: women had their share of public execution. Most of the different methods – beheading, flogging to death, pushing off the Tarpeian Rock, burning alive (vivicombustion), feeding to wild animals or being drowned inside a sack – took place with the victim naked, much to the further delectation of the large crowds that had been summoned to these spectacles by a fanfare of trumpets. As a concession to modesty, however, women escaped the extra humiliation and were executed in private. Even when a Pontifex Maximus scourged a Vestal Virgin for letting the flame go out, he did so behind a curtain. The curtain would have been little consolation to those women who were sentenced to death by strangulation: they were, according to Tacitus and Dio Cassius, raped by the executioner beforehand.[31]

Women were targeted by the *Lex Oppia*. They were also

constricted by the 169 BC *Lex Voconia* in terms of the value of wealth they could inherit. Only sisters of a deceased woman could inherit in cases of intestacy and women were prohibited from inheriting large legacies. Property was allowed so long as the value did not exceed the heir's legacy. This effectively overturned the Twelve Tables law permitting women to inherit and to be named in wills: the presumption now was that the family's money would evaporate if left to a woman and that women frittered away their wealth on frivolous things. Tertia Aemilia (or Aemilia Paulla *c.* 230–163 BC), the mother of Cornelia and husband of Scipio Africanus, exemplifies the ostentatious wealth the law aimed to restrict: 'apart from the magnificence of her personal attire and of the decorations of her carriage, all the baskets, cups and sacrificial vessels or utensils were made of gold or of silver'; when she died in 162 BC she left Publius Scipio Aemilianus enough money and jewellery to pay off the outstanding 25-talent dowries of his two adoptive aunts. Papiria, Aemilianus' mother, lost no time in going out in Aemilia's carriage soon after the funeral wearing Cornelia's famous jewels.[32]

The public clamour (*consternatio muliebris*) for the repeal of the Oppian Laws was by no means the first instance of women exerting independence and political influence in public. After their legendary abduction by the Romans, the Sabine women were assured by Romulus that they, as women now married to Romans, would share all the benefits and privileges that come with Roman citizenship, and that they would be bonded with their husbands by the Roman children they would surely bear. For their part, their new husbands would compensate for the loss of Sabine family and home by being nice to the Sabine women. The men themselves added their own blandishments, protesting that they did what they did for love (*cupiditas*): 'pleas like these are the most effective in influencing a woman'. Later, the wives – now mothers – rose up to form a human wedge between their warring husbands and fathers when the Sabines attacked Rome; they successfully averted the parricide which would have occurred, declaring that they would rather die than allow the conflict to continue and render them widows and orphans. The fighting stopped and the Romans and Sabines became one, thus doubling at a stroke the population of Rome. To honour the role played by women in this early example of empire building the thirty individual political wards of the new Rome were named after thirty of the women.[33]

It was women too who averted the Volscian attack on Rome led by Gaius Marcius Coriolanus in 491 BC. Where envoys and priests had failed to placate Coriolanus, the women of Rome, *ingens mulierum agmen*, sought out his mother and his wife, Veturia and Volumnia. They persuaded them to go into the lines with Coriolanus's two young sons and implore him to withdraw: 'Where men failed to defend the city with their swords, women may be more successful with their tears and petitions.' Moved by the presence of his close family, and by an angry and impassioned Veturia who appealed to his duty as a son and to Rome, Coriolanus relented and withdrew his army.[34] Veturia's success was, no doubt, assured when she reminded Coriolanus how much she had sacrificed for him, providing an education and remaining a *univira* after his father's death, thus making her mother, father, nurse, teacher and sister to him.

It was a crowd of sympathetic women who, in 450 BC, were 'more effective with their silent tears than words could be'. They had congregated to assist Lucius Verginius against Appius Claudius; Claudius had abducted Verginia, Verginius' daughter, on her way to school one day. Although she was already betrothed Claudius maintained that Verginia was in fact just a slave girl whom Verginius had adopted into his family. Despite the pressure from the *matronae*, the story ended unhappily when Verginius exercised his rights as *paterfamilias* and stabbed her in the heart to save her from the shame *(stuprum)* a marriage to Appius Claudius would bring. The women angrily asked if this was the reward they got for bringing up children and remaining chaste: *pudicitiae praemia.* According to Livy, *dolor muliebris,* the grief of women, is so much more powerful, their grief so much deeper due to their lack of restraint.[35]

After the disastrous Battle of Cannae, Livy believed that every *matrona* in Rome was bereaved: to avoid further losses and to win back their captured sons and husbands, the *matronae* banded together to, unsuccessfully, lobby the Senate to accept

Hannibal's ransom demand in exchange for 8,000 Roman prisoners of war.[36]

Side-stepping the *Lex Voconia*, men continued to dress their women up to mirror their own standing and wealth. Although this was nothing less than an early form of 'arm candy', women clearly benefited from the men's vanity, until Elagabalus's eccentric reforms in the early third century AD. He regulated the dress and behaviour of women according to social rank. Possibly apocryphal, the story goes that Julia Soaemias, Elagabalus's mother, convened a *senaculum*, a Senate of women, to decree the kind of clothing women of a certain rank in the *ordo matronarum* could wear; whether they were eligible to ride on a chariot or on donkey; whether in a leather litter or one made from bone, adorned with silver or ivory; whose shoes could be decorated with gold and silver; who was to kiss first.[37] Aurelian later revoked the laws.

In 42 BC the three members of the Second Triumvirate, Lepidus, Octavian and Mark Antony, needed funds to finance their wars with the assassins of Julius Caesar; the money procured from their proscriptions was running out. An easy target was women's wealth: accordingly they levied a supertax on the 1,400 richest women in Rome. The women were outraged and, in another rare example of public demonstration by *matronae*, they marched on the Forum where Hortensia, daughter of the orator Quintus Hortensius, delivered a passionate and eloquent speech at a *contio*, before the triumvirs. Hortensia questioned why women, who had no say in or benefit or glory from the wars, should be required to finance them. Attempts to disperse the women failed. Hortensia's passion won the day and the taxable quota was reduced to 400 women; men with over 100,000 sesterces had to make good the shortfall by loaning money to the Triumvirate.[38] Appian[39] declared that the speech was so good that you would never know that it had been written and delivered by a woman. Valerius Maximus says that Hortensia's father 'breathed through the words of his daughter'.[40]

The clubs and assemblies of Julia Soaemias and Hortensia were not unique. Inscriptional evidence reveals a number of *curia* and *collegia* through the years, mostly involved in funeral arrangements and good works. Gaius Sulpicius Vicor voted a double banquet to the *curia* of women in Lanuvium in the second century AD; Lucius Veturius Nepos in the second century AD at Feltria donated 400 sesterces so that the women could provide roses to celebrate his birthday when he died;[41] in 206 BC when the Temple of Juno was struck by lightning, twenty-five *matronae* were selected to contribute money from their dowries to purchase a golden bowl to dedicate to the goddess;[42] a meeting of married women (*conventus*) witnessed Agrippina the Younger getting a slap from Lepida's mother for trying it on with her son-in-law, the emperor Galba, Lepida's widower.[43]

From the early days of Rome, Livy gives examples where women joined together for collective action: to mourn Brutus for a full year in 507 BC in recognition of how he had restored Lucretia's reputation; to mourn Publius Valerius in 503 BC; and to await news of casualties after the Battle of Lake Trasimene in 217 BC. In 390 BC a council of women met to discuss the tribute to Apollo after the capture of Veii and decided that they personally would contribute their gold and jewellery. The Senate rewarded their munificence with a law allowing them the right to travel to and from the games and festivals in a four-wheeled carriage, and to use standard carriages whenever they liked.

The *ordo matronarum* has its origins in the early Republic although it was in the early Empire that it was at its most influential. Essentially it was the *matronae*'s equivalent of the senatorial order – a hierarchial club of rich women, which met (in a *conventus*) at times of political and social anxiety to exert collective pressure on their husbands. Livia, as first lady, was seen as a figurehead of this early pressure group; all part of the high-profile role she took during the reigns of her husband and son, Tiberius.

Public praise, albeit not always altruistic and not just in funerary inscriptions, started to come women's way in the second century BC. Gaius Gracchus made political capital every time he cited Cornelia, his mother.[44] In 102 BC Q. Lutatius Catulus started the tradition of *laudationes* and funeral orations with his encomium for his mother, Popilia.[45] In 69 BC Julius Caesar famously eulogised his aunt, Julia Caesaris, the virtuous wife of Marius. In the following year, he similarly praised Cornelia

Cinnilla, his late first wife, the first public eulogy for a younger woman – both actions winning him popular and political kudos. At the age of twelve, a young Octavian delivered a *laudatio* for his grandmother Julia; on Octavia's death (the sister of Augustus) two orations were delivered: one by Augustus, the other by Nero Claudius Drusus, followed by a period of public mourning.

In literature, women were the subject of the *epicedion*, the funeral ode. In one respect this is something of an extended funerary inscription, where much of the praise is obviously conventional. The effect, nevertheless, is, like that of the tombstone, to bestow eternal recognition on the subject; Propertius's Cornelia and Statius's Priscilla both benefited from *epicedia*. Cornelia, as we have seen,[46] was a *univira* to Paullus; she brought no shame to his *res gestae*; indeed, she was a credit to his lineage; she was the perfect *matrona*. The image of Priscilla would be 'a grateful keepsake for her husband'.[47] She was *quies*, calm, *modesta*, her table was *modica* and she looked after Abascantus well, untouched by his success – he was very close to Domitian. She was a veritable *matrona*.

The opportunities to men for reflected glory offered by their fine women is also evident in imperial coinage where wives and mothers feature on coins minted by emperors; they often take the form of such personifictions as *Pax, Securitas, Fortuna, Concordia* or *Iustitia* – propaganda for their husbands and sons. Statues of women started to go up in the late Republic, despite the best efforts of Cato the Younger to stifle the practice; Tiberius later advised moderation. Augustus honoured Livia with the Portico of Livia and the shrine of Concordia. In the provinces, a diluted version began to appear when the wives of governors were celebrated in statuary.

Many men were absent from home for long periods of time and for much of their careers due to the demands of military service and provincial administration. This would also have fostered a degree of independence among wives left behind at home. In time, the statues were replaced by the real thing: Caecilia Metella led the way when she accompanied her husband, Sulla, to Athens in 86 BC; in 49 BC Cornelia went with Pompey to Lesbos and Egypt. Aulus Caecina Severus adopts an extreme view, exaggerated in his unsuccessful speech of AD 21, as recorded by Tacitus, but it contains within it the arguments which no doubt moulded the regulations relating to accompanied postings. Severus gets on with his wife and they have had six children together – however, he has left her at home for the forty years he has been away in the provinces. Why? Because women encourage extravagance in peace time and weakness during war; they are feeble and tire easily; left unrestrained they get angry, they scheme and boss the commanders about. He cites instances of women running patrols and exercises, and how they attract spivs and embrace extortion.

Soldiers were not permitted to marry on service but many, no doubt, did, building relationships with local women and starting families with them.[48] One of the fascinating Vindolanda Tablets from around AD 100 shows that wives of officers clearly did accompany their husbands abroad: Claudia Severa sends a birthday party invitation to her sister Lepidina asking her to make her day by coming, on 11 September. The body of the letter is written by a scribe but the postscript is written by Claudia and is the oldest example of a woman's handwriting in Latin in existence.[49]

When women attended dinner parties with their husbands, initially they sat at table, later they reclined like their men. And it was not all jugglers, clowns, dwarfs and Spanish dancers; more serious entertainment such as discussions about rhetorical, grammatical or philosophical niceties were often on the agenda. The post-prandial gladiatorial displays and decapitations that Livy describes must have been quite rare. Apparently, though, it was not always all refined elegance. The jaundiced Christian writer, Clement of Alexandria, is appalled by the behaviour of women at drinking parties: they tilt back their heads exposing bare necks, stretching out their throats to gulp their drink down, as if to show everything they can and belching with the best of the men.

Women were free to attend the races, the games and festivals. Ovid recommends the games as the best place to pick up a sophisticated woman; Valeria 'accidentally' made contact with Sulla there. However, unless you were a Vestal Virgin or a member of the imperial family, you were, as a woman, subjected to a pecking order when it came to seating in the amphitheatre or the theatre; women, along with slaves and foreigners, found themselves at the back, while men enjoyed seats at the front according to their rank.

Women may not have had the vote in the legislative assemblies, the *comitia* and the *concilium*, but graffiti in Pompeii shows that they took an active interest in local politics and electioneering with examples of *programmata*, posters on which they endorsed candidates. Of the 2,500 *programmata* discovered, Savunen indicates that fifty-four (2.16 per cent) were posted by women supporting twenty-eight candidates. There is, though, one striking example of women exercising real political influence. In 1955 an inscription dating from around AD 6 was found in Akmoneia (modern-day Ahat in central Turkey) by Michael Ballance, the English archaeologist. The inscription is now lost but luckily Ballance photographed it and copied it down. What it tells us is that 'the women, both Greek and Roman, honoured Tatia daughter of Menokritos ... the High Priestess who acted as their benefactoress under all circumstances, in recognition of all her virtue'; there then follows the names of the three men responsible for erecting the statue. Remarkably, we have here a unique example of women taking the initiative in, and responsibility for, an act of civic administration within local government, voting to finance and raise the statue of one of their own. We cannot know if this political emancipation was a one-off or if there were other isolated instances now lost to us. What is important is that the women of Akmoneia proved beyond all doubt that women could have been actively involved in politics where the will existed to allow them.[50]

Tatia was not the only benefactoress: Eumachia was a priestess who had married into one of the leading Pompeiian families after inheriting from her father, a successful brick manufacturer; she was patroness of the guild of fullers – a prestigious position in one of the most important local industries. During the reign of Tiberius, Eumachia gifted the fullers a large building for their head office, dedicated to Concordia Augusta and Pietas; it survives today as the Building of Eumachia.[51] The timing of the gift may not have been accidental: it coincided with her son's campaign for public office. Another Pompeian lady, Julia Felix, owned a local estate that comprised baths, shops with rooms above them and flats on the second floor – all available for rent on a five-year lease. Junia Theodora is fondly commended by the citizens of Corinth in AD 43 for her largesse;[52] likewise Flavia Publicia Nicomachis for her total virtue, as benefactoress and founder of the city of Phocaea in the second century AD.[53] Modia Quintia, a priestess in Africa Proconsularis, was honoured with a statue to recognise the fact that she furnished a marble patio in the portico, ceilings and columns, and for paying for an aqueduct.[54]

The emperors' women, of course, were able to assume a public prominence and public profiles far and away above anything possible to women in the Republic. Only a foreign woman, the *fatale monstrum* (that 'deadly monstrosity' to use Horace's description) that was Cleopatra, came anywhere near to the power wielded by the Julias, the Livias, the Agrippinas and the Mesallinas by virtue of their position at the heart of government and in the beds of the men running those governments.

Names are key to personal identity, individuality and lineage – nowhere more so than in ancient Rome. Roman men had two names, sometimes three – *praenomen, nomen* (the family name) and *cognomen.* Up to the end of the Republic, Roman women, however, usually had to make do with one, the feminine form of the family name – an exception was the Caecilii Metelli, who boasted two. This vividly reflects the subordinate role women played in Roman public life and creates the impression that Roman women lacked individual identity and were perceived only as an adjunct to the family.[55] Where there were sisters they, confusingly, had the same name: for example the three sisters of P. Clodius were all Clodias. Adjectives such as *Maior* or *Minor, Tertia* or *Secunda* were sometimes appended to help differentiate them. On marriage, a woman kept her name but it was augmented by the husband's name, an indication of whose property she was.

In the later Republic and Empire women increasingly assumed two names – the first her family name and then her father's third name, sometimes her mother's; for example Cicero's daughter Tullia was Tullia Ciceronis. Maternal lineage assumed importance in the Empire, leading to women taking names from their maternal grandfather, instead of the usual father's. But anthroponymic confusion continued to reign: for example both Vipsania Agrippina, the wife of Germanicus, and Julia Agrippina, her daughter and the mother of Nero, were Agrippina. By the third century nominal inflation, or polyonomy, had set in: for instance, one of the wives of the emperor Severus Alexander, or rather Marcus Aurelius Severus Alexander Augustus (reigned AD 222–235), outdid her husband and went by the name Seia Herennia Sallustia Barbia Orbiana Augusta. She, however, had nothing on Quintus Pompeius Senecio, consul in AD 169, who named himself with a further thirty-five *cognomina*. Hopefully, the man who inscribed his tombstone in Tivoli charged by the letter.[56]

4

EDUCATED WOMEN, THE *PUELLA DOCTA* & THE FINE ARTS

This chapter will describe the education of Roman women, the educated woman and male attitudes towards the educated woman. Initially, Roman education was, to all intents and purposes, Greek education. Until the Romans could provide their own critical mass of poetry and rhetoric, written in Latin, all education was based on Greek works. By the end of the Republic, however, the burgeoning corpus of literature published in Latin allowed Cicero and Virgil, Sallust and Terence, for example, to replace their Greek counterparts providing gold standards in rhetoric, poetry, prose and drama. The ultimate aim of 'primary' Roman education (conducted by a *litterator* or a *magister ludi litterarii* from around age seven) was to perfect self-expression: knowing how to speak properly and to interpret the poets was paramount. Painstaking and laborious work on the alphabet, first with letters, then with syllables was inevitable and unavoidable according to Quintilian (*Inst.* 1, 4, 2; 1, 1, 30) and Dionysius of Halicarnassus (*On Composition* 3).

From the age of eleven the *grammaticus* took over and the equally painstaking and pedantic reading and analysis of literary texts began: the texts were never studied as an end in themselves but as further preparation for the pupil's role as an orator in the courts or in the Senate. Literary criticism, geography, mythology and grammar were on the curriculum. Aptitude in public speaking was the be all and end all. By the end of the Republic a third stage had become established: instruction and practice in rhetoric, under the *rhetor*, which moved the fifteen- or sixteen-year-old boy student yet closer to competence in declamation, that obsessive *sine qua non* of a successful life on the public stage, of a good *cursus honorum.* He discarded the *toga praetexta* and donned the *toga virilis*: the first stage on the *cursus honorum.* He would pursue either the *tirocinium militia* (military cadetship) or the *tirocinium fori* (legal apprenticeship) for a year. If the latter, this may have been complemented by some philosophy, and perhaps a 'grand tour' of Greece or of a Greek colony.

But women were excluded from public life and that naturally obviated the need for their instruction in rhetoric and declamation. The education of girls and young women seems to have been limited to a home-based instruction of the elementary stage under the *materfamilias* or a *litterator*, alongside her brothers. Marriage, too was a limiting force: when a girl married at twelve or thirteen there was little time for education for the fledgling *matrona* – her concern in this regard would be the education of the children she was expected to produce.

Some young women, would, of course, excel and some, in the richer families, did move on to the grammar stage. Cicero (*Brutus* 211) and Pliny (*Ep* 1, 16, 6) remark on the purity of the Latin turned out by some women. The poetry of the love poets, the letters of Pliny and the satires of Juvenal all attest to sophisticated and literate women, indeed also to bluestockings and lady pedants. The Romans, though, faced something of a dilemma when it came to the education of girls and educated women. One of the most highly valued functions of the *materfamilias* was the education of her children, at home; however, the end product – the educated woman (*puella docta*) – also attracted suspicion and scorn, not least among the love poets and the satirists.

Girls were not entirely forgotten, however; while he had his grandsons educated in reading, swimming and handwriting by the renowned teacher Verrius Flaccus, Augustus attempted to inculcate domestic skills such as weaving and spinning in his granddaughters, and in the wayward Julia, in a bid to resurrect traditional values. However, there is no reason to suppose that the girls did not benefit from the tuition provided by Verrius Flaccus as well. Ovid's stepdaughter obviously benefited from a sound education: in a letter from exile (*Tristia* 3, 7), he envisages Perilla sitting with her mother, 'her nose in a book and amongst the Muses', when his letter arrives. He refers to her *docta carmina* and how only Sappho is more gifted; he recalls how they used to read each other's poetry to each other, how he was her critic and teacher; Perilla is obviously *doctissima*. Ovid urges her to keep on writing because, come what may, she, like him, will always be read by posterity.

The home education, in the middle and upper classes at least, threw up a number of exceptionally gifted and talented women among the teachers and the taught. Illiteracy within the upper classes was probably uncommon but, all the same, these women were exceptional. Cornelia, mother of the Gracchi, was an early beneficiary of a more enlightened, Greek-influenced education for women which extended beyond household management and the spinning of wool. She was erudite and attracted Greeks among the 'learned men' in her circle. Carneades of Cyrene found it quite normal to converse with her on things philosophical. It was the education she in turn gave her sons which accounted for their success, not their lineage; Cornelia also hired Blossius of Cuma and Diophanes of Mytilene to help out. She was bilingual in Greek and Latin, well read, a good lyre player, a competent mathematician and could hold a philosophical argument. Quintilian praised her literary style and Cicero reveals that her letters were admired and published. She would certainly have benefited from the Greek library brought home to Italy by her uncle, Aemilius Paullus. Her namesake, Cornelia Metella (*c.* 73 BC – 48 BC) daughter of Metellus Scipio, was similarly gifted: good at the lyre, good at mathematics and good at philosophy.

Sallust grudgingly acknowledges Sempronia's intellectual and artistic gifts: she could compose verse, tell jokes, be reserved, soothing or scatological in conversation, in short, a woman of charm and elegance, a veritable *docta puella*. Cornificia was a contemporary of Catullus and sister of Q. Cornificius, a neoteric poet friendly with Catullus and Cicero; she married a Camerius, another friend of Catullus. None of her work is extant but her reputation as an epigrammist lasted well into the fourth century when St Jerome in his *Chronicle* described her work as 'remarkable'.

Pliny is delighted that Calpurnia, his wife, expresses her love for him by reading and re-reading his books, by closely following his court cases and by singing his verses while playing the lyre. In another letter, a eulogy for the younger daughter of Fundanus, he describes her *anilis prudentia, matronalis gravitas* – her grown-up good sense, her dignity befitting a *matrona*; her affection for her teachers, her avid and studious reading.

Julia Procilla steered her son, Agricola, away from his infatuation with philosophy and helped him become the military and political success he was. Tacitus we know believed that childcare was no substitute for a mother's influence. He cites the examples of Cornelia, Aurelia Cotta, Julius Caesar's mother, and the mother of Augustus, Atia, as role models: 'the mothers of the Gracchi, of Cæsar, of Augustus, Cornelia, Aurelia, Atia, all looked after their children's education bringing up the greatest of sons. The strict discipline produced in each case a pure and good nature which vice could not corrupt'. Other talented and educated women include Helvia, mother of Cicero, and Eucharis, the dancer granted her freedom before she died aged fourteen, and whom was *docta erodita omnes artes virgo*: a clever young girl proficient in all the arts.

Aurelia Cotta was a particularly strong-willed and gifted woman: she defended Caesar against Sulla who had demanded he divorce his wife, Cornelia Cinna; to Plutarch she was strict and respectable. Aurelia also testified in the divorce case of *Julius Caesar* v. *Pompeia*, after Publius Clodius, masquerading as a woman, gatecrashed the Bona Dea festival held at Caesar's house. As for Atia Balba Caesonia, Tacitus relates that swearing in her presence caused great offence, and that she never did a wrong deed. She looked after the serious work of her young charges sympathetically and religiously, even their sport and games.[1]

Quintilian agrees that it was a mother's duty to ensure her children received the best possible education, whatever her own education, also citing Cornelia as the exemplar.[2] He refers to the eloquence of Laelia, the daughter of Gaius Laelius, and the speech Hortensia made to the triumvirs in 42 BC[3] – a speech which has been remembered because it was intrinsically good, and not just because it was, unusually, written and delivered by a woman. Cicero adds that Laelia came from a family of accomplished orators: as well as her father, her two daughters, the Muciae, and her granddaughters, the Liciniae, were also eloquent speakers.[4]

Both Cicero and Quintilian mention letters written by Cornelia; they were considered to be of a high literary standard and revealed her 'educated style of speaking'. If they are genuine, then they reflect caring, informed and resourceful advice she gave to her son, Gaius Gracchus.

Women then had a vital role to play in the education of their children; elite and well-off women were respected for giving them a good start in life. For boys they provided an impetus for the *cursus honorum*. For girls and boys they passed down the all-important cultural heritage of the family, and of Rome.

Agrippina, mother of Nero, wrote her memoirs (*commentarii*) in note form; Tacitus used them as a source for his histories as did Pliny for his *Natural History*.[5] We hear of two female philosophers: Magnilla, whose father, Magnus, and husband, Menius, were both philosophers, and Euphrosyne, versed in the nine Muses.[6] In the first century AD Epidaurian Pamphile was a learned woman and wrote thirty-three books of historical memoirs, summaries of various histories, controversies and books on sex. The courtesans Astyanassa and Elephantis also wrote 'pornography'.[7] Martial recommends the works of Sulpicia to married couples if they want to please each other: like Ovid before her, she teaches *ars amatoria*, the art of love.[8]

Musonius Rufus, the Stoic philosopher of the mid-first century AD, showed an enlightened attitude when he remarked that he could see no reason why women should not study philosophy; indeed, philosophy equips the woman to be a good wife and *matrona*: philosophy underscores everything. It enables her to run the house, rear her children, remain chaste and be a devoted mother and wife. It helps her to keep her emotions under control, be compliant, frugal and modest.[9] Rufus also argues that men and women should be educated in the same way and to the same extent. A pupil of his, Epictetus, noted that Plato was popular with women because they believed that he advocated women's communes and promiscuity.[10] Pliny the Younger is particularly concerned about education in women.[11] Plutarch argues that women should be well educated, if only to stop them filling their heads with all kinds of nonsense: the woman who is studying geometry will have no time for dancing; the woman who is reading Plato or Xenophon will reject magic and other such mumbo jumbo.[12]

In the late Republic home-based education was accompanied by a growing independence among increasing numbers of better-off women, allowing them more freedom outside the home. At the same time a number of male poets were able to eschew the traditional *mos maiorum*, rejecting the *cursus honorum* for a life of *otium* in which they could while away their time penning poetry and pursuing the objects of their affection. Among these coteries we can recognise such poets as Licinius Calvus, Varro of Atax, Valerius Cato, Furius Bibaculus, Helvius Cinna, Cornificius, Ticidas and, most famously, Catullus. Collectively, they went under the name of *poetae novi, neoteroi* or *Cantores Euphorionis*.[13] Traditionalists regarded this otiose lifestyle as frivolous and un-Roman.

Like Sallust's Sempronia, the women put on a pedestal by the love poets, their *doctae puellae*, were diametrically opposed to the *matrona*; they were anything but modest, discrete, *univira*, compliant or chaste, and it seems unlikely that between them they produced very much wool. The poets allowed themselves to be dominated by these women, their *dominae*, even to be enslaved by them in *servitium amoris*; their *cursus honorum* was *militia amoris*, their role in the *domus* and the *familia* bore little resemblance to *patria potestas*: they languished locked out on the doorstep, *exclusus amator*.

As champion of the *mos maiorum* and despiser of things Greek, Cato the Elder (234–149 BC) had spoken out sternly against what he saw as a period of moral decline and the erosion of the sturdy principles on which Rome had laid her foundations.[14] He identified the growing independence of the women of Rome as an ominous ingredient in this.[15] The defeat of Hannibal at Zama in 202 BC, the victory over the Macedonians at Pydna in 168 BC and the final extinguishing of the Carthaginian threat in 146 BC all allowed Rome to relax more and encouraged an unprecedented influx of Greek and Eastern influences and luxuries into a receptive Rome.[16]

Marriage *cum manu* had more or less died out, leaving women to marry in a much freer arrangement where love and affection were sometimes nothing more than a fortunate by-product;[17] divorcing was easy and it seems likely that adultery was on the increase. Widowhood, free marriage and divorce often left women better off financially; certainly they could be more independent.[18] The social climate is well summed up by Horace in *Odes* 3, 6: writing about Rome around 28 BC he describes how the traditional Roman *familia* and *matrona* were corrupted at the end of the Republic: he talks of how 'generations rich in sin first sullied marriage, families and the home' and then focuses on the *matura virgo* who loses no time perfecting Greek dancing and other blandishments. She fantasises about *incesti amores* – illicit love – and at drinking parties indiscriminately and casually seeks out young adulterers; the lights are left on so that her husband, who is taking payments for her services, can see it all, whether she's cavorting with a Spanish sailor or a door-to-door salesman: 'dedecorum pretiosus emptor – the buyer of her pricey shame'.[19]

It is in such an environment that Catullus and his contemporaries flourished. Their women could mix with whomsoever they chose at the games, at festivals, at dinner parties or in the theatre enjoying, if they so chose, a degree of sexual freedom not dissimilar to that enjoyed by a *meretrix*, a prostitute, but with little of the social stigma.[20]

Lesbia typifies the unattached, or readily detachable, sophisticated, rich, intelligent and urbane ladies of the day who could exert considerable influence – sexual, psychological and sometimes political – on their male friends: the recession of the *mos maiorum* allowed them to do that, and to provide the *milieux* for the *poetae novi* to write with conviction about their love for and of their relationships with them.[21] Independent men of means were for the first time able to shrug off the traditional allegiance to bar and battlefield and to write personally and subjectively about independent women of means.[22]

Hitherto, if the surviving evidence is to be relied upon, there is nothing subjective in Roman love poetry. Q. Lutatius Catulus (consul in 102 BC), Porcius Licinus and Valerius Aedituus do describe women and erotic themes in their epigrams but they bear the second-hand stamp of Callimachus, Meleager and Sappho, and are all the more impersonal for that.[23] Catullus and his colleagues wrote the first introspective, subjective and personal poetry about Roman women.

Catullus's poetry is shot through with references to the urbane society in which he moves, the sophisticated company – male and female – which he elects to keep, and the elegant, polished verses he and his associates are expected to pen. His work exudes adjectives such as *suavis*, *elegans* (13, 10), *urbanus*, *salsus* (39, 7–8 and 22, 2), *venustus* (31, 12), *lepidus* (1, 1) – 'in' words all indicative of the exclusive and smart society in which he moved; everything and everyone worth knowing is agreeable, elegant, urbane, witty, charming, smart.[24]

On a typical *dies otiosus* Varus invites Catullus to come over and meet his girlfriend: first appearances show her to be elegant and well mannered, but a later indiscretion on her part that embarrasses Catullus renders her silly and annoying. Flavius's reticence about his girl leads Catullus to assume that she is *illepida atque inelegans*: common and rough, *febriculosum scortum*, a fever-ridden slag no less. When he invites himself over to Ipsithilla's place for an afternoon of sex he sarcastically and sycophantically calls her 'my delight, my clever one': 'meae deliciae, mei lepores'.[25] Both Quintia and Ameana fall short: Quintia is indeed fair, tall and she holds herself well, but beautiful (*formosa*) she is not because she lacks *venustas* and *salis*, charm and wit; Ameana cannot talk posh. As for Caecilius's girlfriend, she has begun reading his *Magna Mater* and is fired with passion for Caecilius as a result. To Catullus, she is thereby more refined than the Sapphic Muse.[26]

It is Lesbia, though, for whom Catullus reserves the highest praise: Claudia Pulchra Prima (b. 94 BC), wife of Metellus Celer, brother of Publius Clodius Pulcher and mistress of Catullus. She was also a lover of Marcus Caelius Rufus, the friend whom Cicero defended against charges of attempted poisoning and, in doing so, destroyed Clodia's reputation such as it was, calling her, among other things, the 'Medea of the Palatine'.[27] Lesbia has the *venustas* and *salis* Quintia lacks, and *veneres* – grace, elegance and charm; this, and physical beauty adds up to total beauty. Lesbia has literary skills: she can identify the 'best bits of the worst poet as she demonstrates' when she hands back the awful annals of Volusius, 'pure unsophisticated doggerel, complete crap': 'pleni ruris et infacetiarum annales Volusi, cacata charta'.[28]

Some twenty-five years separate Catullus's death in the mid-50s BC and the publication of Propertius's first book of love elegies around 29 BC. The gap, though, is artificial because it was occupied by other poets whose work is not extant. One such poet was Cornelius Gallus; he was born around 70 BC and committed suicide after being denounced by Augustus in 26 BC. We know that he wrote four books of elegies[29] and provided some degree of continuity between Catullus and Propertius.

Propertius includes finesse in the fields of dance, music and poetry, as well as intelligence, in the competencies that drive his passion. Physical beauty is eclipsed by these skills; Cynthia's lyre playing inspires his poetry. Cynthia is *docta*; she is a fitting companion to him in Helicon. At the other extreme of the intellectual spectrum, Acanthis the bawd assures her protégé that poetry is valueless.[30] Propertius's (inconsistent) fidelity to Cynthia is secured because she possesses 'the accomplishments of chaste Pallas, radiating the splendid fame of a learned forefather'.[31] Her conversation is fine, particularly when the couple are in bed together. She can compose poetry herself, and Propertius goes so far as to compare her with Corinna, a contemporary of Pindar.[32] Intellectually, Cynthia is on a par with Propertius: it is reasonable to assume that a less intelligent or less accomplished woman would have held little attraction for him. At the same time, though, her *lepor* and sophistication are a double-edged sword: the attention she thereby attracts from other impressionable men, and her care not to be dependent on any one man, may be reasons why he is unable to keep her.[33]

Propertius's contemporary, Albius Tibullus, is noticeably reticent on the intellectual qualities of both Delia and Nemesis. Indeed, not for Tibullus the cosmopolitan life of a Catullus or a Propertius: he 'in his madness' (*demens*) actually desires a bucolic life, embracing *rus* rather than sneering at it, as was the convention – 'I will live in the country, and my Delia will be there to look after the fruits of the earth.' He describes a lifestyle more befitting a country *matrona,* which sees Delia sitting at home in

the evening surrounded by seamstresses who one by one fall
asleep working away at the loom. This itself is reminiscent of
Lucretia, that paradigm of *matronae*.[34] By contrast, the author of
the *Garland of Sulpicia* describes the poetess Sulpicia as *docta
puella*.[35]

For Horace, who was writing around the same time as Propertius
and Tibullus, any appreciation of female artistic accomplishment
is largely limited to the floor shows put on by the dancing girls at
the drinking parties he attended: Damalis is leered at remorselessly,
Lyde is summoned to play her lyre and Neaera is required to sing
– all as a precursor to sex. Phydile is dismissed as simply *rustica*.[36]
In a more general context Licymnia is praised for her *dulces
cantus*, sweet singing, Chloe is skilled on the cithara and is good
at gentle dance rhythms – *dulcis docta modos et citharae sciens* –
while the *eburna* and *curva* lyres of Lydia and the *scortum* Lyde
are much in demand, as are Phyllis and *arguta* (melodious) Neaera
for their singing, and Tyndaris for her lyre-playing and singing.[37]
Horace appreciates accomplishment in the arts – music, dancing
and singing – but he seems quite indifferent to intelligence, wit or
social sophistication in his women.

Paradoxically, he is at his most vituperative with 'the grown-up
girl [who] delights in being taught the Greek movements and is
coached in seduction; all she thinks about now is illicit sex from
top to toe': 'dancing today, adultery tomorrow'.[38] Horace probably
summed up the usual male attitude: an attitude exemplified
by Scipio Africanus, who was flabbergasted by the increasing
popularity of dancing among girls and boys; dancing was so
Greek, not at all Roman. Sempronia was vilified by Sallust because
she danced like a professional. On the other hand, Cornelius Nepos
later admonished Romans for their xenophobic assumption that
other cultures could not possibly like dancing, just because
Romans despised it and consigned it to the demi-monde.[39]

Ovid is even less particular: to him if a woman is *non rustica* – if
she affects the resilience of the Sabine women, if she is bookish
– or if she is common (*rudis*), if she attracts by virtue of her
simplicitas: if she is any or all of these things, she is fine by Ovid.
Shy girls, coquettish girls, tall girls, small girls, fashionable girls,
frumpy girls, blonde girls, black girls – girls, girls, girls – they are

all the same to Ovid. In the same poem however, he does single
out the attractions of a woman who is literate and critical, who can
sing, play the lyre and dance well:

> This girl sings sweetly, she has good range ... this one thrums the
> awkward strings with practised thumb – who could not adore such
> clever hands? This one delights in the way she moves, her arms
> following the rhythm and her soft hips twisting with subtle skill.
> (*Amores* 2, 4, 25–31)

Ovid confirms this in the *Ars Amatoria*.[40] The obsession with
and admiration of dancing girls and singers flew in the face of
convention. Dancers, to many, Horace included, were one short
step up from prostitutes, ancient-world lap dancers.

Ovid can advise where to find all types of girls, including
cultissima femina – the games are literally crawling with
sophisticated women – confirmation that the educated woman was
out and about and generally much sought-after. He acknowledges
that some women appreciate good oratorical style and oratory, and
he himself consorts with women who are able to value his poetry
– not least Corinna. He advises his fellow men to get educated,
because women appreciate intellectual gifts in a man more than
they do good looks.[41] He recommends that men read widely in the
Greek classics and in modern literature, suggesting clearly that
women were similarly well read and enjoyed literary discussion.
Later in the poem, though, he qualifies this when he admits that
doctae puellae are thin on the ground and that, generally, poetry
is held in low regard. Clever women do exist, though, and many
aspire to culture; women can be seduced by verse or a piece of
declamation, be they clever or stupid.[42]

This is Ovid as *praeceptor amoris* – a teacher of love, or 'agony
aunt'. In Books 1 and 2 he teaches men; in Book 3, women. He
is working for both sides: his advice to women covers social
etiquette and sexual technique designed to maximise the pleasure
for both parties.[43] Unfortunately for Ovid, *praeceptor amoris* as a
profession was not exclusive to men. While the love poets were
busy admiring the intellectual and artistic talents of their women,
an altogether less salubrious type of education was being provided

in the seedy Roman demi-monde. The *lena*, or bawd, had a role to play as *praeceptrix amoris*, instructing her girls in seduction and meretricious exploitation.

Propertius's Acanthis poem is an example of the rancour these women excited. It is a litany of invective and abuse, expressing outrage that the *lena* has scuppered his chances of sexual progress with his girl. It starts savagely, setting the tone for what is to follow: a catalogue of all the unhelpful advice given to the girl, all freighted with Propertius's disgust. Acanthis recommends a wholly mercenary attitude – dishonesty and deceit, withholding sex, jealousy – and it gets personal when she scorns poetry and music as worthless gifts.[44] She sabotages Propertius's best weapon – his intellect and his verse.

Sulpicia was a *docta puella*: the six elegies in which she describes her love for Cerinthus as part of the *Corpus Tibullianum* constitute one of the very few surviving examples of poetry composed by a Roman woman.[45] She came from a gifted family: her father, Servius Sulpicius Rufus, was a lawyer of some note who dabbled in love poetry; her uncle, M. Valerius Messalla Corvinus, was a literary patron and a composer of erotic and bucolic verse. It seems probable that Sulpicia was in Messalla's circle, thus confirming for us that women were not excluded from the literary coteries of the day; moreover, one of Sulpicia's slaves, Petale, is a *lectrix*, a public performer of Greek and Latin literature. Just as her male contemporaries, Tibullus and Propertius, lived a somewhat dissolute life, free from the shackles of the *mos maiorum* and the *cursus honorum*, so too did the coquettish Sulpicia, liberated from the modesty and chastity expected of the *matrona*: she loves being naughty – *pecasse iuvat*.

We can add another Sulpicia – Sulpicia Caleni, a poetess who lived during the reign of Domitian and is praised by Martial. Her poems, only two of which survive, are based on her own experience of married life, particularly her sex life with Calenus. Martial declares that they are required reading for wife and husband alike and the key to a happy, one-man, one-woman marriage: all the wives and all the husbands are reading Sulpicia.[46]

She, a *univira*, teaches pure and honest love, 'messing about, teasing and joking'. Sappho, no less, would have benefited from her as teacher, *magistra*. In the fourth century AD her reputation is still sufficiently alive for Ausonius to describe her work as salacious, her manner prim; the less liberal Sidonius Apollinarus in the fifth century includes her in a list of earlier poets ... whom he will not be imitating.

Around AD 130 Julia Balbilla accompanied Hadrian and the Empress Vibia Sabina on tours of the Nile valley, as court poetess and as a kind of royal correspondent. To record their visit she inscribed on the left leg and foot of one of the Colossi of Memnon in Thebes (a monumental statue of the pharaoh Amenophis III) four epigrams in ancient Aeolic dialect – as used by Sappho some 800 years earlier. In so doing, Julia was following a time-honoured tradition celebrating Memnon's amazing early-morning 'singing' – an audible phenomenon emanating from fractures to the statue made by an earthquake. Her first three epigrams dutifully commemorate the royal visit, the fourth Julia's personal experience. Julia's erudition is clearly evident from these inscriptions: she is not only familiar with a long-obsolete ancient Greek dialect and metre, but she displays a working knowledge of relevant Egyptian and Greek mythology. Vibia Sabina added an inscription of her own on the instep of the left foot.

In a similar vein and around the same time, Terentia was touring Egypt when she too paused to make an inscription in time-honoured tradition; she inscribed six hexameters on the Tura limestone that formed the surface of the pyramid of Cheops. It was later quarried to build the modern city of Cairo but luckily in 1935, a German tourist, Wilhelm von Boldensele, had spotted it and made a copy. The lines are essentially a lament for Terentia's deceased brother, D. Terentius Gentianus, and a celebration of his career. Like Julia Balbilla's verses, it displays some erudition with its echoes of Catullus and Ovid in the second verse reflecting their take on the death of a brother; the third verse recalls one of Horace's Odes.[47]

In the first century AD Nero's last wife, Statilia Messalina, studied declamation and was a skilled rhetorician. Dio Cassius tells how Julia Domna, wife of Septimius Severus and mother of Caracella, his successor, at the end of the second century AD, was good at rhetoric and involved in political and philosophical discussions with the powerful and eminent men of the day. She regularly advised Caracella in an official capacity; he delegated to her matters of state with which he could not be bothered – her name appeared with his on correspondence with the Senate.[48]

In the previous chapter we admired Hortensia's spirited speech in the Forum in 42 BC. She was not the only female orator; Valerius Maximus knew of two more in the first century BC who we have also met: Maesia Sentia – Androgyne – successfully defended herself; sadly the charge has been lost to us. Afrania, a senator's wife, regularly declaimed before a praetor and was vitiated for her immodesty, her name becoming a by-word for female wickedness.[49] In AD 203 the Christian martyr Vibia Perpetua gave an impassioned speech before her execution in a North African Roman amphitheatre. As well as showing a good knowledge of Roman literature she delivers an intimate and eloquent account of her life leading up to martyrdom.

We know from Cicero, Ovid and Pliny that women received and sent letters. The letters of Cicero take in a number of female correspondents including his wives Terentia and Publilia, his daughter Tullia, and Pomponia his sister-in-law. Twenty-four letters in the *Ad Familiares* were sent to Terentia. Marcus, his son, wrote to Terentia and Tullia; Pomponia corresponded with her son, Quintus; Pilia, the wife of Atticus, wrote to Cicero's brother Quintus and Atticus himself to Tullia; Terentia corresponded with Atticus and Pomponia. All subjects were covered, not least the news from Rome, which a depressed, suicidal Cicero so craved while in exile in 58 and 57 BC. Pliny's letters are more studied and polished, no doubt with an eye to publication but, businesslike as some of them are, they nevertheless include personal messages to a number of women on a number of different issues. There is a letter to Pompeia Celerina, thanking her for the use of her villa; to the widowed Calvina about Pliny's financial support; to Corellia Hispulla on the matter of a rhetorician for her son; to Calpurnia Hispulla eulogising Calpurnia, his third wife and her niece; and to Calpurnia herself.[50] These letters show not just an obvious literacy among the women with whom Cicero and Pliny corresponded but also the involvement of these women in a range of financial, educational and political activities. Terentia was given a Phoenician scholar as a present; she freed him and he went on to found a school in Rome.

By the end of the Republic, Greek and things Greek had well and truly percolated into Roman education. Dialectic, geometry, astronomy and music were added to the curriculum. Livius Andronicus, half Greek, came to Rome from Tarentum in 272 BC, translated the *Odyssey* into Latin and wrote a number of comedies and tragedies, thereby laying the foundations of Roman literature. We know that he taught the children of M. Livius Salinator, among others, Greek and Latin grammar. Quintus Ennius, Greek by education, followed in 204 BC, introduced, ironically, by the notoriously anti-Greek Cato the Censor. Like Livius Andronicus, Ennius taught the children of the aristocracy. In 159 BC Crates of Mallus, a *kritikos* in the Pergamene School, fell down a drain in the Cloaca Maxima. He broke a leg and stayed on in the city well beyond his recuperation, and during his sojourn he did much to inspire scholarship and education in Rome.

The provision of schools was probably quite sporadic and was concentrated in towns and cities; many were co-educational. Cicero, in the *Republica* (4, 3) tells us that there was no state requirement to provide either an education or public schools. Horace recalls the rote learning he endured at school, especially the epic poetry of Livius Andronicus, drummed into him by *plagosus Orbilius*, 'Orbilius the flogger'. None the worse for his flagellations, he advises a more discerning and critical view of old epics than was often found in his day: 'I'm amazed that they [epics] are considered faultless, beautiful – perfect almost.' The Twelve Tables were learnt by heart. As the Republic drew to an end Latin rhetoric was introduced to run alongside the Greek, and new, contemporary Latin literature in the form of Virgil, Horace and the elegiac love poets began to replace Plautus, Terence and the old epic poets Naevius, Ennius and Livius Andronicus.[51]

After surviving Orbilius, Horace came to appreciate a more subtle approach to education: the power of the bribe or incentive, 'as teachers used to give seductive little cakes to their pupils to make them learn the basics'.[52] Seneca lays down some sensible rules for bringing up children, so as to turn out the well-balanced child – avoid spoiling them, do not tolerate tantrums, give praise where it is due, avoid too much *otium* – basically, tread a middle line.[53] In the *Ars Poetica* Horace gives a typical lesson in arithmetic and money management; by comparison with the Greeks, he says, Roman education was much more pragmatic. Cicero had said as much when he observed that the Greeks studied geometry as an end in itself; the Romans, however, studied it so as to be able to measure out the land.[54]

Home learning from the *matrona* could be supplemented by the appointment of a peripatetic tutor, or by attending school. Minicia Marcella and her sister had *paedagogi* for their elementary education and *praeceptores* for grammar and the arts; Atticus hired a *paedagogus* to teach his daughter, Caecilia Attica, and a *grammaticus*, Q. Caecilius Epirota, for grammar. Epirota introduced Virgil into the curriculum. The children of Pompey were tutored by Aristodemus of Nyssa; we can assume that this included Pompeia as well as Gnaeus and Sextus. When Pompey returned home after years of warring, her tutor had Pompeia show off her learning by reading from the *Iliad*; a more tactless quotation could not have been chosen when she read out Helen's line to Paris: 'You returned from the war; I wish that you had died there.' Excruciating embarrassment apart, the anecdote tells us that by the age of eight Pompeia was bilingual and at the start of the grammar stage of her education. The tuition that Augustus provided for his grandsons was probably shared by Julia and Agrippina, his granddaughters. Indeed, Macrobius mentions Julia's love of letters and great learning. Augustus advises Agrippina to avoid affectation in her grammar work. As we have seen, the daughter of Pontius Aufidianus had a teacher, Fannius Saturninus; that is before Aufidianus killed them both because they were having an affair. On the edge of Empire, in Vindolanda, the fascinating letter of invitation from Claudia Severa shows her literacy.[55]

As for schools, legend has it that Romulus and Remus attended one in Gabii; Verginia went to one in the Forum. The parents paid; Pliny endowed a school in Comum.[56] Horace refers to girl pupils in his advice to bad poets, cheaply implying that it was acceptable for inferior poets to teach girls; Ovid says that Menander was read by girls and boys; Juvenal refers to girls learning the alphabet.[57]

Martial characterises the schoolmaster as *invisus* (detested) by
schoolboys and schoolgirls alike; he reports that the poetry of
Coscomius is suitable for boys and girls and he tells of a *magister*
reading poetry to a grown-up girl. He refers to poetry teaching
in *schola*, in classes attended by girls and boys. His verse is
unsuitable for school use, good only for *nequam iuvenes facilesque
puella* – 'naughty boys and easy girls'.[58] Pliny is only talking about
boys and fathers when he says that everyone's parent was also
their teacher.[59]

From Vespasian's time the state was taking more responsibility
for education; state-funded rhetoricians and *grammatici* in both
Greek and Latin were beginning to appear. Primary schools (*ludi*)
were staffed by a *magister* or *litterator* and covered elementary
education; secondary schools (*schola*), from about age twelve,
were under a *grammaticus* and taught literature, Greek and
public speaking. In his *Brutus* Cicero gives an account of his
education from the age of sixteen when he was learning rhetoric
and philosophy. Suetonius records that there were twenty schools
in Rome teaching grammar by the end of the Republic, and
Quintilian favours schools to home tuition for the children of the
elite.[60] A freedman at Trimalchio's party declares that he learned
no geometry, no literary criticism or other such rubbish, but he
does know his way around advertising posters and percentages.[61]

The education of girls of the lower orders is less clear. We
know that schools were occasionally endowed by the state for the
education and training of poor and orphaned girls – the *Faustinae*
– and we can assume that competence in numeracy and literacy
was achieved by a good number of girls and boys, particularly
those who went into commercial occupations. A tombstone, now
in the British Museum, shows a ten-year-old Roman girl, Avita,
reading, with a bookstand and scroll close at hand. Some girls
were trained, as apprentices, for a career in such jobs as medicine,
midwifery nursing, retail, bookkeeping or hairdressing.[62]

Marriage delimited education for girls – whatever their social
status. An early marriage would have curtailed their education
before the grammar stage. Although some women continued their
education in marriage, most would have been preoccupied with
raising children and running the household. What opportunities

were there for extending education beyond the wedding day? Perhaps the most significant was teaching by the husband. Pliny the Younger records the erudite Pompeius Saturninus, whose wife purportedly composed some very fine letters in the retro style of Plautus and Terence; Pliny congratulates him for making his wife 'tam docta politaque' (so clever, so refined). Pliny's own marriage to Calpurnia offers another example of a learned husband imbuing a wife with a love of learning and literature.[63] Laudable as it is, this 'education by husband' is also, to some extent, indicative of the woman firmly placed in her role as the perfect wife. In the late first century AD the traditional docility of the *matrona* is still very much in evidence: the husband prescribes what the wife reads, assuming, as with Fannius Saturninus's wife, that she had little or no education before their marriage. Plutarch urges the husband to assume the role of philosophical mentor, to prevent the wife having her own independent way of thinking.[64] Husbands reading to wives appear frequently on sarcophagi.[65]

Further education was, of course, available through the same tutor who may have taught the woman before her marriage. Atticus's daughter was tutored by Q. Caecilius Epirota; Fannius Saturninus we know lost his job, and his head, after allegations of improper behaviour – a reflection, no doubt, of the fact that these tutors were often responsible for the moral education of their charges as well as the intellectual and, therefore, an easy scapegoat if and when things went awry.[66] Writing in the second century AD, Lucian parodies what must have been a vogue for hiring Greeks to give the illusion of erudition: the pretentiousness of women exceeds that of men; they are, Lucian sneers, keen to have 'educated men living in their households on a salary and following their litters'; they want to be seen 'to be cultured, to have an interest in philosophy and to write songs that are barely inferior to Sappho's'. They 'listen' to their entourage of rhetoricians, grammarians and philosophers while applying their make-up, having their hair done or during dinner, distracted from the lecture on marital fidelity to read a surreptitious note from a lover.[67] Helvia, the mother of Seneca, was keen to learn but was prevented from doing so by her husband, Seneca's conservative father. She would have received no education from him and would not have been permitted a tutor; when Seneca was in exile he advises her to resume the studies of the *bonae artes* they once shared together, as consolation for his enforced absence.[68]

The relative freedom enjoyed by women would also have had an educational effect. Entertainment at dinner parties was not restricted, as we have seen, to Spanish dancers, dwarfs, magicians and jugglers; gladiatorial displays and decapitations were very much the exception rather than the rule. Cerebral activity was often on the agenda, including recitations, discussions about philosophy, rhetoric and grammar, readings from Menander, Virgil and Homer. Pliny's letters have frequent references to intellectual, prandial entertainment; recitations were *de riguer chez* Atticus.[69] How far women contributed to these soirées is unknown: their presence alone assumes some level of edification, passive or otherwise. Where women did intervene, though, they were sometimes derided for their efforts, as Juvenal shows. Women routinely attended the theatre and would, of course, like the men in the audience, have learnt something from the plays, even the mimes, they saw there.

The love poets focussed their attention on women who enjoyed considerable social independence; these women read their poetry, confirmed for us by the frequency with which the poets, and later Martial, cite women as their audience. Both Ovid and Martial disingenuously try to dissuade respectable *matronae* from reading their salacious verses, but these are no more than publicity stunts: *matronae* were no more likely to avert their eyes than women, 'respectable' or otherwise, are in 2013 from the best-selling *Fifty Shades of Grey* trilogy by E. L. James.[70] The urbanity and sophistication of the women courted by the love poets, the very qualities which attracted the poets in the first place, allow us to assume that they read other genres such as epic, satire, history, tragedy, comedy and philosophy both as leisure reading and for edification; Cicero, Propertius, Horace, Martial and Juvenal all corroborate this.[71] Varro, indeed, dedicated his *Res Rusticae, Country Matters*, complete with exhaustive bibliography, to Fundania, his wife – fascinating reading, no doubt, for the ordinary woman. Whether she ever read it or not we will never know; the point is that she was patently capable of reading it and of understanding its practical applications.

Two recommended reading lists, one aimed at women, exist. The first is compiled by Ovid and is purportedly aimed at lower-class rather than middle-class women; it is nothing if not erudite and includes Greek and Latin texts: Callimachus, Philetas, Anacreon, Sappho, Menander, Propertius, Gallus, Tibullus, the *Argonautica* of Varro of Atax and Virgil's *Aeneid* – as well as Ovid's own work. Quintilian's, for boys learning grammar and rhetoric, is completely different, with examples from tragedy and Virgil the only common author with Ovid's. The lists confirm that women were a serious market for books and that books 'for leisure' were seen as a very different commodity from texts for the serious business of learning rhetoric. An example of a wife 'reading' a husband's work before publication is given by Statius; Claudia, it seems, was sometimes up all night, hearing a first draft of his prolix *Thebaid*.[72]

How far women owned their own books (through copying, ideally from an original to avoid copyists' errors) or had access to private libraries is difficult to know. There is no reason to doubt that Cornelia, Caecilia Attica, Ovid's Perilla, Fundania, Helvia and Pliny's Calpurnia availed themselves of a husband's or father's library. Horace scorns an old woman for her collection of books on Stoicism and, in an early copyright infringement, Caerellia is excused by Cicero (on account of her passion for philosophy and because he was in her debt) for copying his *de Finibus* without permission, from Atticus's original.[73] Sidonius Apollinarus, the fifth-century AD Christian writer, mentions a library in the estate of Tonantius Ferreolus near Nîmes in which the books were shelved according to whether they were devotional Christian literature or Latin classics – the former being located near to the women's seats.[74] Ovid makes no mention of libraries in his list of places for men and women to meet;[75] it may be that the use of public libraries by women was so commonplace that it went unremarked.

At the beginning of the chapter we noted that the *puella docta* sometimes attracted scorn and abuse. Nowhere is this more vivid than in Juvenal's excoriating sixth Satire. His disgust at the vogue for women speaking Greek gives a taste of the vitriol to come: 'omnia Graece ... concumbunt Graece' (everything's gone Greek ... they even have sex in Greek). Women are litigious, taking over the legal system as defendant or prosecutor, writing the transcripts and bossing the male lawyers about. He scorns musical and singing ability and deplores the woman who assumes the role of the (male) grammarian and parades her knowledge of Virgil or Homer at the dinner party: 'so great is the force of her verbiage' that it silences *grammatici, rhetores, causasdici* – even other women. In short, the woman who wants to be *docta* and *facunda*, the pedant and the know-it-all, is a *monstrum* who should just go away and be a man.

No matter how much an Ovid, a Pliny or a Tacitus encouraged education and learning in women, there was always, it seems, a Juvenal lurking round the corner ready to reduce it all to dust.[76] Sallust called Sempronia's morals into question, criticising her dancing skills and other talents, before reluctantly admitting that she was a gifted woman. Likewise, Cicero, in the *Pro Caelio*, includes Clodia's literary skills in a fusillade of attacks on what he saw as a generally sordid character.[77] Persius labels poetesses, *poetridae,* as *picae* – magpies, greedy and plagiaristic.[78] Lucian, as we saw above, continues the unhappy tradition in his *De Mercede Conductis.*

5

SIBYLS & THE DARK ARTS

The previous chapter dealt with the education of women, their accomplishments in the fine arts, their talents as writers, in music, dancing and philosophy and their reception by male contemporaries. This chapter will examine the opposite end of the artistic spectrum and explore women as Sibyls, witches and ghosts, purveyors of magic, and other manifestations of the dark arts.

In Rome, elements of these dark arts were very much a feature of everyday life, separated in some cases only by a very blurred line from state, and 'unofficial' religion, often barely distinguishable from what might be called conventional medicine. They had their roots in folk religions and ancient folk medicine, insinuating themselves in cultures and civilisations in Egypt, Mycaenae, the Middle and Near East and Etruria, as old Italic traditions and practice, before flooding into Rome on the tide of Hellenisation.

Magic was everywhere. The first example of Greek magic comes in the *Odyssey* when the hero meets Circe, a witchy kind of a woman. Circe transforms Odysseus's crew into pigs with a wand and a potion; Odysseus himself is immune, because Mercury has given him *moly*, a snowdrop type of flower with protective and mystical properties.[1] Odysseus nevertheless succumbs to Circe's considerable physical charms and the two embark on an affair during which she provides some useful information about the future, not least Odysseus's forthcoming appointment with the dead in his necromancy. Circe is a *pharmakis* or *pharmakeutrika*; she is *polu pharmakos* and she uses *pharmaka,* and there lies the close tripartite association of drugs, spells and medicine in the ancient world. The Circe episode contains many of the elements of the magical and dark arts we want to examine here in the context of Roman women: magical skill and accoutrements, mystical plants, witches, divine intervention and eschatology. Over the next 500–600 years these motifs were developed and expanded on in Greek literature, religion, philosophy and science; they began to bind themselves to Roman culture and society from the end of the first century BC and to appear in Roman literature.

Other than Odysseus's *nekyia* in Book 11, Homer makes a number of infernal or supernatural references: Proteus predicts Menelaus's destiny in Elysium; the twin gates of dreams are described; Odysseus buries his comrades at sea and in the last book Homer describes the souls of Penelope's suitors, Achilles and Agamemnon in Hades. There is an episode in the *Odyssey* where a *pharmakon* is used to good, recreational end: Helen gives Menelaus and his comrades a drug to take with their wine, guaranteed to make them forget their troubles, however bad, and to cheer them up. In the *Iliad* Homer describes the ghost of Patroclus.[2]

Hesiod, in the *Works & Days* outlines the afterlife of the different ages of man and in the *Theogony* describes Tartarus and its inhabitants. Pindar deals with judgement of the dead and metempsychosis in his second *Olympian Ode*, while two fragments cover Elysium and more on the transmigration of souls. Aristophanes has his celebrated *katabasis* of Dionysus in the *Frogs* featuring Charon, and Euripides has his *Medea*; Sophocles describes Medea's witchcraft in the *Rhizotomoi*; in his *Oedipus* Creon elaborately and at some length describes the setting for a necromancy in which a multitude of ghosts are summoned, including that of Laius. Aeschylus raises the ghost of Darius after Atossa's libations to the gods of the underworld in the *Persae*.[3]

Antiphon describes a daughter of Deianeira who tricked a concubine into poisoning her own son and husband with what she thought was a love potion – a *pharmakon*; the concubine was tortured to death on the wheel. Herodotus recounts Melissa's *nekuomanteion* and Periander's necrophilia. Diogenes Laertius leaves a fragment of Empedocles which refers to a necromancy and Plato expatiates on the immortality of the soul (*Phaedo*);

the nature of death, judgement of the dead (*Gorgias*), Orphism (*Cratylus*) and metempsychosis (*Phaedrus*). His *Myth of Er* describes Er's experience in the underworld.[4]

Lycophron covers Cassandra's prophecy in his *Alexandra* and Theocritus Simaetha's erotic magic. Diodorus Siculus makes use of the mythologising of Dionysius Scytobrachion, a contemporary of Apollonius, in his accounts of Hecate and Medea and, like Seneca later, tells how Deianeira kills Hercules by means of a *philtron*.[5]

The philosophers-cum-miracle workers Pythagoras, Empedocles and Orpheus left their mark; Apollonius of Rhodes developed the witch Medea, Circe's sister, and her *pharmaka* in the epic *Argonautica*. Theocritus wrote the *Pharmakeutria* (*The Sorceress*) on medicinal – and magical – herbs and potions. He describes a love potion in *Idyll* 2, the accuracy of which is confirmed by excavated amulets, curse tablets and magical papyri. A sceptical Pliny the Elder tells us that Menander wrote a comedy, the *Thessala*, about the infamous witches of Thessaly and their ability to draw down the moon. Theophrastus profiled the 'superstitious' type in his *Characters*.

Pliny ascribes the origins of magic in the Greek world to Osthanes who accompanied Xenophon on his expedition. He notes that such luminaries of Greek philosophy as Pythagoras, Empedocles, Democritus and Plato went overseas to learn about magic. On his return, Democritus was responsible for 'seducing the minds of men with the charm of magic'. There were other influences, from the Jews and from Cyprus, from the druids in Gaul and Britain – Britain he marks out as being particularly occult.

From Egypt the *Greek Magical Papyri* comprised a veritable pharmacopeia of potions, arcane knowledge and spells accumulated over the centuries; written down in the late third century AD, they are directories of spells and mystical writings, or the manuals of itinerant magicians, containing potion and spell repertoires, magic formulae and incantations ranging from powerful invovations of infernal gods and daemons to folk medicine and magical tricks, from deathly curses to love charms and remedies for impotence. *Ephesia Grammata* (Greek magic formulae – or meaningless words, mumbo jumbo) were spoken to ward off evil influences, the best-known being ΑΣΚΙ(ΟΝ) ΚΑΤΑΣΚΙ(ΟΝ) ΛΙΞ ΤΕΤΡΑΞ ΔΑΜΝΑΜΕΝΕΥΣ ΑΙΣΙΟΝ. Magical *ostraca*, the damning-to-hell *tabellae defixionum* (curse tablets) and amulets, phylacteries, inscribed with magical formulae – these all added to the rich fund of cabalistic and chthonic knowledge and experience.

In Roman times Ennius adapted Euripides' *Medea*. Plautus contrives a ghost story in the Mostellaria;[6] Apollodorus describes Hercules' *katabasis* and Medea's sorcery in his *Library of Greek Mythology*;[7] Lucretius, in *De Rerum Natura* Book 3, teaches us Epicurean eschatology and Cicero, in the *Somnium Scipionis,* Stoic eschatology.[8] In his *On Divination* he describes a ghost at Megara; there is a necromancy in *In Vatinium*.[9] Strabo, the Greek geographer, pinpoints the oracle of the dead at Avernus as the location for Odysseus's *nekyia* in the *Odyssey*; Varro lists the various forms of divination.[10] Ovid composed a *Medea,* now lost, although she is alive and well in his *Heroides* and his *Metamorphoses*.

Virgil has his underworld in *Aeneid* 6; he also reflects Theocritus with his description of the sorcery of Amaryllis in *Eclogues* 8, and gives his version of the *katabasis* of Orpheus in *Georgics* 4.

Add to this the treatment of one or other of these *topoi* by Tibullus,[11] Horace,[12] the author of the Culex,[13] Propertius[14] and Ovid[15] and we have a theme which is not only rich in terms of literary heritage but dynamic, vibrant, highly topical and contemporary. Later in the first century AD Lucan wrote his *Catacthonion*, also lost, the unfinished *Medea* (according to Vacca) and a work on Orpheus. That Lucan, Statius, Silius Italicus and Valerius Flaccus went on to incorporate chthonic episodes in their epics is hardly surprising given the traditions of the genre, and the ubiquity and popularity of these *topoi*; similarly the novelist Petronius and tragedian Seneca the Younger. The wealth of magical and eschatological material being published undoubtedly reflected an unquenchable popular taste for the mystical, macabre and chthonic which mirrored a preoccupation with the dark arts within corners of Roman society.

By the end of the first century BC, 'sciences' such as magic, astrology, alchemy and daemonology were established as teachable subjects. In his *Natural History* Pliny the Elder records evidence of witchcraft among the Machyles in Africa: apart from being bisexual with one breast female the other male, they induce drought and child mortality on a prodigious scale. The Triballi and Illyrians can kill with just one look from their twin-pupilled evil eyes. Pliny expatiates on magic, denouncing the work of *magi*, magicians, but enumerating all aspects of their suspect arts. He identifies the tripartite link magic makes with medicine and religion, noting how it all started with man's desire to improve his health – and life expectancy – and to know the future, by divination. At best Pliny is ambivalent about the efficacy of magic, admitting that it is *intestabilis* (execrable) but at the same time, when it manifests in poisons, offers *veritatis umbrae* – shadows of the truth. So, for Pliny, the drugs do work, but much of the other magic is all lies.

Some of Pliny's potions and poisons, of course, were to find themselves merging into the respectable and mainstream sciences of pharmacy, pharmacology and medicine.[16] Plutarch's *De Superstitione* suggests, by implication, that obsessive superstition, *deisidaimonia*, was endemic in Roman society. Lucian deplored the ready acceptance of superstition by the gullible: he wrote a satirical account, *Alexander*, or *The Pseudoprophet*, on the founding of a new cult by Alexander of Abonuteichus which was closed to Epicureans and Christians; it did, however, boast a large number of women adherents, attracted possibly by its claim to a new manifestation of the god Asculepius in the shape of a snake, Glycon.

Plutarch probably sums up the typical Roman attitude to magic in his *Moralia* where he offers advice on how to achieve a good marriage. Education of the wife by the husband is an important component of this – he is her mentor, philosopher and teacher and part of his responsibility is to urge the study of Plato or Xenophon, leaving no room for silly and aimless pursuits like dabbling in magic incantations.

By definition it is impossible to gauge just how much occult activity went on in Rome. However, the sheer number of curse tablets found would, on its own, suggest that magic, superstition and cursing were prevalent. The number of women actually, or allegedly, engaging in witchcraft at any one time was no doubt minute, but the frequent appearance of witches in poetry and natural history cannot be accounted for by the exigencies and traditions of genre alone. Roman epic, satire, love poetry and tragedy are populated with witches and other female peddlers of the occult: it seems plausible that audiences will have been familiar with their practices and would recognise them from everyday experience, stories or by traditional superstition.

From the earliest times women were central to the dark arts. Plato observed 'of all wild things, the child is most unmanageable ... the most unruly animal there is. That's why he has to be curbed by a great many bridles.' One of these bridles, reputedly advocated by harassed nurses, was the insinuation of the bogeyman, or rather bogeywoman, into the lives and psyches of children in their charge. She often appeared as a big bad wolf that ate naughty boys and girls alive and always had one freshly devoured in her stomach. The ubiquitous bogeywoman took the shape of Mormo in Ancient Greece – a terrifying donkey with the legs of a woman; she was either queen of the Lystraegones, who had lost her own children and now murdered those of others, or a child-eating Corinthian. Another was Empusa who variously took the form of a cow, donkey or beautiful woman; yet another was Gello, an evil female spirit and child snatcher. To Diodorus Siculus, Empusa was a beautiful child eater. The Roman equivalent was Lamia – a vivacious Libyan woman whose children by Zeus were murdered by Hera; like Mormo she was a cannibal and exacted revenge by murdering other women's babies, eating them alive.[17] Flavius Philostratus in the late second century AD talks of Lamia and Empusa as *phasma* – ghosts, or nightmares. Lucretius was sufficiently concerned about irrational fear and over-active imaginations to attempt to explain it all away; Horace includes the fear of dreams, the terrors of magic, miracles and night-time ghosts in a catalogue of events the strong-minded should have nothing to do with.[18]

Superstition was rife and omnipresent, presumably as much among women as men. Persius singles out god-fearing grandmothers and aunts in his satire on the inefficacy of men's clandestine prayers to the gods. Prayers are expert in averting the evil eye and may predict a life of extravagant wealth, a good marriage, an altogether rosy life: but Persius is far from convinced and no nurse will ever hear a prayer from Perseus. Juvenal too satirises the *anxia mater* at the temple of Venus for optimistically wishing for her daughter's beauty.[19]

In a world where it was considered unpropitious for a black cat to enter your house or a snake to fall from the roof into your yard,[20] where it was unlucky if a statue of a god was seen to sweat blood,[21] where a horse was born with five legs, a lamb with a pig's head and a pig with a human head, where a rampant bull ran up three flights of stairs, and a cow talked,[22] and where a statue laughed uncontrollably, a horse cried hot tears,[23] in a world where it was inauspicious to sneeze in the presence of a waiter holding a tray or to sweep the floor when a guest was standing up,[24] where it was de rigueur to whistle when lightning flashed, in such a world it should come as no surprise to hear what were probably exclusively female superstitions such as only trimming your nails on market days – and then starting with the forefinger and doing it in silence – but never at sea; Pliny records that in certain Italian towns it was forbidden by law for women to walk through the streets carrying a spindle. We have already seen how certain days of the year were avoided by betrothed couples when choosing their wedding day, and how the groom carried his bride over the threshold to avoid any chance of an unlucky stumble.

The Romans were clearly very superstitious, then. But it is important to remember that they were probably no more so than other cultures and societies. Indeed, if we look at the old wives' tales recounted by George Orwell from a rural childhood around 1900 in *Coming Up for Air* can we say they are any less absurd or irrational than those of the Romans? Take for example

> Swimming was dangerous, climbing trees was dangerous ... all animals were dangerous ... horses bit, bats got in your hair, earwigs got into your ears, swans broke your leg ... bulls tossed you ... raw potatoes were deadly poison, and so were mushrooms unless you bought them at the grocer's ... if you had a bath after a meal you died of cramp ... and if you washed your hands in the water eggs

were boiled in you got warts ... raw onions were a cure for almost anything.[25]

Magic, superstition, witchcraft and other manifestations of the mortuary were always viewed with considerable suspicion and concern by the authorities, in public at least. Table Seven, law three of the Twelve Tables specifically outlaws the use of incantations and magical arts to sabotage the grain or crops of another farmer; guilty parties were sacrificed to Ceres. Malicious incantations were similarly outlawed. In 331 BC, 116 women were condemned when they assembled for a mass potion- and poison-fest. In 186 BC the rites of the Bacchanals were severely restricted by the *senatus consultum de Bacchanalibus,* with around 7,000 followers of Dionysus thrown into jail or executed, according to Livy. A number of attempts were made to criminalise magical practices: by Agrippa in 33 BC when he banished astrologers (*astrologoi*) and sorcerers (*goetoi*), fearful that they were polluting established religion and having an unsettling effect on social order; by Maecenas in 29 BC; by Tiberius when he suppressed druids and outlawed clandestine consultations of soothsayers, *haruspices*; and by Claudius in AD 54 when he banned druids. None of these measures were entirely successful; furthermore, Augustus had criminalised divination to individuals and any divination on the subject of death in AD 11; he had also indulged in some judicious book burning when in 31 BC he destroyed around 2,000 Greek and Latin books of an unsuitable nature – prophetic writings – and of questionable authorship even though many were anonymous. Some of the *Sibylline Books* were included in the panic bonfires.

Sulla's *Lex Cornelia de Sicariis et Veneficis* of 81 BC had made it illegal to administer a love potion or abortifacients: the penalty for the lower classes was hard labour in the mines; for the upper classes, it was banishment to an island with property forfeited. If the recipient died it was a capital offence. Bewitching, binding or tying (*obcantare, defigere, obligere*) were punished by crucifixion or by being thrown to wild animals. A similar fate awaited witches or anyone who indulged in human sacrifice; if the convicted were from the upper orders they were simply executed. Magicians were burnt alive. Possession of magic books resulted in the books being burnt and the owner's property confiscated; lower classes were executed, the upper classes were banished. If a drug was given to someone as a palliative or remedy and the patient died then the donor was banished or executed, according to their social status. The *Digest of Justinian* adds that peddling of or possession of *venena* and *medicamenta* – evil drugs – was outlawed, as corroborated by Cicero – a woman who gives a drug to aid conception and kills the recipient is executed – irresponsible distribution by perfumers (*pigmentarii*) of hemlock, salamanders, aconite, pine caterpillars, bubrostis insect, mandrake or Spanish fly was also a criminal offence.

Tiberius presided over the condemnation of Libo Drusus for magical activity. Libo had been seduced by the prognostications of the Chaldeans, magical rites and the interpretation of dreams, oneiromancy; there was also evidence of necromancy. Libo tried to explain it away by a desire to know if he would ever be rich enough to pave the Appian Way the whole distance to Brundisium with money. At the same time Tiberius banished a number of astronomers (*mathematici*) including Lucius Pituanius, who was helped off the Tarpeian Rock, and Publius Marcius, grandiosely executed at the Esquiline Gate to the sound of trumpets.[26]

The actions of Valens in the third century AD show how the paranoia continued to haunt the authorities throughout the Empire. In an act of sociopolitical cleansing ostensibly designed to rid the Empire of sorcerors, Valens executed, mainly by strangulation or by burning to death, all the pagan philosophers in the Eastern Empire. Ammianus Marcellinus gives us a catalogue of murders, informers, evidence obtained under torture, planting of evidence, panic burning of potentially incriminating books (many of which were on the fine arts, or were law books) and the burning of libraries in an attempt to avoid incrimination.[27]

Curses and charms were popular throughout the Roman period, with women handing them out as well as receiving them. Here are a few examples of the around 1,600 curse tablets which have been found; *defixiones* reach back as far as the fourth century BC in Greece and were traditionally consecrated to the gods of the underworld. Predominantly a practice of the lower classes, the curses were often provoked by unfortunate events such as commercial disputes, failures in lawsuits, or unrequited love: they gave vent to the curser's vengeful wrath, malice and vindictiveness. Typically the victim's name was written on a lead tablet, although gold, silver and marble are not unknown; blanks have been found suggesting that there was a ready ongoing trade. The consecration was made and a nail stuck through the name; this was often followed by the name of the target's mother, to avoid any mistaken identity which would invalidate the curse. Magic words and symbols were added to enhance the chances of success. Some tablets feature a portrait of the victim, which is also pierced with nails; the texts were anonymous. In tablets inspired by jilted love, a lock of the intended's hair was sometimes attached. By the Hellenistic period a variant, 'vindictive prayers', appears: these usually bore the name of the author. One of the biggest finds was at *Aquae Sulis* (Bath), where 130 were discovered, many angry retorts to clothes stolen while their owners were bathing.

Typical is the *defixio* that brings down all manner of calamity on the recipient: 'May burning fever seize all her limbs, kill her soul and her heart; O gods of the underworld, break and smash her bones, choke her [arourarelyoth], let her body be twisted and shattered [phrix, phrox].'[28] This incandescent man was leaving nothing to chance. A bitter and broken-hearted Marcus Junius Euphrosynus, obviously torn between grief for a daughter and hatred for her mother, set up a tomb to the eight-year-old daughter, Junia Procula, in the first century AD.[29] On it he curses Acte, his 'treacherous, tricky, hard-hearted poisoner' of a shameful wife, hoping that she gets in the next life as good as she gave in this. He leaves the adulteress a nail and a rope for her neck, and 'burning pitch to sear her evil heart'. A late second-century curse on Rufa Pulica, found in an urn along with her ashes in Mentana near Rome, lists a number of her body parts: the prurient focus on sexual organs suggests that illicit sex was involved somewhere. Ticene of Carisius suffered a similar post-mortem fate on a tablet found at Minturnae, south of Rome; her curser wishes that everything she does goes wrong. His catalogue of her body parts is less sexual than Rufa's and quite methodical, running as it does more or less from head to toe. Philo may have had something to hide when he cursed Aristo: he ties up her hands, feet and soul, condemns her to silence and wishes her tongue be bitten off. The wife of Aristocydes curses him and his lovers, hoping that he will never marry another woman ... or a boy.

It was not all fire and brimstone, however. There are occasional examples of love *defixiones* where a lover will invoke chthonic deities to help him win the love of his life. The optimistically named Successus dedicates his wife in a bid to see his love for her requited: 'May Sùccessa burn, let her feel herself aflame with love or desire for Successus'.[30] Plenty of fire but no brimstone here.

Considerably less romantic, and excessively malevolent and obsessively perverted love charms targeted at women appear in the *Greek Magical Papyri*; it originates from the fourth century AD, but undoubtedly describes practices which were prevalent much earlier. Some men went to extraordinary lengths to ensure the fidelity of their women: the following (*PGM* 4, 296–466) is one of the most notorious and takes a typically prescriptive recipe form: 'Take wax or clay from a potter's wheel and form it into two figures, a male and a female ... her arms should be tied behind her back, and she should kneel.' There then follow directions to write magical words on her head and other parts of her body, including the genitalia, to stick a needle into her brain and twelve others into other parts of her body; tie a binding spell written on a lead plate to the figures, dedicate it to gods of the underworld and leave it at sunset near to the tomb of someone who has died violently or prematurely; invite them to rise from the dead and bring X (the object of the charm), daughter of Y, to him and make her love him. There then follows a litany of instructions to deprive the girl of food and drink, sexual intercourse, sleep and health – all designed to make her make love with the curser forever.

Sarapammon (*Suppl. Mag.* 47) invokes a whole pantheon of underworld gods in his efforts to ensure the fidelity of Ptolemais: he asks the daemon Antinous to tie Ptolemais up to prevent her from having intercourse or from being sodomised 'and give no pleasure to any man but me ... and let her not eat, nor drink, nor be happy, nor go out, nor sleep with anyone but me ... drag her by the hair and entrails until she does not reject me ... submissive for her entire life, loving me, desiring me'. This tablet (the Louvre Doll) was found in a vase which also contained a voodoo-type clay figure of a kneeling woman, her hands tied behind her back and body pierced with needles.

This spell, cast by Akarnachthas, was found in Egypt and probably dates from the early first century AD: the ingredients are the egg of a crow, the juice of a crow's foot plant and the bile of an electric catfish from the Nile; these are to be ground up with honey and rubbed on the penis while chanting the spell, which goes, 'Womb of NN, open and receive the semen of NN and the unconquerable seed of ... let NN love me for all of her life ... and let her remain chaste for me, as Penelope did for Odysseus. And you womb, remember me for the whole of my life.' Have intercourse after this, and the woman will love you and sleep with no one else.

Another papyrus aims to render the woman sleepless until she relents. 'Take the eyes out of a bat and release it alive. Take unbaked dough ... or wax and shape a puppy dog. Put the right eye of the bat into the right eye of the puppy and the left eye of the bat into the left eye of the puppy. Take a needle and stick the magic substance into it. Prick the eyes of the puppy ... Pray: "I conjure you to ... make X lose the fire in her eyes or become sleepless and have no one in mind except me ... and love me passionately."' The Papyri were not exclusively heterosexual: one from the second century AD describes a lesbian curse where Heraias brings and binds the heart and soul of Sarapias.[31]

Love potions in literature appear in Virgil's eighth *Eclogue* (adapted from Theocritus's *Idylls* 2) where Amaryllis concocts a potion (*herbae* and *venena*) and spells to win back Daphnis: 'by these magic rites I'll try and bring Daphnis back to his senses: all I need now are some spells'. A less than idyllic love potion recommended by the *magi* and scorned by Pliny the Elder involved the wearing of an amulet which contained a hyena's anus.

Women were always at the centre of Roman divination by virtue of the Sibyl, her *Sibylline Books*, the *Libri Sibyllini,* and of the *Sibylline Oracles*. The originals of the *Books* were a collection of oracular responses in three books brought to Rome by Tarquinius Superbus, after some haggling about their value with the Sibyl at Cumae. Virgil dignifies them by including them in the list of religious initiatives Aeneas will take when he establishes Rome: 'A great sanctuary awaits you too in our kingdom; for this is where I will put your oracles and the mysterious prophecies told to my people; here I will ordain chosen men, propitious Sibyl.'

The *Books* were kept underground in a stone chest under the Temple of Jupiter Optimus Maximus on the Capitoline guarded by ten men; they could only be accessed by fifteen specially appointed augurs, *quindecimviri sacris faciundis*. Consultation took place by Senatorial decree at a propitiatory ceremony in times of civil strife, external threat, military disaster or on the appearance of strange prodigies or phenomena. Unfortunately, the temple and the oracles were lost in a fire in 83 BC. A new collection was compiled from various sacred sites and kept by Augustus in the temple of Palatine Apollo. They were last consulted in AD 363. The *Sibylline Oracles*, on the other hand, are a random fifth-century AD compilation (of dubious authenticity) of Jewish and Christian portents of future calamities.

The Sibyl achieved prominence in Christian literature and art due to her pronouncements in Virgil's fourth *Eclogue,* the *Messianic Eclogue,* which was assumed by Lactantius and Augustine to predict the coming of Jesus Christ.[32]

Heraclitus, writing in the fifth century BC, gives us the standard definition of a Sibyl: 'The Sibyl, with frenzied mouth speaking words of profound seriousness, plain and unperfumed, yet speaks to a thousand years with the help of the god.' Naevius (*fl.* 220 BC) featured the Cimmerian Sibyl in his *Punic War* and Piso (*fl.* 130 BC), one in his *Annales.* Varro lists ten different Sibyls, the seventh of which is the Cumaean Sibyl, otherwise known as Amaltheia, Herophile or Demophile. To Virgil she is Deiphobe (fear of god), daughter of Glaucus. It is from Virgil that we get our most vivid description when she greets Aeneas at the entrance of Avernus and later guides him through the underworld, revealing the future destiny of Rome. Her pivotal function here demonstrates the reverence with which the Sibyl was held and the political and religious importance of the *Sibylline Books.* She is in control right from the start: while Aeneas and the Trojans scamper around doing her will she raves in the cave's entrance trying to shake off Apollo, but the more she resists the more he tires her foaming mouth, taming her wild heart. She gives her responses, predicting

a difficult and dangerous future for Aeneas and for Rome: 'I
see wars, horrendous wars and the Tiber haemorraging blood';
eventually the *furor* abates and her frenzied lips fall silent. Even to
the prophet Helenus, the Sibyl is mad: *insana vates*. Her authority
as she leads Aeneas through the underworld is unquestioned:
she deals one by one with any problems caused by the locals,
Palinurus, Charon, and Cerberus; when it comes to Dido, the Sibyl
remains quiet, tactfully staying out of the 'domestic'. She is *docta*
in her knowledge of hellish topography. Her role in this pivotal
book of the *Aeneid* is itself pivotal: Dennis Blandford has shown
that she makes more speeches (thirteen) than anyone else in the
book, including Aeneas, and has 157 lines, only seven short of
Anchises, the main character. Her bluff and direct attitude towards
Aeneas only went to show how unimpressed she was even with
the future founder of Rome, and how important the Sibyl was to
the Romans.

Tibullus provides more detail in his elegy celebrating
Messalinus's accession to the office of *quindecemviri sacris
faciundis*, describing her as ever reliable with the truth, a chaste
sister to Apollo.[33]

Echoes of Virgil's Sibyl appear in Lucan's *De Bello Civili* when
the *vates*, Arruns, is consulted and a *matrona*, possessed by Apollo,
decries the stupidity of the civil war: 'Tell us, Apollo, what is this
insanity which makes Romans face each other in battle – a war
without a real enemy?' The *matrona* gets her answers and is able
to deliver the future to the quaking populace, the *pavida plebs*: the
Battle of Pharsalia, the murders of Pompey and Caesar, Philippi.

Arruns and the *matrona* were called on to interpret the series
of terrible omens and repellent portents which appeared in Rome
as Pompey and Caesar prepared to do battle. They included the
births of children with extra and enormous limbs, terrifying to
their mothers, and *dira carmina* from the Sibyl of Cumae. In
Book Five, Appius Claudius consults the Delphic oracle, closed
for a number of years. The sacred oracle here was transmitted
through soothsayers, *vates*; they had been only too pleased at the
closure of the oracle since the price of a divine possession was a
horrible death for the *vates*: 'the human skeletal system caves in
from the shock waves of the frenzy and the blow from the gods

violently shakes the fragile spirit'. The prophetess, Phemonoe, is understandably terrified at the prospect of reopening the oracle and tries in vain to dissuade Appius, even to the extent of feigning her divine possession. Appius is not fooled (he calls her unholy, *inpia*) and orders her into the cave where she finally submits to Apollo and delivers the future to Appius in a truncated and somewhat ambiguous prophecy.[34]

Seneca's Cassandra in the *Agamemnon* recalls Virgil's Sybil in some respects, even though the two are acting in very different situations. Both are in a trance and both struggle against the god. Cassandra, a mad priestess, exhibits all the right characteristics – pallor, tremor, hair on end (*horrescat*), tachycardia, eyes turned inwards in their sockets. [35]

Virgil's Massylian priestess first appears in Book Four of the *Aeneid*; she has distinct witch-like characteristics and is dealt with in the section on witches below; she is reprised by Silius Italicus in the *Punica* as much more of a Sibyl: 'here the priestess in her Stygian robes with hair dishevelled summons up Acheron and the spirit of Proserpina'. The dead are called, sacrifices are made and the priestess reveals the future to Hamilcar and Hannibal in a scene reminiscent of Homer's *nekuia* and the Cumaean Sibyl's prognostication to Aeneas.[36]

Silius Italicus has the grieving young Scipio follow in Aeneas's footsteps to Cumae to arrange a necromancy with the *manes* from the underworld and to learn his future. He meets Autonoe, a Sibyl who teaches him the sacrifices to be performed, adding that the future will be revealed by a greater Sibyl than her, the wraith of the veteran Sibyl who is inspired by Apollo, in fact by Aeneas's Sibyl. She eventually arrives, 'the font of all truth' – and the future is disclosed – but only after Scipio is rebuked on behalf of the Roman people for Tarquinius Superbus's ancient haggling over the *Sibylline Books*.[37]

Manto is a kind of sorcerer's apprentice in her role as assistant to Tiresias, her father, at the necromancy in Statius's *Thebaid*. She helps prepare the necessary sacrifices and, like her father, is inspired by Apollo; the ghosts, however, are reluctant, causing Tiresias to wonder indignantly whether the rabid spells of a Thessalian witch might be more effective. Manto works her magic and she is able to describe the Argive and Theban souls as they arrive, thus assuming the role of a Sibyl, a virgin priestess.

Plutarch tells us something about Pythia, the priestess of Apollo at Delphi. For him Pythia was the genuine article – none of that singing, cithara music, perfume, cassia, laudanum or frankincense, or purple robes. She still used the traditional laurel leaves and barley and is all the more effective for that.[38]

There may be a tenuous link between the love *defixio* and witchcraft in the ancient world. It is a short step from putting faith in a spiteful dedication to a reluctant lover to the production of love potions and spells – the preserve of sorceresses and witches. Virgil ascribed to witches the power to draw down the moon, Martial and Tacitus thought them responsible for lunar eclipses. Martial describes the clashing of pots and pans in a bid to ward off their evil influence: 'when the eclipse of the moon is lashed by the Colchian magician's wheel (rhombus)'. The *rhombus* was a four-spoked magician's wheel often used to attract women: a cuckoo was attached and whipped like a top, the object of desire was then drawn by some invisible force to the wheel, and to the man. Pliny records that men were so unsettled by witches that they resorted to fixing a wolf's beard, good for and against spells, to their doors to deter them.[39]

An encounter with Roman witchcraft survives from Horace in his satire on the *garrulus*, the chatter-box, written sometime around 35 BC. While trying to shake him off, Horace pretends to recall the old Sabine maid, a witch, who sang her prophecy to him when he was a boy: Horace was not going to die from the usual deadly drug or by the sword, or from an illness; Horace was going to be talked to death by a *garrulus*.

His Canidia and her colleagues appear in a horrifying description of a cabal of witches intent on performing a live hepatectomy: making a love potion from the liver of a terrified young boy. Canidia, Sagana, Vera and Folia are described in equally odious and repellent terms: Canidia with her serpentine hair brings eggs dipped in the blood of filthy frogs, and the teeth of a ravenous bitch; Sagana, her hair on end like a sea urchin or a bristling boar, sprinkles water from Hell; Vera digs the boy's grave in which he will be buried up to his neck, tantalised by an endless succession of meals until his eyeballs melt; and Folia who lusts like only a man lusts. The boy retaliates with the threat of a curse: he will haunt them as a Fury from Hell.[40] The frogs' blood and the use of a human liver are unique to Horace; they do, however, feature in the *Magical Papyri*, demonstrating their prevalence at the end of the Republic. At the same time, the poem vividly reflects the horror, contempt and disgust in which magic and witchcraft were held.

Evidence for a real-world child kidnapping comes from an early first-century AD epitaph which describes how the three-year-old son of Iucundus 'was snatched by a witch's hand' (*saga manus*). Despite their obvious grief, the parents have the little boy warn other parents to 'look after their children well' lest they too suffer a similar fate. Iucundus was the slave of Livia Julia (Livilla) wife of Drusus Caesar; she was executed for allegedly poisoning her husband in AD 23.

Canidia and Sagana make a second appearance in Horace's *Satires*. Here they are ridiculed through Priapus, the narrator of the piece, erected as a wooden statue in a redeveloped park on the Esquiline, which was formerly a paupers' cemetery infested by witches. Priapus describes the witches as 'those who turn mankind's minds with their spells and potions'. They are *horrendae aspectu*: horrid to look at, as they perform a necromancy with the blood of a ripped-apart lamb. The repugnant scene is prematurely ended when Priapus breaks wind and sends the two running: Canidia's false teeth fall out, Sagana loses her wig and they drop their herbs and enchanted love chains.

For Horace, Canidia is synonymous with poisoning: elsewhere he associates her poisons with garlic, defence against the evil eye. Canidia threatens her enemies with the poison of Albucius, and Fundanius flees from a feast as if Canidia had breathed all over the food with her toxic breath.[41] However, *Epodes 17* finds Horace taking it all back. He concedes that her 'science' works, acknowledges her spell books and requests her to draw down the stars from the skies. Her spells have reduced him to a sallow bag of bones, he has aged prematurely, his hair is white and he cannot sleep; his breathing is laboured, his chest burns with pain and his head feels like it is exploding. He enumerates an infernal catalogue for Florus: nightmares, the terrors of magic (*terrores magici*), miracles (*miracula*), ghosts and Thessalian rites. Canidia, though, is having none of it and turns the tables on Horace, calling *him* a sorcerer and promising him a slow and lingering death. She ends by listing her credentials as a witch: she can bring wax effigies to life, draw down the moon, raise the dead and mix love potions.

Ovid describes Tacita, a witch who performs imitative magic to 'stop hostile tongues wagging and close the mouths of enemies'. We find her teaching three young girls; she places three pieces of incense under the threshold, she then binds magic threads onto lead and rolls seven black beans around in her mouth. She fries the head of a small fish whose mouth has been sealed shut with tar and sewn up with a bronze needle, pouring some wine over it. She and the girls drink the rest; she announces their success in silencing the enemy and departs drunk.

In the *Heroides* he describes Medea, ascribing to her the typical witchy characteristics: she is is not remembered for her beauty 'but rather her incantations'. Notably, he dwells on her skills with *simulacra cerea* – waxen effigies – and the needles she drives into their livers.[42]

The voodoo theme is taken up in the *Amores* when Ovid describes the enervation he suffers through love: was it due to 'being addicted to Thessalian drugs, – spells and herbs, or did a witch bind my name with purple-red wax and prick my liver with sharp needles?' Whatever the cause, one of the symptoms of Ovid's malaise was erectile dysfunction – a condition ascribed by his disappointed girl to some voodoo work by a Circean witch ... or to sex with another woman. His Dipsas, in the *Amores*, is both witch and *praeceptrix amoris*. She 'is conversant with the magic arts and the spells of Aeaea'; she can manipulate the way of the world and make the moon bleed; she knows her poisons and herbs and can work the *rhombus*; she flies like a bird in the night; her eyes dart out twin beams of light, and she knows all about necromancy.[43]

In Book 4 of the *Aeneid* Virgil gives a very different picture of sorcery and infernal communication.[44] Betrayed by Aeneas and sidelined by his dedication to his mission to found Rome, Dido is incandescent with rage and in a pit of misery and despair:

'she rages, out of her mind, and rushes through the city, mad as a Bacchant'. She confronts the treacherous Aeneas and promises to haunt him for eternity in a threat reminiscent of a *defixio*: 'When I'm gone I'll follow you into the black fire of Hell, when icy death draws out the spirit from my limbs; my ghost will be everywhere; you'll pay the price, you traitor, and I will hear about it – the news will reach me deep down among the deadmen.'

Dido had seen the future and the future frightened her; when she made offerings to the gods on the incense-burning altars, the milk turned black and the wine she poured congealed into an obscene gore. *Horrendus dictu* – shocking to say it – she resolved to take her own life. She can hear the ghost of Sychaeus, her late husband, and a solitary owl wails its song of death; Dido recalls the warnings of the *pious* priests who predicted that it would all end in tears. She instructs her sister, Anna, to build a pyre and enlist the services of the remarkable Massylian priestess; she will wipe out the memory of Aeneas with her spells; his things will burn on the pyre. By implication, Aeneas is *impious*; he is subjected to a kind of *damnatio memoriae* in which he is erased from Dido's memory, as befits a traitor.

This Massylian priestess possesses the powers of a witch: she can stop rivers flowing and change the course of the stars; by night she raises and communes with the dead; the ground below her groans and trees tumble down from the mountains. Dido is ashamed for resorting to the magic arts; the pyre is raised and the *sacerdos*, her hair in disarray, booms out her invocation to 300 gods, notable among whom are Erebus, triple Hecate (Luna and Diana) and Chaos – all denizens of Hades. She recreates the waters of Avernus; herbs, toxic black milk and a love charm from the forehead of a foal, *hippomanes*, are all added to the infernal mix.

Virgil's audience would have understood the efficacy of Dido's threats: Rome did indeed pay the price for Aeneas's duplicity, with three devastating Punic Wars; Aeneas was indeed haunted by Dido, in their frosty meeting in the underworld. The Dido episode works on three levels: it showcases the black magic arts of witch-like women, evident from real life and in literature – descendants of the Circes and Medeas of epic and tragedy; it extends the epic chthonic tradition by recalling the *nekuia*, initiated by Homer, as a precursor to the *katabasis* in Book 6; and it resonates uncomfortably with the political upheaval caused so recently by Cleopatra, a foreign queen eerily reminiscent of Dido, whose facility for global power-play would be viewed as comparable to the unnatural skills of a sorceress.

Propertius's mistress ascribes the poet's infidelity to the machinations of some woman who possesses all the credentials of a witch; Cynthia feels she is confounded by her rival's potions and the magic wheel, her fat frogs and snakes; screech owl feathers and the head band from a corpse make up the ghastly picture. Acanthis the bawd in Book 4 boasts many witchy qualities: to Propertius she is a natural enemy because of the obstructive advice she gives his mistress designed to deflect him. He describes her magical skills: the demagnetisation of magnets, the flooding of a crop-filled field with her magic herbs, and disguising herself as a wolf, she gouges out the eyes of crows and uses *hippomanes* against him. *Lewis & Short* defines *hippomanes* (literally horse rage) as 'a small black membrane on the forehead of a foal, used in making love potions'; it can also be 'a slimy humour which flows from a mare when in heat, and which was used to excite desire'.

Tibullus describes two witches. In a poem bemoaning the loss of Delia, Tibullus himself is accused of being possessed and Delia of being a witch; indeed it is her beauty that bewitches him. He goes on to compare Delia's *lena* to the sordid existence typically led by witches: surrounded by ghosts and a screech owl, eating blood soaked food, desperately scrabbling for herbs and the graveside leftovers of wolves, shrieking through the city pursued by dogs.

His other witch actually sides with Tibullus; she can confound natural phenomena, call up the dead and call down the stars, creating chaos on land and in the skies; she is well versed in the *malae Medeae herbae,* the evil herbs of Medea, and has tamed the wild dogs of Hecate. Most crucially for Tibullus, though, she has concocted a *cantus*, a spell for Delia which will enable her to deceive her husband who, even if he sees he and Delia in bed together, will literally not believe his own eyes. Significantly, Tibullus adds that the *cantus* will only work with him; if she uses it with other men it will be quite ineffective and all will be laid bare.[45]

Witches and magic do not escape Juvenal's vitriolic sixth Satire: women use *magici cantus* and *Thessala philtra* to vex their husbands, to drive them mad, fog their brains and induce short-term memory loss. Caligula's wife, Caesonia, started a craze for the aphrodisiacal *hippomanes* when she drove him insane with it; less damaging though than the mushroom (*boletus*) with which Agrippina induced a heart attack in Claudius, reducing him to a trembling, slobbering wreck. Such is the damage wreaked by a single poisoning, *veneficium*.[46]

Tacitus tells of the suspicious death of Germanicus, the adopted son of Tiberius, in AD 19. The assumption was that Germanicus had been poisoned by Gnaeus Calpurnius Piso and his wife, Plancina; some, though, suspected black magic – a suspicion that was confirmed when workmen searching Germanicus's quarters made a sinister discovery under the floor and between the walls. There they found human remains, spells, *defixiones* inscribed with Germanicus's name, bloody ashes and other magic paraphernalia. In a related story, a Syrian witch, Martina – famous for her *veneficia* – is summoned to Rome by those preparing charges against Piso and Plancina. However, before she can get there she is found dead at Brundisium, poisoned it seems by her own poison, knotted in her hair.[47]

Witches feature in Seneca's *Medea* and *Heracles on Mount Oeta*. In *Heracles*, Deianira, Heracles' wife, is carried away by Nessus, a centaur who, when he attempts rape, is shot by Heracles with poisoned arrows. Slyly, Nessus convinces Deianira that she must make use of his blood as a love potion to keep Heracles true; the blood is of course toxic and slowly kills Heracles. The magic theme is enhanced by the fact that Deianira's nurse and confidante is a witch. Interestingly, the witch observes that it is quite common for women to attempt to save their failing marriages by resorting to magical arts and prayers. She enumerates her own skills: what she says goes – the earth, sea, sky and Tartarus all bend to her will; she has turned spring into winter, day into night, stopped thunderbolts dead, controlled the seas, rolled rocks, opened doors, stilled ghosts and made them talk, emasculated nature with her spells. She draws on her poisonous herbs and on many of these superhuman powers, but to no avail.[48]

Like Dido, Seneca's Medea is spurned in love; she curses Jason and wishes death on his family and the family of his new wife. In a cauldron of occult materials, tools and incantations, she unleashes a menagerie of reptiles and dragons and draws down animals and snakes from the constellations to vent their poison on Earth; she herself mixes toxic herbs and other venoms, invokes Dis and the shades of the dead and releases the eternally damned – Tantalus, Ixion, Sisyphus – from their infernal punishments. Like Deianira's witch she can turn the world and nature upside down and set it in reverse.[49]

In Valerius Flaccus's *Argonautica* we first meet a less malicious Medea, transfixed by the recently arrived Jason – and he by her. She is virginal and fearful. Later, much has changed. Her father has set Jason some awesome, life-threatening tasks in exchange for the coveted golden fleece; Medea reluctantly accepts that all is lost with Jason. Venus disagrees and visits her, in the guise of Circe, her aunt, to rekindle her love for the hero. Medea, like Dido before her, sees death as the only way out: should she side with Jason or with Aeetes, her father? Medea selects her most potent potion, moves through the city to the sound of magic – the mountain spirits have to look away – and meets Jason to tell him of the labours – the *pericula*, the *monstra* set for him by her father. She gives him the drugs that will help him to beat the bulls and sow the dragon's teeth, and to defeat Aeetes' army by throwing a helmet spiked with Medea's poison into their midst, causing them to turn on each other. In Book 8 she rejoins Jason and proceeds to dope the serpent guarding the golden fleece with 'the toxins of Tartarus', and with spells.[50]

In Petronius's *Satyricon*, an old lady, Proselenus, with magical powers, is brought by Chryseis to Eumolpus to (successfully) cure his impotence with her potions, an amulet and magic stones. His dysfunction presented itself when he was consorting with Circe, Chryseis' mistress; to Chryseis, Circe is nothing but a witch who draws down the moon. Proselenus later returns, her hair in disarray, all in black: she questions if it was witches who emasculated him and subjects him to a bout of flagellation in the room of Oenothea, priestess of Priapus. Oenothea comes in, is told by Proselenus that Eumolpus is flaccid, and sets about an elaborate magical process to restore him 'as stiff as a horn'. She too displays distinctive witch-like qualities with her powers to confound nature.

Earlier in the novel, Trimalchio tells how the recent death of his master's son attracted screeching witches; a Cappadocian slave goes out to deal with them and stabs one of them with his sword. The mourning mother then goes to her son's body only to find there a straw effigy; the witches had stolen his corpse and left the straw doll in his place. The Cappadocian – much the worse from having been touched by the evil hand of the witches – goes mad and dies soon after.[51]

First century AD epic poetry is a rich source of chthonic material, particularly witches. Lucan in the *de Bello Civili*, Statius' *Thebaid*, the *Punica* of Silius Italicus and the *Argonautica* of Valerius Flaccus all display elements of the occult and female representations thereof. Witches and other female chthonic agents were, of course, stock epic themes, with, it seems, each poet vying with their predecessors to produce the most frightening and abhorrent cabalistic characters. Lucan's Erictho is a witch surpassing even Seneca's Medea in her repulsiveness.

Sextus Pompey, driven by fear, wants to learn the future; he eschews conventional forms of divination, electing instead to deploy the ungodly, 'the mysteries of the furious enchantress'. Being in Thessaly he is local to the world's most dreadful witches and their *herbae nocentes, pernicious herbs*; when the witches here cast their spells even the gods above stop to listen, and are sometimes persuaded to do the witches' will. Lucan describes their *noxia pocula, noxious potions*, their theft of the *hippomanes* to pervert the natural course of love, and their *venena*. The usual physical, astronomical and meteorological calamities are in their powers; lions, tigers and snakes submit.

Wild Erictho takes even their evil excesses to new extremes: she communes with the dead and is an expert in all things eschatological. Where she goes contagion follows; she buries the living and brings the dead back to life; she snatches burning children from their pyres for occult experimentation and assaults the corpses of the dead, scooping out eyeballs and gnawing at their nails. She tears flesh from corpses crucified on crosses, harvests the black putrid congealed gore suppurating from the limbs of the decaying; she steals the meat ripped off putrefying bodies by wolves. She is a serial murderess, performing crude caesarean sections on pregnant women whenever a baby is required for the pyre; she rips the faces off young boys; at funerals she opens the mouths of the dead with her teeth, bites their tongues and thereby communicates with Hell. Erictho is just the witch for Pompey, and he seeks her out. Once found, she prepares her squalid necromancy and Pompey duly learns his fate.[52] In her horrific revivication of the soldier, Erictho may well have inspired Mary Shelley's *Frankenstein*: she would have been familiar with the episode through her husband, the poet Percy Bysshe Shelley, who was a great admirer of Lucan.

The *Apologia*, or *De Magia,* by Apuleius is a mine of information on magic; it forms the basis of his real-world defence against charges of practising magic, of being a *magus*, brought against him by the family of Pudentilla, a rich and attractive widow whom he had married. The in-laws were anxious not to lose Pudentilla's fortune to a foreigner and Apuleius accordingly found himself in the dock, defending himself for his life. He makes the point that, over the years, a trumped-up charge of witchcraft has often been used to dispose legally of one's enemies.[53]

Apuleius introduces two witches in his *Metamorphoses*. In the story of Aristomenes, Lucius meets two men in Thessaly, one of whom rubbished the belief that magic can blank the sun, reverse the flow of rivers, freeze the ocean. Aristomenes' old friend, Socrates, was down on his luck and had had an affair with Meroe, an aging innkeeper who possessed magical powers, and could do all the things his companion had just scorned, and more.

When one of her previous lovers had been unfaithful to her Meroe turned him into a beaver on the grounds that beavers, when hunted, bite off their own genitals leaving them lying around as a decoy to put hunters off the scent; the clear intention was for her unconstant lover to do likewise. She also changed rival innkeepers into frogs, prosecuting lawyers into rams and condemned the wife of another lover to perpetual pregnancy:

unable to give birth, her bump grew to such a size that it looked as though she was carrying a baby of elephantine proportions. When Meroe's evil deeds became known she was sentenced to death by stoning; Meroe wasted no time: she dug a trench, performed the requisite rites and cast a spell on the townsfolk which effectively consigned them to house arrest. Meroe only released them when they promised never to persecute her again. She relocated the house of the ringleader to a town on a barren hill 100 miles away.

Aristomenes was worried that Meroe had overheard their conversation: she had, and sure enough, that night she smashed into their locked bedroom accompanied by Panthia, her sister. The two debate whether to murder Aristomenes straightaway or after they have castrated him, but decide to let him live so that he can bury Socrates. Socrates, it turns out, had previously cruelly abused Meroe and was planning to desert her. He pays the price: she drives a sword into his neck and severs his windpipe, catching the blood that spurts out, and then gropes down into his chest to pull out his heart, plugging the cavity with a sponge. The two urinate over Aristomenes and leave the room; the smashed-down door repairs itself. Aristomenes appreciates the predicament he is now in and attempts to leave, but the doorman refuses to let him out, even suggesting he may have murdered Socrates. Socrates wakes up, apparently none the worse for his ordeal. The previous night's exploits were put down to nightmares caused by excessive food and wine, during which Aristomenes wet his bed and Socrates dreamed that his throat had been cut and his heart removed. They go on their way but, after lunch, Socrates' wounds re-open as he drinks from a river, and he dies. It would seem that Socrates' temporary revival was due to magical reanimation: Meroe had exacted her revenge after all.

In the story of Milo's house, Lucius is staying with Milo when he happens to meet Byrrhaena, his mother's foster sister. They go back to her splendid house where she warns him about Milo's wife, Pamphile, a well-known witch accomplished in necromancy and other magic arts. She only has to breathe on some twigs to transfer the light of day to the underworld. Worse, she falls for every good-looking man she meets and ensnares him in boundless eroticism, a true nymphomaniac. If spurned she turns the lover into stone in her rage, or into a wild animal, or kills him. Undeterred, Lucius sees this as an opportunity to learn the magic arts, a secret ambition of his, from Pamphile, astutely deciding to avoid her physical charms and seduce Fotis, their vivacious slave girl, instead.

In the *Story of Thelyphron*, Lucius attends a dinner party thrown by Byrrhaena where he confides in her his fear of the notorious Thessalian witches and their penchant for body snatching. Another guest, Thelyphron, is cajoled into telling his experiences of witches and their repellent assaults on the living and the dead. When in Larissa he answered an advertisement for someone to guard a corpse that night – locally, the witches frequently chewed off the faces of dead men to use in their potions. The job entailed guarding the corpse against these witches, or any of the birds, beasts or insects they may have metamorphosed themselves into. Anything lost from the corpse was repayable in kind from the guardian's own body. Thelyphron takes on the commission with relish and, when the corpse is certified as intact before witnesses, he begins his vigil. After scaring off a weasel he falls asleep; nevertheless the corpse and Thelyphron apparently survive the night unmutilated and Thelyphron receives his fee. In the funeral procession which follows, the deceased's grieving widow is accused of his murder, poisoning him to conceal an affair and inherit his estate. Assuming that she is a witch, the mob threatens her with vivicombustion, stoning or hanging. A court is convened under the aegis of an Egyptian soothsayer who recommends a necromancy to establish the truth; to get it straight from the dead man's mouth. The corpse, restored to life, confirms his wife-widow's guilt at which some of the crowd recommends she be buried alive with her husband; others side with the widow. The corpse reveals what really happened that night: while Thelyphron was asleep the witches summoned the corpse, also called Thelyphron; however, Thelyphron the guardian answered the call. The witches sliced off his nose and ears and, to hide the mutilation, performed some emergency cosmetic surgery, fitting wax prostheses to replace the originals. Horrified at this revelation Thelyphron feels his face: his new nose and ears drop off, much to the hilarity of the crowd.

In a later story, the *Festival of Laughs*, Fotis corroborates Byrrhaena's warnings and cites examples of Pamphile's occult powers: threatening the sun with extinction, for example. She describes her paraphernalia which includes, apart from the usual incense and *defixiones*, wreckage from sunken ships, flesh torn from corpses, the neatly arranged noses and fingers of crucifixion victims, the nails that transfixed them matted with flesh, and the skulls of men salvaged from between the jaws of animals.

Lucius succeeds in his desire to learn the magic arts when Fotis announces that Pamphile is to transform herself into a bird to enable her to secure the object of her desire. Lucius is amazed when he sees Pamphile fly off as an owl and persuades Fotis to change him into a bird, reassured that she knows the antidote and will restore him to normal. Unfortunately, he uses the wrong ointment and turns into a donkey; the antidote is simple, but before Fotis, now recognised by Lucius as a witch, can gather the roses she needs, he is stolen by robbers.[54] Ultimately, Lucius abandons his youthful dabbling in magic and is converted to the cult of Isis.

Apuleius's first concern in the *Metamorphoses* would have been to tell a good story, full of sex, drugs and magic; this he achieved. However, given that Apuleius had been charged with being a magician, he surely intended his novel to warn people away from the unpredictable and tragic consequences of magic.

Lucian, in a scene from *De Mercede Conductis,* describes two prostitutes, Melitta and Bacchis, employing the services of a Syrian witch to win back Charinis, a former lover. The witch's reputation precedes her: 'They utter incantations and can make a woman loved, even if she is deeply hated before.' Unusually, the witch is still attractive, not the usual old hag. She comes cheap, but does require a bowl of wine, reinforcing the stereotype of the drunken witch seen in Horace and Ovid. All that she needs is seven obols, salt, sulphur and something that belongs to Charinis – his boots are available; these are strung up and fumigated. The *rhombus* is put to work and some mumbo jumbo is chanted.[55]

Heliodorus of Emesa, in the third century AD, describes a necromancy conducted by a witch, an old woman of Bessa, in his *Aethiopica*. Calasiris, a priest of Isis, and Charicleia, the heroine of the novel, come across the aftermath of a battle between the Persians and the Egyptians, a battlefield strewn with corpses. The only living soul is an elderly Egyptian woman mourning her dead son; she invites them to spend the night there. During the night Charicleia witnesses a shocking scene: the old woman digs a trench, lights two pyres on either side and places the body of her son between them. She pours libations into the trench and throws in a male effigy made from dough. Shaking, and in a trance the old woman cuts her arm with a sword and drips her blood into the trench uttering wild and exotic prayers to the moon. After some magic she chants into her son's ear and makes him stand up; she then questions him about the fate of her other son, his brother. The corpse at first says nothing but, because his mother persists, he rebukes her for sinning against nature and breaking the law when she should have been organising his burial. He reveals not only that his brother is dead but that she too will soon die violently because of her life of unlawful practice. Before collapsing again the corpse reveals the awful truth that the necromancy had been witnessed not only by a priest *beloved by the gods* but also by a young girl who has travelled to the ends of the earth looking for her lover. A happy outcome is promised for both, however the old mother is outraged by this intrusion and, while pursuing Calasiris and Charicleia, is fatally impaled on a spear.[56]

The line between what was considered conventional medicine and malevolent magic potions is often blurred. Pliny gives an example in his *Natural History* when he prescribes a potion that makes sex repugnant to women: it involves smearing the genitalia of the woman with blood from a tick that resides on a wild black bull. If she then drinks goat's urine she will find love repellent too. Smearing blood had a similar effect on Faustina, the wife of Marcus Aurelius: she was smitten by a gladiator and finally confessed her passion to her husband. On advice from the Chaldeans the gladiator in question was executed and Faustina was made to bathe in his blood, and then have sex with her husband still covered in the blood. All thoughts of the gladiator apparently vanished.[57]

Ghosts were a fact of life in Rome and are variously called *di manes*, *Lares*, *Lemures*, *umbrae*, *imagines*, and *species*. Evidence of women either experiencing ghosts or appearing as a ghost is relatively rare. What ghosts there were were often wicked. We have already encountered Empousa, Mormo and Lamia, ghost-like spirits who frightened naughty children in their guise as bogeywomen. Plautus wrote his *Mostellaria*: the story of a haunted house; Pliny the Younger describes a haunted house in great detail in a letter; Lucian relates the exorcism of a haunted house in his *Philopseudes*.[58]

During the frantic escape from Troy, Aeneas is separated from his wife, Creusa. He is beside himself as he searches high and low for her in the burning city. Eventually her ghost appears to him, larger than life, and stops him in his tracks: 'The unhappy image of Creusa appeared before me – her very ghost, she looked bigger. I couldn't believe it, my voice caught in my throat, my hair stood on end.'

Creusa sensitively reassures Aeneas that her death was the will of the gods and that she was never intended to accompany him, reminding him of his *pietas* and his obligation to the future of Rome. Her parting shot is to remind him of his duty to Ascanius, their son: Creusa, even as a ghost, acting the *matrona*, concerned with the interests of her child and supporting her husband. The ghost retreats back into the invisible air; three times he tries to embrace her, three times the ghost eludes him: 'just like a breeze, just like fleeting sleep'.

In the underworld Aeneas encounters the ghost of Dido, still smarting from the hurt he dealt her in Carthage. She appears 'silhouetted in the shadows; he's like the man who sees, no, thinks he sees, the moon rising early in the month through the clouds'. His desperate appeals to her are in vain: she is adamantine in her refusal to talk, as hard as a rock. Dido has fulfilled her promise to haunt Aeneas and returns to the comfort of Sychaeus, leaving the hero distraught and powerless.[59]

Cynthia's ghost returns to lambast Propertius for being unfaithful to her after her death. The poet describes her dress and beryl ring both scorched from the funeral pyre, her lips chapped from drinking in the waters of Lethe when she passed through the underworld. Some things have not changed, though: Cynthia's voice and her anger are still the old Cynthia. She spends over forty lines nagging him and then declares that she will not nag. She berates him for an unconvincing performance of grief at her funeral and insinuates that Nomas, allegedly complicit in her murder, has magical skills and that Chloris, her replacement in Propertius's affections, uses potions to control him. After a brief description of the underworld and some of its denizens, Cerberus and Charon, she ends by pointedly reminding the poet that they will soon meet again when they will, in an excruciating image, grind bone on bone.[60]

Julia, daughter of Julius Caesar and wife of Pompey, died in 54 BC. In Lucan's *De Bello Civili* her ghost appears to Pompey:[61] 'Julia, an image full of horror and foreboding, appeared – her sad face visible over the gaping earth, standing on her flaming tomb, raging like a Fury'. She ominously declares that Hades is getting ready to receive casualties from the war. She has received special dispensation from the kings of Hell to haunt Pompey: her *umbra* and *manes* will be there in the battle, ominously reminding him that 'the Civil War will make you mine'.

Nero arranged the murder of his mother, Agrippina, in AD 59 appropriately near Lake Avernus in Baiae. Suetonius relates how he, fuelled by drink, paid an unhealthy level of attention to his mother's corpse thus substantiating allegations of incest. Her ghost haunted him and in a bid to rid himself of this spectre he enlisted magicians to call up her ghost and exorcise the evil.[62]

In Apuleius's *Metamorphoses,* a witch hired by his unfaithful wife is used to send a ghost to a cuckolded miller. The witch can either reconcile the couple or else murder him through the ghost or some other such demon. She fails in the former and angrily resorts to the latter by sending the ghost of a woman recently murdered to kill him. Dressed in rags, bare-footed, sallow, hair dishevelled, covered in ashes from her pyre and emaciated, the ghost appears to the miller. Some time later he is found in a locked room hanging from a beam. Things get even worse when the miller's ghost then appears to his daughter and in so doing gives her the first horrific news of his own death, revealing her stepmother's adultery, her recourse to witchcraft, and how the ghost bewitched him.[63]

A number of *versipelles*, werewolves, of indeterminate sex, prowl and howl through the literature. Pausanias and Ovid tell the story of Lycaon, transformed into a wolf for murdering a child. Virgil described lycanthropy in the *Eclogues*, human beings transforming into wolves. Pliny the Elder tells two tales of lycanthropy: a man hung his clothes on an ash tree and swam across a lake in Arcadia, turning him into a wolf. The deal was that if he refrained from attacking any human being for nine years he could swim back across the lake and turn back into a human. Then there was the story of a man who was turned into a wolf after eating the entrails of a child, but was restored to a human being ten years later.[64]

Petronius describes an attack by a werewolf in his *Satyricon*. Nicarus, accompanied by a soldier, leaves his house by moonlight intent on visiting his mistress, Melissa; when they get to the out-of-town tombstones the soldier strips, urinates around his pile of clothes – and promptly turns into a wolf, howls and flees into the forest; his clothes turn to stone. Nicarus reaches Melissa's house; she tells him that a wolf had just savaged her sheep and that a slave speared it through the neck. Nicarus returns home, via the stone clothes which had been replaced by a pool of blood, only to find a doctor tending the soldier for a neck wound. At this point Nicarus realises he has been dealing with a werewolf (*versipellis*).[65]

WOMEN & RELIGION

Roman religion was predicated on an extensive and incestuous pantheon, the gods in which were held responsible for everything that happened to Romans in the Roman world, in this life and in the next. Women and women's issues were fully represented by the deities, male and female, in that pantheon. Women had recourse to female divinities; they could see them all around – painted on walls, in statuary, on their coins, in mosaics on the floor. If they could read they could learn about them from, for example, Lucretius's *De Rerum Natura,* Cicero's *On the Nature of the Gods,* or Ovid's *Metamorphoses*; if illiterate then the theology or mythology could be read to them verbatim or communicated in stories; they could see them on the stage. Some of the most powerful gods were goddesses: Venus, Juno, Diana and so on; women would also see their gods at countless festivals and in temples – in short, female gods were, as with all Roman gods, omnipresent and ubiquitous. Both Cicero and Virgil say so: 'God covers all things: the earth, the open seas and the vast skies.'[1]

State religion had become rather staid, dilapidated and impersonal by the end of the Republic.[2] Varro in 47 BC was so concerned by the contemporary decline and indifference that he wrote it all down, lest it be forgotten. His *Human and Divine Antiquities* contains sixteen books describing the festivals, rites, priests, temples, divinities and institutions. Ovid, too, describes the various festivals and liturgies in his *Fasti.* Within this malaise a woman's religion was, in one respect, considered irrelevant: on marriage women were expected to renounce their own religions and follow that of their husbands.

Women had a place in the cultivation of the household and

family gods, the *penates* and the *lares*, but the *paterfamilias* was really in charge.[3] In the prologue to Plautus's *Aulularia*, Lar Familiaris, the household god, bemoans the fact that successive male generations of the family have neglected him and how it is only the daughter of the current *paterfamilias* who pays him any attention. Organisation and management of the broader religion, the priesthoods, was largely a man's work. State religion was inextricably bound up in politics; the priesthoods were held by politicians and sacerdotal responsibilities were invested in men. They, not women, consulted the *Sibylline Books* and reported back on the results of divination. Caesar was a Pontifex Maximus; Cicero was an augur. Men represented the Dea Dia as flamines, as they did other female deities: Ceres, Flora, Pomona and Furrina. The responsible and respectable practitioners of state-sponsored divination, interpreting bird flight, dreams, weather, natural phenomena, entrails and a whole host of other omens, were men. The more nefarious, witchlike and chthonic end of the business was, as we saw in the previous chapter, the preserve of women. Women were excluded from sacrifices, which were nearly always performed by men. In abridging second-century AD Festus, Paulus Diaconus tells us that women and girls were banished (*exesto!*) from sacrificial rites along with convicts and foreigners. The concessions made to Sabine women after their abduction by the Romans included a ban on grinding corn or preparing meat – tantamount to a ban on preparing sacrifices.[4] The prohibition on women drinking *temetum*, sacrificial wine, reinforced this exclusion.[5]

There is a case for arguing that the role played by women in public religion may not have been quite so insignificant; recent work by Lora Holland and by Celia Schulz demonstrates a more proactive and important place for women in aspects of Roman religion.[6] The cults of Fortuna and Ceres, the College of Vestal Virgins and the female priesthoods – the flaminicae and the regina sacrorum – demonstrate this clearly. Moreover, our knowledge of the role of women in Roman religion is somewhat restricted because it comes to us through male authors who naturally focus on the bits that interest them as men, not least the sometimes scurrilous stories about not so virginal Vestal Virgins.

So, women did have a role to play in various festivals, and in temples and cults exclusive to female worshippers. Vestal Virgins apart, this gave women a rare public and official role outside the *familia* and the household, and a visibility, albeit limited, through which they were able to exert their matronly qualities and, indeed, a level of independence from men.

Official Roman religion was essentially founded on and catered for an agricultural society. For example, Jupiter made the crops grow with his rain and sun; Saturn encouraged sowing; Ceres promoted growth. As Rome colonised more, and became more urbanised, then, with the syncretisation of foreign gods and goddesses, traditional religion gradually lost some of its relevance to changing Roman life and culture. It is hardly surprising then that it became staid and unappealing; it is even less surprising that men and women turned to and embraced the new, oriental, mystery religions that began to emerge. With the exception of Mithraism, which was exclusively for men, these cults, particularly the cult of Isis, offered women an active role in the priesthood; the cults could be personalised and customised to meet the needs of individuals, be they man or woman, and because their eschatology often enshrined birth and rebirth they offered hope of life after death, immortality.

The state pantheon featured numerous deities specific to women. The goddess who looked after virgins was *Fortuna Virginalis* to whom young girls dedicated their togas when they reached physical and sexual maturity around the age of twelve, exchanging it for the *stola*, the garb of a *matrona*. Diana too, along with other divine functions such as hunting, was responsible for pre-nuptial girls in her guise as Diana Nemorensis, named after her most celebrated shrine at Nemi. Ovid tells how girls crave her help in marriage and childbirth.[7] She is also adopted by girls who died before they were married, offering their grieving parents solace with an image of their daughter hunting in the afterlife.[8]

On marriage the girl passed to *Fortuna Primigenia* of Praeneste, the goddess of mothers and childbirth, whom they shared with men in her capacity as goddess of virility, material wealth and financial success. Indeed, as Augustine observes, the bridal chamber seems to have been rather overcrowded with well-intentioned divine intervention: Mutunus Tutunus, related to Priapus, was a phallic deity on whom virgins practised before consummating their marriage: Lactantius says 'brides sit on this god's organ to make the first offering of their virginity'.[9] His temple on the Velian Hill was visited by women wearing veils, according to Festus. Both words in the god's name are slang for penis.

Augustine has more: [10] Virginiensis, or Cinxia, is there to loosen the bride's girdle (*cingulum*), along with Subigus who surrenders the bride to the groom; Prema, goddess of the sex act itself and Inuus or Pertunda who helps with penetration; Venus provides the passion and Priapus the erection. Juno is the goddess for women's sexual function and has a multifunctional role in marriage: as Iterduca she is specifically responsible for leading the bride to the groom's house and, as Unxia, oversees the anointing of the bride; she is a bridesmaid as Pronuba, and performs a midwifery role as Lucina. Janus opens the way for the semen to enter, leading to conception, while Saturn looks after the semen. Consevius is the god of insemination; Liber Pater enables the man to ejaculate, Libera does likewise for the woman.[11] Mena (Juno) produces menstruation which in the pregnant mother is diverted to feed the foetus. Fluonia is Juno who keeps the nourishing blood in the womb. Vitumnus gives the foetus life; Sentinus or Sentia introduce perception in the newborn.

Venus, of course, was goddess of love, of *matronae* and marriage, and, at the other end of the social spectrum, of prostitutes. Liber was the god of wine, growth and fertility: each year a wooden phallus representing the god was carted through various towns of Italy, Lanuvium being the most famous, and crowned by the most *pudica matrona* to ensure a successful harvest and to avert the evil eye. His female equivalent, Libera, is closely associated with Ceres. The phallus, or *fascinum*, was much more than a sexual symbol; it was a catch-all charm against the evils of magic, often worn as an amulet. Hence its ubiquity and its presence in all manner of public places, and the large number found in Pompeii: it was even worshipped by Vestal Virgins. Priapus, essentially a phallus with a face, was often called upon by couples experiencing sexual problems.

Servius Tullius, the sixth King of Rome, reputedly owes his

birth to a mock bride and a phallus. The exceptionally beautiful and modest Ocresia was captured at Corniculum, and became a slave, working for Tanaquil, wife of Tarquinius Priscus. She was ordered one day to pour wine on the embers of a fire left burning for the household gods: a phallus rose from the ashes. Tanaquil told Ocresia to dress as a bride and sit on the hearth; she was taken by the phallus, a representation of Vulcan, and subsequently gave birth Servius Tullius.[12]

Fortuna Virginalis had links with Mater Matuta; their temples were built close to each other in the Forum Boarium in Rome and they shared the same dedication day, the Matralia, 11 June. Mater Matuta was the *univira*'s special deity; it was, therefore, exclusive to respectable *matronae*: this is demonstrated by the rite which involved introducing, then expelling, a lowly slave girl amid a fusillade of physical violence and abuse. Ovid gives us all the details.[13] Aunts, who held their sisters' children during the ceremony, were also protected by Mater Matuta. There was a connection with the cult of Pudicitia Patricia (Patrician Chastity) also templed in the Forum Boarium; this contained a veiled statue, touchable only by *univirae*. Livy records that in 296 BC the patrician Verginia was excluded from the cult because she had married a plebeian. Verginia indignantly responded by founding the corresponding cult of Plebeian Chastity, Pudicitia Plebeia, reminding the religious authorities that plebeian *matronae* had the same ideals, the same *pudicitia* as their patrician counterparts.[14] The following year, however, a number of *matronae* were convicted of adultery; this led to the dedication of the temple of Venus Obsequens – Venus the Compliant – which stood as a permanent warning to women to watch their ways. The cult of Fortuna Muliebris was also exclusive to *univirae*, established in 491 BC after the demonstration of woman power which dissuaded Coriolanus from attacking Rome at the head of the Volsci.[15] The women's reward was a temple dedicated to Fortuna Muliebris built on the site with the rare right to sacrifice there.

Fortuna Virilis, or Fortuna Balnearis, also had a say in the sexuality of women. Each year, 1 April saw women invading the men's baths; it seems that the celebration was confined to plebeian women, possibly even just prostitutes and other such socially inferior women (*humiliores*). For some men this was all a bit decadent so the *Sibylline Books* were consulted: they recommended that adulteresses receive a permanent warning with the establishment in 215 BC of the cult of Venus Verticordia – the Heart Changer – also celebrated on 1 April at the Veneralia, and attended by Vestal Virgins. Verticordia promoted fidelity and harmony in marriage, the essence of *univira*-ness; the antithesis to prostitution. Her statue was dedicated by Sulpicia, wife of the Senator Q. Fulvius Flaccus, the most *pudica matrona* in Rome, chosen by a committee of one hundred of the most chaste Roman *matronae*.[16] Statues of Verticordia were ritually washed and garlanded; the *matronae* then bathed, adorned themselves with myrtle and drank a *cocetum*, a concoction of milk, honey and poppies – all to sex themselves up for their husbands and revivify their marriages.

It is impossible to tell just how effective these cults were in inculcating real *pudicitia* and matronly values and virtues in Roman women. Juvenal would have us believe that they were spectacularly unsuccessful and describes how Tullia and Mauria stop their litters to urinate on the Temple of Pudicitia: this 'is where they piss, filling the goddess' statue with their long streams'.[17]

In vivid contrast to the more relaxed and objective account by Plutarch,[18] Juvenal launches an excoriating attack on the patrician women performing the rites of the Bona Dea, describing them as drunken maenads, crazed with desire for sex, which, if it cannot be satisfied by an *adulter*, can be sated by the *adulter*'s son, or by slaves, or the water carrier; as a last resort an ass will take them in the arse: *inposito clunem sumittat asello*.[19] The cult first appeared in Rome around 272 BC, during the Tarentine War; Bona Dea was associated with chastity and fertility and the protection of Rome; as Fauna she could prophesy the fates of women. She had two festivals: one at her temple on the Aventine, the other at the home of the Pontifex Maximus. Her Aventine cult, in which a blood sacrifice took place on 1 May, was re-dedicated in 123 BC by the Vestal Virgin Licinia, but this was annulled as unlawful by the Senate: Licinia was later charged with unchastity, and entombed.[20]

Although Bona Dea was celebrated by men and women alike,[21] in the domestic rite which took place on 3 December all males were banished, even male animals and pictures or statues of males. Only *matronae* and the Vestal Virgins were present. The Vestals brought in Bona Dea's image from her temple and a meal of sow's entrails was eaten, sacrificed to her on behalf of the Roman people, along with sacrificial wine. The fun (*ludere*) lasted all night with female musicians, games and wine, euphemistically called 'milk', from a 'honey jar'. This was not a weak attempt to conceal clandestine drinking; rather, it came about when Faunus, married to the Good Goddess, caught her drinking surreptitiously and beat her to death with a myrtle branch. Myrtle was also associated with Aphrodite and with sex; as such it was alien to the rites and banned. The *matronae* refrained from sexual relations in the run up to the festival. According to Cicero, any man caught observing the rites could be punished by blinding.[22]

Bona Dea was jealously protected by its adherents, so when the high-profile rites of 62 BC were infiltrated by a high-profile man, the ensuing scandal was huge, not least because Caesar's mother, Aurelia Cotta, Pompeia his wife, his sister, Julia, and the Vestals were all there. According to Juvenal, any sexual propriety that remained in Rome evaporated that night: Publius Clodius Pulcher (Juvenal's 'lute girl with a penis' – 'psaltria penem ... intulit') sacreligiously gatecrashed the rites which were being held chez Caesar, that year's Pontifex Maximus. The scandal led to Caesar divorcing Pompeia; she was implicated, and Caesar's wife must not be under suspicion.

The *Nonae Caprotinae,* in honour of Juno Caprotina, took place on 7 July and were exclusively celebrated by and for women, particularly female slaves. They ran about hitting themselves with their fists and with rods. One derivation has it that, after a damaging siege by the Gauls in the fourth century BC, various unscrupulous neighbouring Latin tribes demanded Roman women in marriage, on threat of destroying the vulnerable and weakened city. A slave-woman, Tutela, along with other slave-women dressed as *matronae,* approached the enemy armies, and, pretending to be out on a hen night, got the Latins drunk. When the soldiers were sleeping it off the slave-girls relieved them of their weapons, and Tutela climbed a fig tree (*caproficus*) – a symbol of fertility – to wave a torch signalling the Romans to attack. As a reward for the resulting victory, the Senate awarded each slave-woman her freedom, and a generous dowry. To commemorate this, the *Nonae Caprotinae* were celebrated: fig-branches and the milky sap of the fig tree were offered to Juno, and rites were held in the fig grove of the Campus Martius.

Other festivals involving women included the Terminalia, a family affair which was originally celebrated at the limits of Roman territory, or on the last day of the old Roman year. The Lupercalia took place in February: here women offered themselves up to be ritually whipped with goatskin to promote fertility, banish sterility and ease childbirth; the Vestals handed out *mola salsa*.

Plutarch has some interesting details regarding the role of women in various other rites. In the Bacchanalia, for example, frenzied women go straight for the ivy and chew it to bring on 'a wineless drunkenness and joyousness; [it] has an exciting and distracting breath of madness, deranges persons, and agitates them'.[23] The temple of Carmenta may owe its origin to women who refused to sleep with their husbands pending the repeal of a law prohibiting them from riding in horse-drawn vehicles.[24] Carmenta was the patroness of midwives; she invented the Roman alphabet. Women who sacrifice to Rumina, responsible for breastfeeding as the she-wolf that suckled Romulus, do so with milk and not wine because Rumina knows that alcohol is harmful to babies.[25]

Rumina was by no means on her own. Alemona presided over the foetus and was akin to two of the Parcae, the Fates: Nona and Decima, responsible for the ninth and tenth months of gestation, Parca or Partula watched over the delivery. At the birth, Parca establishes the limit of the baby's life in her guise as a goddess of death called Morta. The *profatio Parcae*, prophecy of Parca, signalled the child as a mortal being; Vagitamus opens the baby's mouth to emit the first cry; Egeria brings out the baby. Postverta and Prosa avert breech birth, considered unlucky; Lucina is the goddess of the birth; Diespiter (Jupiter) introduces the infant to the daylight; Levana lifts the baby from the ground, symbolising contact with Mother Earth; Cunina looks after the baby in the cradle, protecting it from malevolent forces and magic; Statina gives the baby fitness; Candelifera is the nursery light kept burning to deter the spirits of darkness that would threaten the infant in the crucial first week of birth and to banish the bogeywomen – child-snatching demons such as Gello. On the *dies lustricus*, the *Fata Scribunda* were invoked; the 'Written Fates' was a ceremonial inscription of the child's new name. The giving of a name was as important as the birth itself: receiving a *praenomen* established the child as an individual with its own fate. Potina allows the child to drink, Edusa to eat; Ossipago builds strong bones, Carna strong muscles, defending the internal organs from witches; Cuba is there to ease the child's transition from cradle to bed; Paventia deflects fear from the child; Peta attends to its first demands; Agenoria bestows an active life; Adeona helps it learn to walk. Iterduca and Domiduca watch over it as it it leaves the house and returns home again; Catius Pater makes the child clever; Farinus teaches it to talk; Fabulinus gives the child's first words; Locutius helps it to form sentences; Mens provides intelligence; Volumnus makes the child want to do good; Numeria is there for counting, Camena for singing; the Muses bestow an appreciation of the arts, literature, and sciences – and so it went on with a host of *indigitamenta* – spirits – or gods, attending every single stage of life, and also death.

The hearth was literally the *focus* of the Roman household, traditionally tended by the daughters of a family. Vesta was the goddess of the hearth, traditionally attended by virgin priestesses, the Vestal Virgins, who kept the sacred flame, *ignis inextinctus,* alight in the Temple of Vesta. This flame symbolised the nourishment of the Roman state; the *Virgo Vestalis Maxima* symbolised the wife of old Roman kings (represented in turn by the Pontifex Maximus) while the others, the College, were the symbolic daughters of the king. The kings were said to originate from sparks in the ground. Any Vestal careless enough to allow the flame to go out was whipped; tending the flame occupied the Vestals for around eight hours every day. Sarah Pomeroy points out the paradox whereby Vesta was also associated with agricultural productivity and with fertility.[26] The Vestals' virginity embodied the safety of Rome: Rome was safe while their virginity remained intact, and when it was violated, Rome was under threat. When a Vestal was ill, she was treated by a *matrona* away from the temple.

Romulus and Remus were reputedly the offspring of Rhea Silvia, a Vestal Virgin, and Mars. In the early Republic there was possibly just one Vestal Virgin but this increased to a college of six, of various ages. Recruitment took place every five or so years: candidates were originally elected by lot from a group of twenty or so aged between six and ten; they served for thirty years (ten in an apprenticeship, ten as a Vestal, ten as a teacher) after which they were let go, given dowries and were free to marry should they so wish. Not many did: hardly surprising when the gods apparently took such a dim view of this by making it a life-shortening move for any husband. To be considered for election, their parents not only had to be alive but their pedigree had to be above question: in AD 19 when two girls were competing for one vacancy, the unsuccessful candidate was the one whose parents had divorced;[27] the successful girl's mother was a *univira*. The candidates themselves must have neither a speech impediment nor a hearing defect.[28] Perhaps because of the understandable shortage of prospective husbands some Vestals served for longer than thirty years: Occia did, for fifty-seven years, while Junia Torquata was a Vestal for sixty-four years. Initiation bore similarities to the regular marriage ceremony with initiates delivered to the Pontifex Maximus; they wore a red headdress (the *flammeum*) and the six braids.[29]

As well as keeping the flame alight and thereby ensuring the endurance of the Roman state and the purity of public sacrifices, the Vestal Virgins had a number of exclusive festal responsibilities.[30] In mid-May they threw straw figures (*argei*) into the Tiber from the Pons Sublicius; on 9 June, the *penus* – their storehouse symbolising the storehouse of the state – was opened for women to bring offerings at the Vestalia; the blood from the slaughtered 'October horse' was stored in the *penus* in October; calves' foetuses were ripped from the wombs of thirty-one slaughtered cows in April at the festival of Fordicidia, cremated and their ashes stored in the *penus* until the Pales (21 April) when they were scattered to purify the people; people ritually jumped over a mixture of the blood and the ashes that had been poured over burning straw at the feast of Parilia. *Mola salsa* were made in May ready for the Vestalia and the Lupercalia on 15 February – an instance of the Vestals' special dispensation to help in the preparation of sacrifices, hence our word immolation. They each had a *sescepita* – a sacrificial knife. On 15 June they ritually swept and cleansed the temple.

During the Vestalia donkeys were celebrated to mark their valuable role in the making of bread, a staple. The donkey was Vesta's saviour when Priapus attempted to rape her: this accounts for the presence of a donkey in some depictions of the goddess. Its sexual prowess forms part of the paradox that surrounds the Vestals, as is the phallus which is sometimes shown in the flames of their fire. In a more secular context both Julius Caesar and Augustus deposited their wills with the Vestals.[31] The fact that Vestals, as virgins, enjoyed privileges reserved for married women, *matronae*, and for men, highlights even further the sexual ambiguity of their status and throws into relief their vulnerability and the fragility of their reputation.

Vestals received a payment on joining and a yearly stipend thereafter; as much as 2 million sesterces were paid out – twice the dowry of a rich girl. The remuneration came to be as much a bribe as anything, given the increasing difficulty in finding candidates. If a Vestal died intestate then the estate went to the treasury, supposedly to pay for sacrifices; Vestals could make wills and they were free to dispose of their property.

The last known *vestalis maxima* was Coelia Concordia, appointed in AD 380. The Vestals were finally disbanded in AD 394 but not before ten or so had been entombed alive, the awful penalty for a Vestal who lost her virginity (*incestum*), or was suspected of having lost it. The entombment took place in a cellar under the Campus Sceleratus; the male partner was flogged to death in the Comitium like a slave, *sub furca*. The rationale behind entombment was that Vesta would still be able to rescue the 'Virgin' if she were innocent. Vesta never did. Plutarch wonders if entombment was decided upon because the Romans thought it somehow inappropriate that one charged with looking after the flame should be cremated, or that one so sacrosanct should be

murdered.[32] He graphically describes the solemn process where
the condemned Vestal is bound and gagged and carried to her
subterranenan prison in a curtained litter; she is then unbound
and, after a prayer, the Pontifex Maximus puts her on a ladder
which leads to the small chamber below. The ladder is hauled up,
the entrance closed and covered with earth. The chamber has a
bed, lamp, bread, water, milk and oil. To Plutarch this is the most
shocking spectacle in the world; when it occurs it is the most
horrific day Rome has ever seen.[33]

Vestal Virgins sometimes took the blame when catastrophe
struck: for example their alleged *incestum* was held responsible for
the slaughter that was the Battle of Cannae in 216 BC.[34] Two Vestals,
Opimia and Floronia, were duly convicted: one was entombed, the
other committed suicide. Lucius Cantilius, the secretary of the
Pontiffs who had deflowered Floronia, was beaten to death.

On the other hand, their sacrosanctity was clearly evident in
their role as intermediaries between Claudius and Messalina,
and as envoys for Vitellius during the battles in AD 69, the year
of the four emperors. Important state papers and the wills of
eminent statesmen and emperors were kept in their building, the
Atrium.[35] The Vestal Virgins were the stuff of legend and provided
a fertile source of copy for the historians. One Vestal, Aemilia,
let the flame go out, provoking questions about her chastity;
she reacted by praying to Vesta and threw a cloth onto the cold
embers; when this burst miraculously and spontaneously into
flame all questioning ceased. Tuccia endured the same calamity
but absolved herself by fetching a sieveful of water from the Tiber
without losing a single drop.[36]

Domitian was particularly suspicious of the moral rectitude
of the Vestal Virgins: he brought a number to trial in AD 83 and
AD 90 in a bid to improve the moral climate – *correctio morum*,
particularly as it seems the Vestals had lost their moral compasses
under Vespasian and Titus and were running what was virtually a
brothel. In AD 83 the Oculata sisters and Varronilla were given the
option to commit suicide – *liberum mortis arbitrium* – while their
lovers were exiled. Seven years later, Cornelia, the Chief Virgin,
was condemned to the living death that was entombment, while
her lover was whipped to death.[37]

Vestal Virgins were sometimes sacrificial lambs in games of political intrigue. In 114 BC, three were charged with *incestum* and running a brothel – one was convicted; the other two were condemned the following year after a retrial was demanded by Sextus Peducaeus who accused the Pontifex Maximus, L. Metellus Delmaticus, his political rival, of partiality.[38] In 73 BC two Vestals were embroiled in the Catiline conspiracy: Fabia, the half-sister of Terentia, Cicero's wife, was accused of having an affair with Catiline, while Licinia was similarly accused of consorting with Crassus, her cousin. Both were acquitted,[39] but mud sticks: soon after, neither Vestal was present at a religious event described by Macrobius[40] although their four colleagues were; no doubt they were selected to stay back at the temple and fan the flames. In AD 215 Caracella seduced a Vestal and had her, and two others for good measure, entombed. In AD 220 Elegabalus divorced his wife and married a Vestal, Aquilia Severa, after arranging special dispensation for her to renounce her vows of chastity.[41]

In other ways the Vestal Virgins enjoyed a certain emancipation; they were, according to the Twelve Tables, unique among women in that they were free from the power of the *paterfamilias* and they were not bound by *tutela*, guardianship; the Pontifex Maximus could punish them for transgressions or negligence but his power ended there. Their emancipation from guardianship allowed them to make wills and dispose of their property – a privilege usually only extended to men or later to women who had had three children, or four if a freedwoman. They could testify in court and they were exempt from the sumptuary *Lex Voconia* of 169 BC. They were permitted to ride in a two-wheeled wagon, the *carpentum*, which demonstrated their status; they were preceded in the street by a *lictor*, just like magistrates and priests, who cleared a way through the crowds. Should they encounter a prisoner *en route* to his or her execution then it was in their gift to deliver a pardon. They could sit in some of the best seats at the theatre or in the amphitheatre when other women were up in the 'gods'. The privileges enjoyed by Vestal Virgins were held in such esteem that Imperial ladies were said to have 'the rights of Vestals'; Imperial women were often portrayed on coins as Vestal Virgins. Other perks included attendance at sumptuous religious banquets. Four Vestals attended one in 69 BC to celebrate the appointment of a new flamen martialis; the thirty courses included asparagus and oysters. Unlike most people the Vestals could be buried within the city walls of Rome. Pliny tells us that even in his day some people believed that a Vestal Virgin could root a runaway slave to the spot with one glance, provided he was still within the city of Rome.[42]

Not surprisingly, the prospect of thirty years of celibacy, or of being entombed alive if suspected and convicted of *incestum*, did not always deliver a ready supply of Vestals: Augustus attempted to increase recruitment by allowing the daughters of freedmen to serve.[43] He also excused the daughters in families that had three children; while this did nothing for the shortage of Vestal Virgins it probably made a small contribution to increasing the faltering birthrate.[44]

While the Pontifex Maximus was at liberty to marry whomsoever he wished, there were conditions relating to the wives of other priests. For example, the priests of Jupiter, Mars and Quirinus were required to marry only women whose parents had married under *confarreatio*; the wives of the rex sacrorum (the regina sacrorum) and of the flamen dialis (the flaminica) were priestesses in their own right. The flaminica was not allowed to climb three steps of a ladder (unless it was a Greek ladder), she could not bathe in May or comb her hair in the first weeks of June or when the Priests of Mars (the Salii) were dancing in March. If she died, the flamen was forced to resign; he could never divorce her. Like the Vestals, and unlike women in general, the flaminicae and the regina sacrorum could partake in sacrifice: the flaminica dialis sacrificed a ram every market day (*nundinae*) while the regina offered up a sow or female lamb on the first day of every month; they too possessed a *sescepita*.[45] The flaminica had a girl assistant, a little priestess, in the same way as her husband had a boy assistant.

The Salian Virgins (Saliae Virgines) also enjoyed special privileges. They were the female equivalent of the Salii who officiated at the ceremonies marking the opening and end of the campaigning season (19 March to 19 October). The Virgins wore a pointed hat (*apex*) and the *paludamentum* – a crimson cloak fastened at one shoulder, usually worn by military commanders and troops, and they sacrificed at the Regia, the home of the College of Pontiffs.[46]

Women were active in the cult of Ceres – goddess of agricultural and female fertility. In the early days of the Republic, Ceres, and divorced women, benefited if a man divorced his wife for reasons other than adultery, making copies of his keys or poisoning the children: the wife got half of his estate, Ceres the other half. After the Battle of Cannae, celebration of the annual rites of Ceres were compromised because those tainted with death were excluded from the ceremonies and every Roman *matrona* had reputedly been bereaved after the battle. Over time the cult was Hellenised by association with Demeter and women took over completely – even to the extent that Greek priestesses were brought to Rome from Naples and Veleia. The myth of Proserpina became a central feature and was re-enacted every year at the *sacrum anniversarium Cereris* and the *initia Cereris*, the mysteries of Ceres, by *matronae* and *virgines*.

The cult of Bacchus was also, at first, exclusively female, and notorious for the frenzy and shrieking of its adherents, the beating of drums and the clashing of cymbals. It had a hugely popular appeal even before men were admitted: Livy described its spread as an epidemic; it excited the sexual emotions in women.[47] Officially, it was regarded as an unsettling conspiracy against Rome, the Etrurian initiate was suspected of secret and mysterious nocturnal sacrifices and soothsaying. Originally, it was relatively harmless with daytime rites three times a year and *matronae* as priestesses; we know from Cicero that nocturnal rites were illegal, as was initiation, except in the rites of Ceres.[48] Things changed dramatically when a priestess called Paculla Annia started initiating men – the rites were moved to night-time and took place a frequent five times every month. The heady mix of wine, darkness, women and then men was explosive, with *orgia* on a grand scale involving hetero- and homosexual sex, and providing a platform for perjury, forgery, poisoning and murder. The initiation of men was seen officially as tantamount to removing them from the sanctity of the *familia* and of the state.

It all came to a head in 186 BC when Publius Aebutius was

targeted by his greedy stepfather who, with the boy's mother, Durenia, conspired to dispose of him by enrolling him in the Bacchanalia. Aebutius's girlfriend, Hispala Faecina, a reforming prostitute who had witnessed the orgiastic rites as an initiate, was horrified when she heard this and dissuaded Aebutius from going along with it. Such was the notoriety of the cult and the hazards involved: routine ritual male rape, with any opposition resulting in summary sacrifice. On the advice of his aunt, Aebutia, Aebutius reported the matter to the consul, Spurius Postumius, whose wife Sulpicia then interviewed both Aebutia and Hispala to establish their integrity; Hispala, understandably reluctant at first, eventually agreed to reveal all, taking up residence in Postumius's house for safety. The outcome was that, according to Livy, 7,000 Bacchantes were prosecuted under the *Senatus Consultum de Bacchanalibus*, many of whom fled Rome or committed suicide.[49] A manhunt ensued and imprisonments and executions followed; many of the convicted women were handed over to their *paterfamilias* for the family to dispense justice. Most of the Bacchic shrines in Rome and throughout Italy were then destroyed. As we have seen,[50] both whistle-blowers were handsomely rewarded: a measure of the deep concern the rite caused the authorities and of their determination to stamp it out.[51]

There is inscriptional evidence of women as priestesses. Mamia, public priestess, set up a small temple using her own money on her own land near the portico of Concord in Pompeii; Tullia, priestess of Hestia from the first century AD in Ephesus; Alexandria, priestess to both Bacchus and Isis in Rome; Tata, lifelong priestess of Hera in the second century AD in Aphrodisias; Cassia Victoria, priestess of the Augustales in Misenum; and Paulina, a priestess who kept her options open in this life and in the next by serving as a priestess in Rome in AD 384 for Dindymene, Attis, Hecate and Ceres.[52]

An early, and officially sanctioned, import from Asia Minor was Cybele, or Magna Mater – a deity with obvious relevance to and association with women; she was a universal earth mother who looked out for all things maternal and represented rebirth and immortality through the resurrection of Attis. The couple are celebrated in Catullus 63; Ovid describes Attis in detail in the *Fasti*.[53] Cybele was brought to Rome in 204 BC after consultation of the *Sibylline Books* revealed that victory over the Carthaginians could be ensured by her presence – according to Livy the *Books* decreed that any foe will be expelled if the Idaean mother is brought from Pessinus to Rome. A delegation was promptly despatched to Phrygia to bring back a meteoric stone symbolising the deity.[54] The stone had originally been brought from Pessinus to Pergamum by King Attalus I, and lodged in the Megalesion shrine there.[55] Publius Cornelius Scipio (the future Nasica) was the official receiver at Ostia, chosen as the noblest man (*vir optimus*) in Rome at the time; he handed the 'goddess' over to a delegation of *matronae* who took her on to Rome. One of these was Quinta Claudia, a *matrona* whose *pudicitia* had been questioned; however, she scotched all rumours and emphatically restored her reputation that day: the boat carrying the delegation ran aground in the Tiber and soothsayers declared that it could only be refloated by a *matrona* whose reputation was above doubt. Claudia grabbed the rope and refloated the boat, and her reputation. The Magna Mater was duly installed in the Temple of Victory on the Palatine; she received her own temple there in 191 BC and games, the Ludi Megalenses, were set up in her honour.

Once the cult was established, however, the Roman authorities must have regretted not having taken more care over what they had wished for. The orgiastic, frenzied rites, the eunuchs, the dancing, the self-castration and other acts of self harm by adherents – the Galli – were all quite alien and objectionable to the Romans: measures were taken to control the cult and to marginalise it as far as possible. Lucretius has a fine and vivid account of a display of Cybelean rites where he describes the Galli as 'crazy eunuch priests', and their 'violent frenzy'.[56]

The oriental cult of Isis spread to Italy from Egypt at the end of the second century BC and had immediate appeal to women, not least because Isis was associated with a number of other female deities such as Athena, Aphrodite, Hera, Demeter and Artemis. She was also seen as being caring and compassionate, with time for each of her initiates. Moreover, Isis was flexible and versatile: she was all things to all men, and all things to to all women. One inscription describes her perfectly: 'Goddess Isis,

you who are one and all.'[57] She was a woman and a mother who
had known grief and bereavement, and she had been a prostitute
in Tyre; she therefore appealed to the whole gamut of female
Roman society. She was beneficent and came to be associated with
fertility – every year when she saw famine encroaching on Egypt,
she wept in sorrow so that her tears replenished the Nile and
irrigated the flood plains. She was responsible for the Egyptian
practice of honouring queens above kings, as exemplified by
Cleopatra; most crucially, 'she made the power of women equal
to that of men'.[58] Women would have sympathised with Isis' role
as a mother, depicted as she often is with a baby in her arms,
Horus, the offspring of her incestuous relationship with Osiris,
her brother. Death and resurrection could be recognised in the
rejuvenated Egyptian lands and the death and rebirth of Osiris,
also her husband.

Tibullus is frustrated with the time his Delia spends worshipping
Isis – all that clean-water bathing, and sleeping alone in clean
sheets.[59] Propertius too is indignant and resents the fact that Isis
separates him from Cynthia;[60] Ovid hints at the freedom women
enjoyed when pretending to be out celebrating the cult, out of
bounds to men, when they were really living it up at the races or
the theatre.[61] Elsewhere he recommends that Isis be given as an
excuse for a headache, and no sex.[62] Juvenal[63] mocks and ridicules
women adherents to this and to other oriental cults. Apuleius has
a colourful description of the initiation of Lucius into the rites of
Isis in his *Metamorphoses*.[64]

Men and women of every age and rank were involved in the cult
of Isis. The women, all dressed in white, sprayed their hair with
perfume; they strew the road with flowers and perfumes (notably
balsam) and had mirrors on their backs to reflect Isis as she
approached; with ivory combs they pretended to comb her hair.

The inclusiveness of the cult set it apart from official Roman
religion: it allowed women to aspire to high religious office
and become priestesses. One inscription shows us six female
Isis *sacerdotes* (out of twenty-six), one of which was a woman
of senatorial rank, another the daughter of a freedman, Usia
Prima.[65] Around one-third of Isis devotees mentioned in Italian
inscriptions are women.

As the popularity of the cult spread and grew, so did the official suspicion and paranoia. Augustus saw in Isis a worrying reincarnation of Cleopatra and a threat to his license-curbing, moral legislation: in 28 BC he banned the building of temples of Isis within the city of Rome and in 21 BC extended this to an exclusion zone outside the city. The anti-Isis fever reached its zenith under Tiberius after a scandal involving a well-to-do *matrona*, Paulina, and the equestrian Decius Mundus. The priests of Isis had told Paulina that Anubis, the Egyptian god, wanted to have sex with her in the temple; Anubis, of course, was played by none other than Decius Mundus who had paid the priests to assist him. The tactless equestrian boasted of his conquest and word inevitably reached Tiberius: Mundus was exiled, the priests were crucified and thousands of Isis worshippers were expelled from the city to Sardinia.[66] The scandal is interesting because it not only shows that it was quite usual for a Roman *matrona* to visit a temple of Isis but also it vindicates, to some extent, Juvenal's scorn for the gullibility of women involved in such cults. Caligula was the first to spot the political kudos to be gained from support for such a popular cult: he built a temple to Isis in the Campus Martius within the walls of Rome and the goddess never really looked back thereafter.

Judaism too held attractions for women. One of the first skirmishes with the authorities came when three Jews embezzled money given by a rich lady called Flavia – the donation was intended for alms in Jerusalem but it never reached there:[67] thousands of innocent Jews accordingly followed the followers of Isis on the one-way trip to Sardinia. Nero's wife, the Empress Poppaea Sabina, a well-known customer of astrologers, was an adherent; Titus had an affair with the powerful Cleopatra-lite Berenice, daughter of Herod Agrippa I and a Jewish queen; popular opinion persuaded Titus not to take her as his empress.

Christianity too had its attractions. The wife of Aulus Plautius, Pomponia Graecina, *insignis femina* – a distinguished lady according to Tacitus – was a convert. Aulus Plautius was the Roman commander of the invasion force that conquered Britannia in AD 43 and became first governor of the province; Pomponia spent most of her life mourning Julia, a relative of hers and grandaughter of Tiberius, executed by Claudius, her maternal uncle. Her public mourning was an outward show of defiance against the Imperial household: after fourteen years of this she was charged in AD 57 for harbouring an *externa superstitio*, a 'foreign superstition'. A family court was convened by her husband: she was acquitted and left to get on with her brave act of disobedient mourning for another twenty-six years.[68]

7

WOMEN'S MEDICINE & WOMEN'S HEALTH

We noted in the chapter on women and the dark arts the often blurred distinction between magical spells and potions and what may be termed 'conventional' medicine. The medicine practised in Rome, particularly from around the last hundred years of the Republic, was heavily influenced by Greek medicine and by Greek physicians. Before that it was very much a domestic affair reflecting the largely rural society that Rome was; family medicine was administered by *pater-* and *materfamilias* and was largely reliant on traditional and folk remedies.

Homer, in the *Odyssey* (17, 382–384), places doctors on a social standing equal to seers, shipwrights and musicians, in other words, useful and valuable; in the *Iliad* (11, 514–515) he values military surgeons highly. His depiction of the terrible trauma suffered by Erymas with his brain cleaved, his teeth knocked out, and blood spurting from his eyeballs, nose and mouth is typical of the vivid descriptions in the *Iliad* of battlefield injuries.

The *Hippocratic Corpus* collects a number of medical treatises dating mainly from the fifth and fourth centuries BC. The around sixty texts are written by up to twenty authors: they comprise textbooks, lectures, notes, research papers and numerous case histories, many of which, like a Google symptom search today, conclude with the death of the patient. The content is aimed both at the specialist and the layman. The Hippocratic Oath – a key tenet of which is 'help, or at least do no harm' – endures today as a cornerstone of ethical medical practice.

The *Corpus* covers eleven gynaecological subjects out of a total of around sixty: they include *Semen* or *Generation* or *Intercourse*; *the Nature of the Child* or *Pregnancy*; *the Diseases of*

Women; *Sterile Women*; *the Diseases of Young Women* or *Girls*; *Superfoetation*; *the Nature of Woman* and *Excision of the Foetus*. Although much of the *Corpus* was written when the Roman Republic was in its infancy, its authority and currency persisted well into the Empire, and beyond.

Aristotle (384–322 BC) expatiated on human medical matters in his *History of Animals* and *Generation of Animals*. The *Historia Plantarium* compiled by Theophrastus around 300 BC provided a taxonomy of plants and contained information on medicinal herbs and other plants.

Both Diocles of Carystus and Cleophantus wrote a *Gynaecology*. Fourth-century Diocles coined the term 'anatomy' and was also celebrated for his work on diet and nutrition, as well as for a book on comparative anatomy. Cleophantus's brother, Erasistratus (born c. 304 BC), is noted for his work on anatomy, cardiac physiology, and, particularly, the vascular system. Herophilos (335–280 BC) produced nine medical books (all lost) including a *Maiotikon* – a midwifery text; he pioneered human dissection and founded the medical school in Alexandria, a centre of excellence which was particularly important around the Mediterranean because the dissection of cadavers was illegal in Rome, banned on religious grounds. This obviously had implications on the understanding of deep structures and the workings of internal organs – only Alexandria had special dispensation to dissect.

A medical practitioner in Greece was viewed no differently from any other craftsman; he would learn his trade by attaching himself to an experienced practitioner, for a fee, having spent time in one or other of the medical schools, for example Cyrene, Knidos and the Asclepieion of Kos. As a pupil he, or she, would help attend to the patient and assist in operations, handing over the instruments. On completion of the training the novice doctor would practice as a peripatetic to gain experience; after this, the best trainees would be hired by the State. In common with other crafts, guilds of doctors were set up (*collegia*), for example at Ephesus, Turin, Beneventum and Aventicum, providing social gatherings, medical competitions, advice and instruction, and provision for funerals.

The surgeon was very much a generalist with a list that

would have taken in fractures and dislocations, trepanning of the skull, cataract operations, maxillofacial surgery, ENT procedures, lithotomy, and obstetrics and gynaecology.

The Greek god of medicine, Asculepius, was imported from Epidaurus into the Roman pantheon in 293 BC, on the advice of the *Sibylline Books* during an outbreak of plague. A snake slithered out of the temple at Epidaurus and took up residence on the mast of the ship which was to bring a statue of the god to Rome – hence the familiar British Medical Association logo which survives today. At the Epidaurus temple, supplicants habitually carved cures on the walls or erected monuments to help subsequent sufferers of various ailments. The snake jumped ship, landing on Insula Tiberina where a temple to Asculepius was promptly built: the plague soon subsided and the temple became a clinic attended by the sick and dying, its reputation constantly enhanced by reports of miraculous cures. The insular site may have been chosen because it facilitated the quarantining of infectious diseases; a temple to Vejovis, another god of healing, was also built there. Over time Galen and Rufus of Ephesus both endorsed the temple. Telesphorus, the god of convalescence, is sometimes seen at the foot of statues of Asclepius, depicted as a hooded dwarf.

In early Rome, with the absence of formally trained and qualified doctors, the norm was for the *paterfamilias* to take the lead in the provision of family medicine. Old Italic folk remedies, magic and divination formed the basis of early Roman medical practice with the focus on remedies for symptoms rather than anything sophisticated related to diagnosis, history taking or prognosis. The gods and the spirits looked after all of that: there was one for every stage of life. Things began to change with the influx into Rome of Greek culture and science in the second and first centuries BC; this brought with it scientists, including Greek doctors. In the first century AD, 90 per cent of doctors in Rome were of Greek origin.[1] Access to libraries such as Alexandria and the medical school there led to improved surgical technique and progress in anatomy, physiology and pathology. Later on, Galen attributed the shortcomings in Roman medical training to the lack of practise on cadavers and urged students to visit Alexandria;

failing that, to make good use of the corpses of robbers to be found on the roadside, or of bodies washed up on river banks.[2]

The first Greek physician to come to Rome to practise, Archagathos, arrived around 219 BC. He was an experienced battlefield surgeon, originally called the wound healer, *vulnerarius*, but later earned the sobriquet *carnifex*, the butcher; this probably says as much about the suspicion in which he was held as it does about his surgical expertise. Aulus Cornelius Celsus, the first-century encyclopedist, compiled his *De Medicina*, a work in eight parts covering *The History of Medicine, General Pathology, Specific Diseases, Parts of the Body, Pharmacology, Surgery* and *Orthopedics*. Alexander Philalethes authored another *Gynaecology*.

Asclepiades of Bithynia (c. 120 BC – c. 70 BC) arrived, and with him a good bedside manner: he practised medicine 'tuto, celerites ac iucunde' (safely, swiftly and with a smile). Allegedly, he had raised a man from the dead; he repudiated much of the Hippocratic teachings, was admired by Cicero and Lucretius but was later considered a charlatan by Galen. When Julius Caesar was fatally stabbed, a doctor, Antistius, was called to perform a post-mortem in what may be history's first recorded example of a pathologist assisting in a murder case; only one of Caesar's twenty-three stab wounds had proved fatal.[3] In 46 BC Caesar had moved things forward for the profession when he granted Roman citizenship to immigrant doctors working in Rome;[4] in Ephesus doctors were immune from tax, as was Antonius Musa when he shot to fame after curing Augustus of a serious illness with a form of hydrotherapy in 23 BC.[5] Caius Stertinius Xenophon is another example of a doctor made good: he came from Kos to become court physician to Claudius, and he also ran a lucrative practice in Baiae where he financed new public buildings including a library. Tacitus spoils the picture, though, when he gossips that Xenophon poisoned the Emperor.[6] Apart from private practice, there was a form of public medical care where doctors (*archiatriae*) worked for the civil authorities to provide care on demand in the fourteen regions of Rome: the poor received free treatment. Benefits for these doctors included exemption from tax and military service. So popular was this state work that Antoninus Pius in AD 160 capped the number of doctors employed, and in the fourth century doctors had to be selected by a panel of seven other physicians.

Pliny the Elder, for whom medicine was no more than a down payment on death (*mortis arra*), reflected what was perhaps a universal Roman distrust of Greek doctors and medicine, deploring their venality and the legal impunity under which they worked. He cites Cato the Elder as a fervent opponent of Greek medicine: Cato believed that Greek doctors were conspiring to wipe out all foreigners – that is, Romans. Cato himself was a good health-care provider, thus ensuring that his slave force was working at maximum efficiency (an unproductive slave was a burden); cabbage, it seems, was the panacea of choice in the Cato household. The best way, it seems, to ensure a healthy child was to bathe him in the urine of a man who existed on a diet of cabbage. Cato lived until the age of eighty-five so it is reasonable to assume that his suspicions of Greek physicians stemmed more from xenophobia than from a distrust of medicine. Pliny also cites cases of outrageous negligence, an example being where Indian cinnabar was frequently confused with red lead – *cinnabaris nativa* and *cinnabaris Indicus* – the former being a noted poison.

Inscriptional evidence, he darkly asserts, bears out his concerns: 'a throng of doctors did for me' being a common epitaph. Pliny is somewhat disingenuous though: medical science was an important part of his expansive *Natural History* – it covers thirteen out of the thirty-seven of his books. His ambiguity is reflected in his attitude to women, both as writers of medicine and as sources of medical information. The cure for a rabid dog bite reported by the mother of a Roman soldier wins his approval; on the other hand, the authority of two female Greek medical authors, Elephantis and Salpe, is considered dubious, simply because they disagree on certain matters; best then not to believe them at all.[7] Indeed, Pliny adds, what they write is also told by midwives and prostitutes – which repudiates not only the skills of midwives but women medical writers in general. Socles in the *Greek Anthology* would have done little for any doctor's reputation: in trying to cure Diodorus's scoliosis, Socles piled three rocks each four feet square onto the patient's spine, and crushed him to death. The only consolation was that he died straighter than a ruler.[8]

1. Funerary Relief of a Potter and His Wife. Late first/early second century AD. Women often shared in the running of the family business. This relief shows what is probably the potter's wife helping out in the production of some pots. The man is glazing, while the woman holds a palm fan and a piece of bread – symbolising her domesticity. The characters were almost certainly freedman and woman, possibly brought to Rome with the numerous slaves who came as skilled craftsmen after Rome's conquests of Greece and Spain. See J. J. Dobbins, 'A Roman Funerary Relief of a Potter and His Wife', Arts in Virginia 25:2/3 (1985), 24-33. With permission from Virginia Museum of Arts, Richmond, Adolph D. and Wilkins C. Williams Fund; VA (object # 60.2).

2. L. Vibius and His Family. This fairly typical funerary relief shows Lucius Vibius, his freedwoman wife Vecilia Hila, and their son Lucius Vibius Felicius Felix, his last name a pun on his *cognomen*. They all attempt to display 'Romanness', *Romanitas*, with father styled like Julius Caesar, mother with Livia-type hairstyle and son like an Augustan boy. End of first century BC; originally published in A. Hekler, *Greek and Roman Portraits* (New York 1902); now in the Vatican Museum.

3. Polychromatic floor mosaic of a typical lady from Pompeii. Note the earrings and the stylish hair. Naples Archaeological Museum. Courtesy of Andante Travels Ltd, Salisbury.

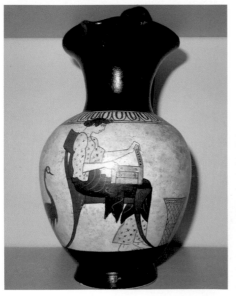

4. Working the Wool. The making of wool by women was a powerful symbol in both Greece and Rome, beginning with Penelope in Homer's *Odyssey*. In Rome it came to be an emblem of the good *matrona*, indicating chastity and fidelity and proper home-keeping. This is a copy of an Attic white ground *oinochoe* (wine pitcher) from around 475 BC, hand-painted by P. Vasglis; the original is in the Athens National Museum. It shows a Greek woman about to start working at her wool, with her basket (*kalathos*) to the right.

Above, right and next page: 5., 6., 7. Women of the Bardo. Fascinating scenes of everyday life from the fourth century AD estate of Julius found in a house in Carthage. This shows the *domina* selecting jewellery to wear from a box held by a slave; the next shows a woman exhibiting her credentials as a *matrona* with one of the articles of faith: she is telling the world that *lanam fecit* – she works the wool. The third is from baths at Sidi Ghrib near Tunis: here the *domina* is being offered a mirror by one of her slave girls as she completes her toilette. 5. and 6. by kind permission of Inga Mantle who took the photographs and Caroline Vout who published them in *Omnibus* 65 (2013). 5–7 are now in the National Museum of the Bardo, Tunis.

Early 1st Century A. D.

Early 2nd Century A. D.

Mid 2nd Century A. D.

End of 2nd Century A. D.

End of the 2nd Century and early 3rd Century

8. Three Hundred Years of Hairdressing. This page, originally published in *Roman History, Literature and Antiquities* by A. Petrie (London, 1926), depicts changing styles from the beginning of the Empire to the early third century AD. The fashionable, extravagant style top right is similar to the Fonseca bust in the Capitoline Museum, Rome. The crown was built up with fillets of wool, and was worn on the back or the front; the hair was combed into two parts, the front was combed forwards and built up with curls, while the back was plaited and made into a bun.

9. Fortunata. Not all wives were paragons of virtue; not all were beautiful; this flattering portrait of Fortunata is taken from the *Satyricon* by Petronius, translated by W. C. Firebaugh, published in 1922 in New York, in a lavish ($30) limited edition, by Horace Liveright.

10. A Wedding Scene. The crucial point in the ceremony where the couple join hands (*dextrarum iunctio*). The bride's matron of honour (*pronuba*) is behind the couple with her hands on their shoulders while the bride's father is on her right. Originally published in the *Universal History of the World Volume 3*: edited by J. A. Hammerton and now in the British Museum. Gods representing Valour, Victory and Fortune are on the left and right for good luck.

11. Aurelius Hermia and Aurelia Philematio. A first-century relief showing the monument erected by the butcher Aurelius Hermia in memory of his dutiful, modest and chaste wife. Originally published in the *Universal History of the World Volume 3*. The relief can be found in the British Museum. See page 15.

12. Out Shopping. This French postcard from the 1920s shows a group of well-to-do Roman women out shopping (and flirting) in a busy street. Note the old lady in the bottom right corner selling her vegetables. The painting, *Dans la Rue*, hangs in the Petit Palais, Musée des Beaux-Arts de la Ville de Paris.

Middle and bottom: 13., 14. Cornelia Africana (*c.* 190–100 BC), Mother of the Gracchi. Two contrasting pictures of Cornelia – the iconic *matrona* – with her three surviving children: Tiberius, Gaius and Sempronia. In the first she is proudly showing off what she famously described as her 'jewels'; in the second, by Rafaelle Sorbi, she seems to be giving the 'jewels' a good telling off. Originally published in *The Comic History of Rome* by Gilbert Abbot á Beckett (London, 1852) and in *Augustus – His Life and Work*, by Rene Francis (New York, 1914).

15. The Rape of the Sabine Women. An amusing take on this famous legend, also originally published in *The Comic History of Rome*.

16. The Sabine Women Intervening Between the Romans and Sabines. By Jacques-Louis David, 1799. Centre stage is Romulus's wife Hersilia – the daughter of Titus Tatius, leader of the Sabines, positioning herself between her husband and her father with her babies: Romulus is about to spear Tatius, but hesitates. The Tarpeian Rock can be seen in the background. Hersilia's brave act was intended to prevent further bloodshed; David's subtext was to encourage unity after the Revolution. Taken from *The Harmsworth Encyclopedia*, 1921; this was edited by John Hammerton, published as a fortnightly part-work and sold 12 million copies throughout the English-speaking world. See page 59.

17. 'Romulus and Remus Discovered by a Gentle Shepherd'. Originally published in *The Comic History of Rome*. Faustulus is the shepherd. The Latin for she-wolf is a *lupa*; *lupa* was one of around fifty Latin words for prostitute.

18. Flaminius at the Isthmian Games. Even the cricket stops when in 196 BC Titus Quinctius Flaminius, at the Isthmian Games, restored freedom to the locals releasing them from Macedonian rule; the women are again out in force in the midst of this rapturous crowd. Another scene from *The Comic History of Rome*.

19. *Above left*: Woman poet or bookkeeper? The so-called 'Sappho' is in the Naples Archaeological Museum. Courtesy of Andante Travels Ltd, Salisbury.

20. *Above right*: 'Lucretia Spinning with Her Minions'. This shows Lucretia, a paragon of feminine virtue, spinning wool with her slave girls, late at night. The scene, described by Livy, predates her rape by Tarquinius, the repercussions of which led to the end of the kings and ushered in the Republic. Her husband, Collatinus, can be seen in the background; they and the Tarquins had left a drinking party to establish which of the *matronae* were the most virtuous; the Tarquin ladies were found living it up at a party (*in convivio luxuque*), while Lucretia won hands down with this show of matronly rectitude, making a cloak for Collatinus. Originally published in *Rome Regal and Republican: A Family History of Rome* by Jane M. Strickland (London, 1854).

21. *Left*: Minerva, goddess of learning. This beautiful Minerva, gracefully reclining on a pile of books and accompanied by an owl and a theatrical mask, can be seen in York where Stonegate meets Minster Gates and Petergate. It was sculpted by John Wolstenholme in 1801.

22. *Doctae puellae* being pursued by their lovers. The scenes are reminiscent of descriptions by Catullus, Propertius, Tibullus or Ovid. The card on the left is of a painting, *Idylle d'Amour* by Henri Daudin from 1914. That on the right was posted in 1906.

Above left: 23. Pompeian Portraits. From P. Gusman's *Pompeii: The City, It's Life and Art* (London, 1910).

Above right: 24. A Roman Dancing Girl. One of a series of 'dancing women of the world' cigarette cards given away by W. S. Kimball & Co, cigarette manufacturers of Rochester, New York in 1889.

25. Women at Home. An idealised picture of a Pompeian nursery showing women and children relaxing and playing. 'And what lovely homes they were! ... the gardens to these palaces were wonderlands wherein gaily-plumed birds caroled amid the bewildering maze of odiferous and magnificent flowers and plants ... here the ladies whiled away the sunny hours'. From an early twentieth century card published by Arbuckle Bros, New York City promoting their coffee, in a series giving a pictorial history of the *Sports and Pastimes of all Nations*.

26. 'Dido Showing Aeneas Her Plans'. By Giovanni Francesco Romanelli (1610-1662). The enthusiasm and optimism exuded in this scene is tragically short-lived: rejected by Aeneas, Dido commits suicide aided by a priestess and reappearing to Aeneas as a ghost during his journey through the underworld. With kind permission of the Norton Simon Foundation, Pasadena, CA.

The Witches *(page 138)*

Above left: 27. Ladies Who Breakfast. A scene from Menander's comedy *Synaristosae, Ladies Who Breakfast,* adapted for the Roman stage and featuring a crone peddling spells and magic. The silver cup no doubt contains some potion or other; the thurible and box of spells add to her odious paraphernalia. Discovered in Pompeii, this animated scene is now in the Museo Archeologico Nazionale di Napoli; originally published in the *Universal History of the World Volume 3: Hellenistic Age to Roman Empire* edited by J. A. Hammerton (London, 1930).

Above right: 28. The Witches. The frontispiece from Volume 6 of the *Satyricon* by Petronius, translated by W. C. Firebaugh, showing the witches attacking the Cappadocian slave before they steal a corpse and replace it with a straw doll. *Satyricon* 63.

29. The *Atrium* and *Lararium.* This is where the household and family gods – the *lares* and the *penates* – held sway in the bigger and wealthier Roman houses. Here we see the women and children of the house bringing offerings to the gods. The idealised scene is taken from a Liebig trade card issued by the Compagnie Liebig (later OXO), manufacturers of meat extracts with factories in Fray-Bentos in Uruguay and Colon in Argentina.

30. Vestal Virgins. The Vestal Virgins keeping the flame burning in the Temple of Vesta in Rome. The flame represented the stability and continuity of Rome – when it went out the Vestal responsible was flogged and there were suggestions of Vestal immorality and ominous times for Rome. Vestals found guilty of no longer being virgins were entombed alive, although this bit is euphemised in *Aunt Charlotte's Stories of Roman History for the Little Ones* by Charlotte M. Yonge (London, 1884), where the picture was first published.

31. Appius Claudius Punished by the People. Appius Claudius getting his comeuppance from the men and women of Rome. He had bothered Verginia on her way to school; her father exercised his *patria potestas* and killed her to avoid the shame a liaison with Appius Claudius would bring. Originally in the *Comic History of Rome*.

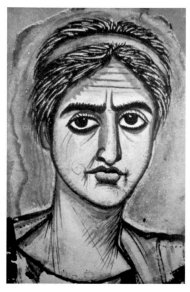

Above left and right: 32. and 33. The Older Woman. Two striking mummy portraits of women from Fayum in Egypt, both showing an astonishing degree of modernity. The first, from the third century AD has an almost Picasso-like quality emphasising the woman's grey hair and wrinkled face. It is now in the British Museum. The second, a portrait of Aline from the early first century AD, now in the Egyptian Museum and Papyrus Collection in Berlin, could have been taken today. Aline was the daughter of Herodotus (not the historian!); she died aged thirty-five years. Her hairstyle corresponds to the fashion under Tiberius; her mummy was found together with the mummy of the husband and three children. Originally published in *Ancient Painting from the Earliest Times to the Period of Christina Art* by M. H. Swindler in 1929, and *Chefs d'Oeuvres de la Peinture Greque.*

34. The Mysteries. A detail from the frescos in the Villa of the Mysteries in Pompeii, showing an earnest looking young acolyte. Originally published in *Chefs d'Oeuvres de la Peinture Greque* by G. Meautis in 1939.

Father Time
Outwitted

Time cannot leave his marks on the woman who takes care of her complexion with Pompeian Massage Cream. Wrinkles and crow's-feet are driven away, sallowness vanishes, angles are rounded out and double-chins reduced by its use. Thus the clear, fresh complexion, the smooth skin, and the curves of cheek and chin that go with youth, may be retained past middle age by the woman who has found what

Pompeian Massage Cream

will do. The use of this preparation keeps skin, flesh, muscles and blood-vessels in a healthy, natural condition, which resists the imprints of time, work, worry and care.

FREE SAMPLE TO TEST

Simply fill in and mail us the coupon and we will send you a large sample, together with our illustrated book on Facial Massage, an invaluable guide for the proper care of the skin.

POMPEIAN MFG. CO., 28 Prospect St., Cleveland, O.

35. Pompeii as a Health Brand. This advertisement from 1910 would suggest that the women of Pompeii had won a reputation for having healthy, youthful complexions. 'Pompeian Massage Cream', with its anti-aging qualities, is clearly responsible for this: by 1909 it was the world's best-selling face cream, with 50,000 dealers selling the 10,000 jars that were made and sold daily. In 1912 Carle Blenner was commissioned to find the perfect Pompeian woman and paint a picture of her: 'a woman who embodied the beauty and poise the users of *Pompeian* products aspired to'. The result is on the advertisement but it would be interesting to know how he came to his conclusions.

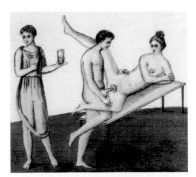

36. The Ultimate Drinking Game? Two plates showing wall paintings from Pompeii copied and published in *Musée Royal de Naples: Peintures, Bronzes et Statues Erotiques du Cabinet Secrète* in 1871 by Colonel Famin (Stanislas Marie César Famin, 1799–1853). These images were locked away from the public in the 'Cabinet Secret' for many years. The one on the right comes from a bar in Pompeii's Via di Mercurio (V, 10, 1): 'The actors in it, placed on two outstretched ropes, caress each other without losing their equilibrium, and drink without spilling a drop of the liquor contained in their glasses. This fresco ... is obscene to a degree.' That on the left is described thus: 'The drawing of these figures is rather incorrect, and the expression cold'. The originals are now sadly lost.

Similar suspicion and distrust is evident in Plutarch in his *Instructions for Health*, written around AD 80. The work is explicity aimed at men, and specifically at men of Plutarch's social class: he preaches a life of moderation in which women have a role, but only as exemplars of *im*moderation, leading men to excess.[9]

Martial too was particularly dismissive: 'Now you're a gladiator; before that you were an ophthalmologist. What you did as a doctor you now do as a gladiator'; or, better still, 'Diaulus was a doctor once; now he works in a mortuary where he does exactly what he used to do when he was a doctor.'[10] Seneca observed with some distaste that the diseases caused by increasingly luxurious lifestyles were suffered by women as well as by men: they lost their hair and suffered gout.[11] He does, nevertheless, go some way to restoring the reputation of the profession when he praises his own doctor for the excellent care he gave, his empathy and his friendly conscientiousness.[12]

The influence and reputation of the Hippocratics continued, although they were not without healthy criticism: for example, at the end of the first century AD the *Gynaikeia* by Soranus of Ephesus was published in which the author disputed Hippocrates' claim that male foetuses incline to the right of the womb, female to the left.[13] Bedside manner and the patient–doctor relationship found a place in the Hippocratic writings. With regard to women, the authors emphasise the close relationship necessary between patient and doctor; with women and girls self-control must be exercised at all times.

Agnodice was reputedly the first professional midwife of Ancient Greece, practising around 500 BC. As a native of Athens, where it was illegal for women or slaves to study or practice medicine, Agnodice was forced to dress as a man while attending medical lectures. On qualifying, women rejected her (as a man) until she revealed that she was a woman; she then incurred the wrath of the Areopagus, who accused her of corrupting her patients, and was charged with practising illegally. Influential Athenian ladies protested and had the law abolished, after which women were permitted to practise medicine, and to be paid for it.

Soranus was the author of around twenty books on biological

and medical science, including the *Gynaikeia*, one of the first illustrated medical textbooks, later abridged and translated into Latin probably in the sixth century by Muscio to produce his *Gynaecia*. The first part is an early multiple-choice questionnaire with questions and answers on anatomy, embryology, childbirth and neonatal care; the second part covers disease. Soranus's original book establishes the qualities that make the best of midwives. She should be experienced in theory and in practice, including therapy, dietetics, surgery and infection control; she will be calm, reassuring and sympathetic; always sober, as she never knows when she might be called to an emergency; she will be discreet (as she will share in many secrets of life) and she will not be subject to vulgar superstition. All very professional, and indicative of the fact that in obstetrics and gynaecology much of the care and treatment was the preserve of the midwife rather than of the doctor; the midwife was, in effect, as much a doctor as a midwife, assuming a high level of literacy and scientific knowledge. We know of Claudia Trophima and Poblicia Aphe who probably met those criteria;[14] the former lived to see seventy-five years whereas Poblicia Aphe from Gaia lived only to her twenty-first birthday. The aptly named thirty-year-old *obstetrix* Hygiae is commemorated on a tombstone by two of her tentmates (*contubernales*) – Marius Orthrus and Apollonius.[15]

Soranus knew what made a good wet nurse too, even though he believed that a mother's breast is best. She should be between the ages of twenty and forty and should have had two or three children herself; she should be big, and of a good complexion. Her breasts should be of medium size, not rigid but soft with no wrinkles, the nipples neither big nor too small; she should be calm, a Greek and well turned out. The insistence on a calm temperament perhaps indicates a concern regarding the physical abuse of infants; Soranus says that angry women are like maniacs; they drop the babies or handle them roughly when they cry endlessly. A letter has come down to us from the end of the second century BC advising a new mother on how best to select a competent wet nurse: she should be Greek, modest, clean, alert and sober; she will offer the breast when *she* thinks it's time, *not* when the infant demands; she should be calm and induce a suitably equable environment for the baby, bathing him or her from time to time, not all of the time.[16]

Inscriptional evidence for nurses and nursing includes that by Athenian Apollodorus grieving for his nurse daughter, Melitta.[17] Two contracts for the hiring of wet nurses for foundling slave children have survived from 13 BC Alexandria: Theodote signs up for eighteen months to provide her pure and unadulterated milk to Tyche; if Tyche should die (it goes on in a matter-of-fact way) then Theodote will nurse another child, agreeing all the while neither to sleep with her husband nor get pregnant. Didyme has a similar sixteen-month contract, suggesting that these were standard agreements.

Scribonius Largus (*c.* AD 1–50), court physician to Claudius, compiled a list of 271 prescriptions, many of them apparently original, in AD 41 in his *Compositiones Medicamentorum*; these were later plagiarised by Marcellus Empiricus around AD 410, for his *De Medicamentis Empiricis, Physicis, et Rationabilibus*. Taking a topographic approach Scribonius also covers plasters (*emplastra*), analgesics (*acopa*) and emollients (*malagmata*). He reinforces the Hippocratic dictum banning abortion and the use of abortifacients. Unlike Pliny and Polybius, Scribonius is happy to include women to support the efficacy of his pharmacy, citing a *matrona* and a little African lady.[18] The *matrona*'s compound for the treatment of epilepsy (*morbus comitialis*) is interesting, not so much for the ivory scrapings, Attic honey, tortoise blood and fresh wood pigeon, but rather for her insistence that where the epileptic is a girl then the specimens should be female, and male where the patient is a boy.

The Greek physician Pedanius Dioscorides (*c.* 40–90 AD) came to Rome during Nero's reign; he was also an accomplished botanist and pharmacologist. Dioscorides stressed the importance of experiential medicine, testing and retesting, and the value of the post-mortem examination. His five-volume book *De Materia Medica* is our first pharmacopeia, comprising 1,000 or so natural drugs, nearly 5,000 medicinal applications for drugs, and 360 medical properties for agents such as antiseptics, anti-inflammatories and stimulants. Plants and minerals used specifically by women are recorded – particularly in skin lotions, depilatories, perfumes, even love potions. A contemporary was Thessalus of Trales (*fl. c.* 65–95), court physician to Nero; Thessalus is notable for his use of vegetables, emetics and fasting to restore health.

In the next century Galen of Pergamon (b. around 129 AD) assumed the mantle of leading light on all things medical. A prodigious amount of his work is extant – nearly 3 million words in Greek alone – making him responsible for about 10 per cent of all surviving Greek literature. Galen, an exceptional eleven years in the training, was very much in debt to the Hippocratic authors: 25 per cent of his surviving work is devoted to Hippocrates, either in the nineteen commentaries (thirteen survive) on Hippocratic works, or the *Glossary* of Hippocratic terms, the *Elements According to Hippocrates* and the *Opinions of Hippocrates and Plato*.

Galen came to Rome in AD 162 and lectured, wrote and demonstrated extensively, particularly on anatomy, using the cadavers of pigs and other farm animals, apes and an elephant. His findings were published in a number of books, including *Anatomical Procedures* and *On the Dissection of the Muscles*. In the latter he is quite exhaustive, ascribing, for example, musculature to the penis but not to female genitalia or to the womb. He started out as a very successful doctor to gladiators and later became physician to Marcus Aurelius and Commodus. Central to his teachings was the belief that women were inferior to men, because women are physically colder; women possess all the bits that men have, the only difference being that in women the parts are internal whereas in men they are external. His *On the Order of his Own Books* is a useful *vade mecum* to his own prodigious oeuvre, and is one of a few such guides he wrote in which he stresses the importance of methodology and of 'demonstrative knowledge'. He advocates that preclinical medicine be learnt first – anatomy and physiology – through his *On Pulses for Beginners* and *On Bones for Beginners*, followed by the clinical *On the Usefulness of the Parts*. Galen believed that women had no need for facial or for extensive body hair because they did not need to look impressive or *august* in the way that men do; women did not need hair to keep them warm either, because they spent most of their time in the house.

This of course takes no account, for example, of women working in the fields or in shops, or going out to the theatre or the games.[19]

Galen leaves us the names of numerous other *pharmaka* specialists, for example Heras the Cappadocian, Andromachus the Younger, T. Statilius Crito and Asclepiades Pharmakion. Aretaeus of Cappadocia produced valuable work in eight books on the symptoms and characteristics of various diseases.

After Galen, Athenaeus, in his *Deipnosophistae* written at the end of the second century AD, keeps up the attacks on Greek doctors; he has one diner say that if there were no doctors, the next most stupid group would be teachers; Galen was supposedly present but, such was his arrogance, that the remark made no impression on him whatsoever. Indeed, for Galen the more the merrier: there was room in Rome for all medical and surgical specialists, including dentists, otolaryngologists and proctologists.

Our last known *Gynaecology* was published by Philumenus, also at the close of the second century. After him Oribasius (*c.* AD 320–400), physician to Julian the Apostate, compiled what must have been a useful compendium of excerpts from Galen and the writings of earlier medical authors in his extensive work, the *Collectionum Medicarum Reliquiae*. Alexander of Tralles wrote an encyclopedia of medicine in the sixth century AD; he was the author of the first textbook on parasitology, *Letter on Intestinal Worms*, and made progress in the diagnosis of angina and in ophthalmology.

The practice of medicine in Roman times was an amateurish affair. Medical training seems to have been alarmingly short and somewhat hit and miss – six months trailing someone a bit more experienced as part of an extremely large firm, or attendance at a lecture or dissection, or rather a vivisection, was about as good as it got; no licence to practice was required. Martial, exaggerating no doubt, but revealing a germ of the grim truth, complains about the 100-strong firm prodding him with their cold hands and leaving him with a fever he never had before they arrived.[20] There were plenty of textbooks and pharmacopeias for those who wanted and could afford them, but precious little practical training or professional standards to aspire to. Anyone, it seems, could set up as a doctor (*iatroi, medici* or *medicae*).

Nurses were responsible for a wide range of what today we

would class as medical work; midwives (*maiae* or *obstetrices*), as we have seen, were crucial in obstetrics; wet nurses were very popular with those who could pay them. Pliny the Younger exemplifies the high regard and affection in which some nurses were held; he is anxious to ensure the good management of a farm he has left to his nurse, and that it produces a good yield for her – her pension, in effect.[21] For Quintilian[22] it was essential that a nurse spoke well, as hers is the first voice and hers are the first words the child will hear, and imitate.

Doctors were forever in professional competition with each other in terms of successful outcomes, probably to the detriment of patient care. They also fought a continuous battle against the ubiquitous amulets, potions and incantations of the fringe and folkey medical practitioners, the quacks, root cutters (*rhizotomoi*), the practitioners of magic (*herbarii*), the *magi* and other unscrupulous pretenders who did nothing for the reputation of the profession. An example of the paraphernalia comes in the shape of an Egyptian haematite fertility amulet excavated near Welwyn; it bears a picture of a uterus, a scarab beetle and the inscription 'Ororiouth' – the name of the spirit which protected against women's diseases.[23] Soranus has no time for superstition but is circumspect enough to appreciate the psychological benefits of amulets and other magical paraphernalia.

That is not to discredit the Romans' use of phytomedicine or herbal remedies: some potions were admittedly the product of irrationalism, fantasy and quackery but others were undoubtedly efficacious: some are still in use today. Examples of naturally occuring medicines obtainable from any modern pharmacy include atropine (belladonna) used in bradycardia and ophthalmology, quinine (malaria), aspirin (originally an analgesic and antipyretic, now used in the secondary prevention of cardiovascular disease; 40,000 tonnes of it are taken every year), metformin (type 2 diabetes) and taxol, indicated for treatment for breast, skin and pancreatic cancers. Indeed, according to the World Health Organisation, 25 per cent of drugs dispensed today in pharmacies to the 4 billion users worldwide contain at least one active ingredient derived from plant material. The Greeks and Romans were on the right track.

Doctors were the preserve of the wealthy; the less so would have stuck with their traditional folk and sometimes phoney remedies and put their faith in the gods. Pliny the Elder said it very well when he declared that thousands of people lived without doctors, but not without medicine.

Some public baths were reputed to have healing qualities. For example, at *Aquae Sulis* (Bath) the Temple of Sulis Minerva was a magnet for the sick and infirm; a prescription for an eye salve has been found there belonging to Titus Janianus. That women routinely visited the shrines dedicated to Sulis Minerva there, and other such temples around the Roman world, is evidenced by the discovery of curse tablets, and *ex votos* – models of parts of the female anatomy (breasts in wood, terracotta, bronze, and ivory) – such as the one discovered at Wroxeter indicating a possible case of mastitis. Every body part and organ is represented: female breast and uterus votives probably indicated gratitude for the birth of a child; a large number of male and female sexual organs (compared to an untypically small number of the usually copious hands and feet) may well indicate the prevalence of sexually transmitted infections, for example at the Campetti sanctuary in Veii. Concentrations of children and pregnant women votives at Massigny-les-Vitteaux near Dijon, and of swaddled infants and men and women with exaggerated genitalia at Essarois may be a sign of temples dedicated to fertility and childbirth.

Most doctors were men, but there were female doctors, *medicae*, many of them slaves or freedwomen. We know a number from the funereal and inscriptional evidence; many of them come from medical families. In the first century AD Antiochis, daughter of physician Diodotus, was so highly appreciated for her medical expertise by the people of Tlos in Lycia that they set up a statue celebrating her; Galen credits her with the discovery of effective drugs for sciatica and rheumatism.[24] Aurelia Alexandria Zosime was also honoured with a statue by her doctor husband in Adada, Pisine. There is Primilla, a physician who died at the end of the first century AD at the age of forty-four in Rome, four more Roman doctors: Iulia Pye, Minucia Asste and Venuleia Sosis, all freedwomen, and a slave, Melitine – and Secunda Livilla and Terentia Prima. Wealthy *medicae* include Metilia Donata from

Lyons.[25] Indeed, there is evidence of female physicians from all over the Empire: Hulia Sabina from Italy, Flavia Hedone from Gaul, Asylla Polia from Africa, Himertos of Marathon, and Iulia Saturnina from Merida in Iberia – she was not only a wife beyond compare, but the best doctor.[26] The husband of Pantheia, a second-century AD physician from Pergamum, is generous in praise for his doctor wife; apart from being 'the rudder of life in our home' she did much to enhance the family's medical reputation: 'even though you were a woman you were just as accomplished as me'. Naevia Clara was also married to a doctor, in Rome in the first century BC. Later in the second century AD Domnina from Neoclaudiopolis in Asia received virtual apotheosis because she 'saved her native fatherland from disease'. Theodore Priscianus[27] in the fourth century AD dedicated his book on gynaecology to Victoria, the 'sweet teacher of my art'. Aspasia was a second-century obstetrician and gynaecologist; we have an inscription referring to a 'medica a mammis' (breast disease specialist).[28]

Most medical writers were men, but there were female authors. Metrodora was a second-century AD author of a treatise on gynaecology, diseases of the kidney, uterus and stomach. She is noted for the advances she made in gynaecological pathology and her expertise in digital examination and the use of the vaginal speculum. According to Galen, a lady called Cleopatra wrote *On the Composition of Medicines by Place* (*Kosmetikon*) which included, among many other things, a remedy for baldness involving the topical application of pulverised mouse skulls (an alternative therapy required the use of mouse droppings), Cleopatra is more likely an example of clever branding than of Ptolemaic provenance. Pliny's *Natural History* names female practitioners as sources for his work: Elephantis, Lais, Olympias of Thebes, Salpe and Sotira. Galen quotes Elephantis's cure for alopecia; she was also the author of a famous book on sexual positions – a Roman *Kama Sutra*. Suetonius tells that Tiberius packed a copy when he left for his retreat on Capri; Martial says it is[29] '[a book] with intriguing new ways of making love'. Aspasia in the sixth century AD wrote works on gynaecological surgery and abortion; she was reputedly even more empathetic with her patients than Soranus.

Despite the influx of doctors, the texts, the increasing medical knowledge and the libraries and medical schools, the gods continued to provide a powerful alternative, if not parallel, recourse. As we have seen, there was a divine entitity responsible for every stage of life – from conception through to death. The suspicion surrounding the medical profession, the disagreements on the best possible course of clinical action, the cost, and the prospect of enduring surgery and other painful procedures in an anaesthesia-free, septic world would be quite enough to steer the patient away from the doctor towards the gods in a bid for a pain-free, survivable option.

The second-century AD orator Aelius Aristides gives a good example of this route when he describes the confusion among his doctors over the best treatment for a huge tumour in his groin. Aristides ignores all the conflicting advice and puts his faith in the gods who prescribe a certain drug – the tumour shrank and all was well.[30] Indeed, the Hippocratic writings and the *Oath* are predicated on the patronage of Apollo the healer, Asculepius and Hygieia, Panakeia, Sequana and all the other healing gods and goddesses. It was Asculepius who pointed Galen toward a career in medicine; Asculepius was also the doctors' god – thus forging links between secular medicine and temple medicine.[31]

We can only speculate on the role women played in the medicine relating to their own bodies and their minds. It is impossible to know how far the mainly male authors of books on obstetrics and gynaecology based their findings on patient consultations, examination and patient history – actually talking one to one with the women about their health issues, about how they felt regarding their symptoms and what they themselves knew about their condition. However, if we can assume some level of patient–doctor communication this gives a rare voice to women: Doctors Soranus and Galen surely did take patient histories to support findings and diagnoses extrapolated from physical examination. The treatments recommended by Soranus, for example, are often empathetic and enlightened, possibly reflecting time he spent with his patients teasing out symptoms and looking for important signs.

Much of Graeco-Roman gynaecology was focussed on the womb, *hystera*, and woman's ability to bear children – the essential medical difference between man and woman. Hippocrates[32] puts it succinctly: 'the so-called women's diseases, the womb is the cause of them all'. The Hippocratic authors believed that women's bodies comprised flesh which was softer and more porous than that of men,[33] an example being the female breast in which the woman's nourishment is converted into milk.[34] This porosity was caused by the absorption of moisture in the form of blood, released each month during the woman's period. The concept of porosity is linked to the knowledge that women leak, through the vagina, with menstrual fluid, sexual lubricant, locheal discharge and discharges from various infections.[35]

On conception, to produce a male child rapid thrusting during sex at the end of the woman's period is recommended; for a girl things are slightly less vigorous or spontaneous and involve tying up the right testicle for sex in the middle of the period.[36] Blood clogging up the venous system in the breasts signifies that the woman is going mad – a physiological explanation for the age-old stereotype that women are naturally neurotic, erratic and unpredictable. Menstruation as a purging agent was, then, a good thing, as indeed was epitaxis (nose-bleed) which performed a similar purging role. Amenorrhœa caused all manner of physical and psychological illnesses; virgins were particularly susceptible, which explains their tendency to hang themselves or jump down wells to their deaths. In essence the physiological differences between men and women supported the belief that women were physically and mentally inferior to men.

The views of the pre-Socratics and Aristotle would likewise have prevailed in the fusion of medical knowledge that the Roman doctor, and their female patients, absorbed. Empedocles (b. *c*. 493 BC) believed that men were hotter than women.[37] Aristotle taught that men were more perfect than women; because women were less able to produce the heat that was vital for generation of the species – due to the debilitating effect of menstruation – women were incomplete, deformed males. In contrast to his Hippocratic contemporaries Aristotle believed that menstruation was not a good thing. Aristotle championed the long-standing myth that the womb comprised two separate compartments, often used to explain the birth of twins; males were born from the right (hotter) chamber, and females from the left with all its sinister implications. He rejected the Hippocratic belief that hysteria in women was attributable to the movements of the womb and made tentative steps towards an understanding of the Fallopian tubes, largely unknown in antiquity. Some 600 or more years later Galen also subscribed to this temperature-based theory and the notion of the incomplete woman.

Herophilus, in his *Midwifery*, differed from the Hippocratics in that he believed the womb to be no different from other internal organs. However, thanks no doubt to the knowledge acquired through dissection of cadavers while in Alexandria, he furthered the understanding of the female and male reproductive systems. Herophilus was able to highlight the analogous relationship between the male testicles and the female ovaries; he believed that menstruation was the only physiological contribution women made to conception, and considered menstruation to be a cause of illness in women.[38]

Women's medicine involved many remedies made up from various potions. Some of these were applied topically via salves and plasters; others were administered internally as fumigants, nasal clysters, enemas or pessaries. Fumigation involved the burning of agents such as human hair, medicinal herbs and bitumen in a pot; a lead tube was led from this into the woman's vagina. It was not without its hazards, if Soranus's warning about the dangers of burning the vagina is anything to go by.[39] Enemas were introduced for disorders of the bladder, rectum, vagina and uterus – vaginal douches via vaginal clysters were often used. Pessaries were deployed for a wide range of conditions including inducing menstruation, inflammation of the womb, expelling dead foetuses and relieving hysteria.[40] Pessaries were also used in cases of a prolapsed uterus,[41] while tents were administered to staunch uterine haemorrhage and suppurating wombs.[42] Celsus pioneered the use of metal tubes that were introduced into the vagina to channel medication after operations for occlusion of the vagina. Eviscerated puppies stuffed with spices and cooked were used as fumigants.[43]

One of Celsus's treatments for disease of the womb, based on Numenius, entailed the use of a pessary made up of ¼ denarius of saffron, 1 denarius of wax, 8 denarii of butter, 12 denarii of goose fat, 2 boiled egg yolks and less than 1 cyathus of rose oil. The rose oil and lion's fat cannot have been easy to obtain. Other remedies include pomegranate rind in water for the evacuation of dead foetuses and snails' shells crushed with honey (an anti-bacterial) for women who suffer fits from diseases of the genitals. Pliny recommended the application of tree moss from Gaul as therapy for gynaecological infections; bramble berries are excellent for gums, tonsils and genitals. If aconite comes into contact with female genitalia the woman dies the same day, and a good aphrodisiac was produced by rubbing the genitalia with a donkey's penis plunged seven times into hot oil. He describes the use of calcinated lead in ophthalmic medicines, especially in the treatment of proptosis, bulging eyes, often a sign of hyperthyroidism and Graves' disease, and in the treatment of ulcers, haemorrhoids and anal fissures – even though he knows that the fumes are harmful to dogs. Other aphrodisiacs involve wearing an amulet made from the right part of a vulture's lung in a crane's skin, drinking the yolk of five duck's eggs mixed with pig fat and honey, and wearing an amulet made from a cockerel's right testicle wrapped up in ram's skin. A lizard drowned in a man's urine had the opposite effect.[44]

Medical instrumentation reflected academic and clinical progress: vaginal *specula* (*dioptra*) were, among other tools of the trade, found in the House of the Surgeon in Pompeii; they would have been used to dilate the cervix in the treatment of hysteria.[45]

Soranus reminds us that it was a Roman wife's first duty to produce children, ideally boys, to populate the ranks of the Roman military and administration, 'since women get married to bear children and heirs, and not for fun or pleasure'. To promote this Soranus teaches that successful conception is all down to timing. 'The end of menstruation, when the urge and desire for sex is present, when the body is not full nor the partners drunk, after light exercise and a light snack, when the mood is right' – these are the most promising conditions for making babies. Before him, Lucretius had taught that the best position for conception was for the woman to have 'coitus more ferarum' (sexual intercourse like wild beasts do it), or *a tergo (kubra,* in Greek).[46]

Soranus went some way to recognising the dangers caused by alcohol in pregnancy. He advised women to be sober during intercourse if they wanted to avoid foetal abnormalites: the soul is afflicted by strange fantasies when the woman is drunk. Women who digest their food readily, do not have loose stools and who are of a good and happy disposition are most likely to conceive. He goes on to offer treatments for excessive morning sickness (hyperemesis gravidarum), and pica – a condition that involves eating non-foods such as soil, charcoal, vine stems and unripe fruit. He specified the ideal diet for the pregnant woman and ruled out 'eating for two'. Also out was sex during pregnancy – it leads to superfoetation. Pliny recorded that the best time to conceive was at the beginning or the end of a period; a promising indicator of conception (*fecunditas*) was when traces of drugs used as eye drops appear in the woman's saliva. Soranus believed that the optimum time for conception was at the end of the cycle, a confusion caused by ignorance of ovulation among the Greeks and Romans.[47]

The life expectancy for women was, on average, just shy of thirty years, somewhat less than that for men. Mortality caused from 'too soon to marry, too soon to carry' no doubt accounted for some of the difference: women could be married from the age of twelve and, in some cases could have been subjected to constant sexual activity before menarche, which would typically occur around age fourteen. The serial childbirths that often soon followed would, over time, also have a deleterious impact on a woman's physical – and mental – health. Add to that dystocia, or difficult labour of one kind or another, the chances of haemmorrhage, infection, puerperal sepsis, eclampsia, obstructed labour, thromboembolism, and the fact that precocious sex possibly led to cases of cervical cancer, then there is little wonder that the life expectancy was generally short. There are many epigraphical and funerary inscriptions for women who died in their twenties. Evidence from the Roman cemetery at Poundbury in Dorset may not be conclusive but it shows that fifty-one out of 281 females died in or around childbirth. Pliny the Younger writes about the tragic death of the Helvidiae sisters, who both died in childbirth giving birth to daughters (who survived): 'two great girls cut down in the bloom of youth by their own fertility'.[48]

Obviously, there are long-lived exceptions: in Britain alone funerary inscriptions reveal that Tadia Vallaunius survived until she was sixty-five, Julia Secundina saw seventy-five, and Claudia Crysis lived until the age of ninety. Context is important too: such desperate mortality figures are by no means confined to the Roman age. Recent statistics show that 90 per cent of adolescent births (2.8 million) in 2006 occurred in developing countries where 28 per cent of females gave birth before the age of eighteen, the age at which a girl is deemed biologically fit for motherhood. In the UK, as everywhere, geographical location and deprivation influence neonatal death: in the most deprived areas infant mortality is 85 per cent higher than in the least deprived.[49]

There is inscriptional evidence for maternal mortality, pain in childbirth, and a *matrona*'s concern for her offspring: at the end of the first century BC in Egypt Dosithea, aged twenty-five, died in childbirth; she died 'in pain, escaping the pangs of childbirth'. Rusticeia Matrona died in childbirth and from *malignant fate* at the same age in Mauretania; she urges her husband to look after their son. Also twenty-five, Daphne, from Carthage, died giving birth; her epitaph records her aching concern for the baby: 'who will feed him, look after him for the rest of his life?' Socratea died of a haemorrhage in childbirth aged thirty-six. This fifteen-year-old died giving birth, with her baby, in Tusculum in the first century BC: 'The tomb [holds] two deaths in one body, the [urn] of ashes contains twin funerals.'

The situation, of course, cannot have been helped by the conjecture and ignorance about the length of gestation. Aulus Gellius inclined to the view that babies could be born in the seventh, ninth and tenth months – but never in the eighth. Strenuous work in the fields and a poor diet was the lot of many women and this can only have exacerbated the problem.

Soranus is particularly sensitive about complicated labour. He dismisses the crude and cruel methods of other doctors which involve such hideous practices as tying the mother to the bed, lifting it up and letting it fall, and shaking the mother violently. Instead he advocates a reflective approach – calmly assessing the situation and establishing if the causes are psychological, foetal or physical, and consulting with the midwife. Lubricants, catheters and enemas are deployed as required for the comfort and safety of the parturient, which is paramount.[50]

Breech births were to be avoided and much manipulation went on to ensure a normal delivery. Pliny declares that breech deliveries are unnatural and explains why babies born feet first are called Agrippa – *aegre partus* – born with difficulty, and are unlucky. Marcus Agrippa was blighted by lameness and constant warring; his legacy was the two Agrippinas who left to the world Caligula and Nero. Nero too was born feet first.[51] Where manipulation failed, a truly horrible array of procedures – embryotomy – came into play to evacuate the foetus as soon it was presumed dead, to ensure the survival of the mother. Hooked knives were used to dismember the foetus and thus facilitate delivery; likewise, decapitating instruments enabled the head to delivered first.[52] Soranus recommended amputating parts of the foetus as they presented, rather than internally, to avoid cutting the vagina with the blade.[53] Unusually large foetal heads were crushed with a cranioclast (a bowed forceps with teeth) or split with an embryotome; both instruments are still in use today. Traction hooks were also used; samples have been found in Pompeii. Their use is described in Hippocrates, and by Celsus and Soranus.[54]

Iberia, it seems, was not the ideal place for a woman to go into labour: Strabo, in his *Geography*,[55] reports that when a Spanish woman gives birth her husband lies in bed 'and she looks after him'. Pliny recommends a way of concluding a protracted labour. What it lacks in expediency it more than makes up for in creativity: get a stone or similar projectile which had killed three living things – human, bear, wild boar, say – in three blows and throw it over the roof of the house where the woman is in confinement; she will then give birth immediately.[56] Potions were available to help in the evacuation of the placenta and in encouraging lactation, as indeed they were for keeping breasts firm or for inhibiting their growth. The ability to delay puberty in girls was a valuable asset in the slave markets.

Infant mortality may have been as high as thirty deaths in every 100 pregnancies, compared with 9.1 per 1,000 in Western Caucasian populations today.[57] It is worth noting that improvements in the

Roman statistics only came about relatively recently: the London Bills of Mortality for 1762–1771 show that 50 per cent of infants died before the age of two. Susan Treggiari has usefully compiled some revealing statistics extrapolated from an assumption that female life expectancy at birth was twenty-five years. A woman, of course, would not expect to die at that age, rather it means that 30 per cent of all babies died before the age of one and 50 per cent by the age of ten; these survivors would then have a 50 per cent chance of reaching the age of fifty. A further 17 per cent would see seventy. This reveals a lot about the demographics of women in Roman society, and the number of women available for marriage, and for remarriage.[58]

Pliny gives some of the reasons suggested to explain the very high rate of maternal and infant mortality. Babies born before the seventh month do not survive and babies born in the seventh month survive only if they are conceived the day before or after a full moon or during a new moon; eighth-month babies are common, despite what Aristotle says, however, they are vulnerable until they are forty days old. For mothers, the fourth and eighth months are the most critical; abortions at that time are fatal. In a normal pregnancy the ninth day after conception sees the onset of headaches, dizziness, blurred vision, loss of appetite and nausea, indicating that the foetus is forming; male foetuses produce a healthier complexion in the mother and make for an easier delivery; movements in the womb begin on the fortieth day with males, for females after ninety days. Babies are particularly vulnerable when they start to grow hair and during the full moon, if the pregnant mother eats too much salt then the baby will be born without nails, excessive maternal yawning can be fatal during delivery. It has been estimated that the average early Empire Roman woman had to give birth to five babies if she was to ensure the survival of two and to do her bit to maintain the required birth rate.

The main causes of neonatal mortality, death within the first twenty-nine days of life, were insanitary conditions at the birth, and trauma; infant morbidity and deaths were often caused by intestinal disorders, particularly enteritis and dysentery. Celsus recorded that the latter was particularly virulent in children up to the age of ten and in their pregnant mothers, where the unborn baby was also lost.[59] Over-zealous swaddling – where the limbs are confined and the heartbeat slowed down dangerously – dirty laundry, and mastication of baby foods by wet nurses who themselves might be carrying an infection may also have taken their toll. As indeed would goat's and cow's milk which contain infectious organisms and would have been used not just by reluctant breast-feeders but by poorer, undernourished women who were unable to feed and could not afford a wet nurse.

Humans have sexual intercourse during pregnancy, and this, the Romans believed, led to superfoetation – carrying more than one foetus at a time. It is actually very rare. Pliny the Elder scurrilously cites cases: a woman bore twins, and one baby resembled her husband while the other looked like her lover; a slave from Perconnesus who had sex twice in one day produced twins, one like her master, the other like the estate manager; a mother gave birth after five months and then again at full term; a woman produced a seventh-month baby and then twins some months later.

Pregnancy could have definite advantages other than the chance of a healthy child: Julia, Augustus's daughter, is alleged to have said that being pregnant allowed her to pursue her extra-maritial affairs without fear of getting pregnant: 'I never take on a passenger unless the ship is full.' Unfortunately for Julia, another type of ship was to take her into insular exile on Pandateria for her adulterous behaviour. Juvenal, in his sixth-satire rant against women, tells us that some women prefer potent eunuchs or *cinaedi* – to avoid pregnancy and a need for abortion.[60]

Pliny the Younger's wife Calpurnia miscarried; sympathy and concern for Calpurnia apart, Pliny as much as anyone would have felt the all-round disappointment when so much pressure was on wives to produce an heir. In his letter to her grandfather Calpurnius Fabatus, Pliny writes, 'The news that your granddaughter has had a miscarriage will be even sadder for you to hear when you so much wanted a great grandchild. Being very young she did not know that she was pregnant and so failed to take certain precautions and avoid things she should have avoided. She paid for her mistake with the warning that she had put her life in mortal danger.' The girl's ignorance of her own pregnancy (at a stage when Pliny obviously thinks she should have known more) highlights the obvious shortcomings in sex education among even more educated families; it certainly demonstrates a failure on the part of the wife's mother or even the nurse to provide appropriate care and advice.[61]

Causes of miscarriage can be found in the *Hippocratic Corpus*: carrying too heavy a weight, being beaten, jumping up into the air (an occupational hazard for dancers), lack of food and fainting, fear, loud shouting, flatulence and too much drink. Pliny the Elder disparages the claims of the *magi* when they say that miscarriage can be avoided if a woman wears the white flesh of a hyena's breast in gazelle leather, along with seven hyena hairs and the genitals of a stag.

Menstruation exercised physicians and scientists alike. Celsus tells us that when *menses* ended it removed much of the protection menstruation afforded women: headaches and a range of diseases ensued, while the protection against *podagra* (gout in the feet) and *chiragra* (gout in the hand) disappeared; night vision was impaired while pre-existing *tabes* (consumption) became very difficult to treat.[62] A girl's first period will cure childhood epilepsy. Menstruation, along with other forms of blood discharge such as nose bleeds and therapeutic bleeding, was to Celsus essential for good general health. Soranus recommends that women lose their virginity only after the onset of menstruation.[63]

Dioscorides describes over 100 agents which stimulate menstruation, while Pliny lists over ninety. Pliny addresses the marvellous powers inherent in menstruation: 'it would be hard to find anything that produces as many amazing effects (magis monstrificium) as menstrual discharge'. The onset of a period during a solar or lunar eclipse spells disaster for the woman, and for any man who has sex with her during that time. If, however, a woman, during her period, walks naked through a field that is filled with pests, those pests will die as she walks past; he cites Metrodorus of Scepsis as evidence: this is what he says happened in Cappadocia during a cantharid beetle plague and accounts for the fact that women there walk in the fields with their dresses hitched up above their buttocks. Ironically, cantharidin was to become a popular aphrodisiac in the nineteenth century. Sprinkling the ashes of menstrual blood onto clothing took away their colour and spoilt purple dyes. A menstruating woman will turn grape juice sour, make seeds sterile when they are touched by her, make grafts wither away, dry up garden plants and cause fruit to fall from the tree. Her look will cloud mirrors, blunt the edge of steel, and dull the sheen of ivory. If she looks at a swarm of bees, they will drop down dead; brass and iron will instantly go rusty, and smell offensively; dogs that taste the discharge will go mad, their bite will be poisonous and incurable.

Soranus describes the physiological changes that take place at the start of menstruation: lethargy, aching, sluggishness, flushes and excessive yawning, nausea and lack of appetite. He advises that each woman do what is best for her during her period: rest, or light activity. Women approaching menopause should ensure that their periods cease gradually, extending them, if necessary, through the use of suppositories or injections. Soranus rejected the view that menstruation was a beneficial, healthy purgative, believing instead that its only use was in facilitating conception. Virginity, on the other hand, was good, as it obviated the stress and trauma caused by childbirth.[64] Roman women, in common with women of other civilisations, used menstrual cloths; a sixth-century AD philosopher and mathematician gathered some of her used ones up to put off an unwanted admirer. The alternative to cloths was to bleed into one's clothes, as described by Pliny.[65]

Both Pliny and Dioscorides list various agents that will determine or alter the sex of a foetus: Pliny recommends thistle, hare's testicles, rennet or uterus or a cock's testes for generating male babies.[66]

Contraception was somewhat makeshift. Aristotle had advocated smearing cedar oil, white lead or frankincense on the female genitals while the *Hippocratic Corpus* swore by drinking *misy*, dilute copper sulphate: how far these methods were adopted by Roman women it is impossible to tell. Lucretius taught that women should wriggle their hips to divert the semen – but not all women: not *matronae*, just prostitutes. Pliny the Elder, quoting Caecilius, recommended the use of an amulet made from the worms that inhabit the large head of the hairy spider (*phalangium opilo*); they were to be attached to the woman with deer skin and worn before dawn to prevent conception for up to one year.[67] Pliny seems somewhat embarrassed by advocating contraception, no doubt on account of the obsessive Imperial pressures on women to conceive; he explains it away by a concern to offer fertile women some respite from serial pregnancies and childbirth. Non-vaginal sex could be a form of contraception: graffiti from Pompeii confirms its prevalence – with examples of sodomy[68] and fellatio – Romula 'sucks her man here, there and everywhere', while Sabina sucks but doesn't get it quite right. Seneca[69] alludes to anal sex taking place on the wedding night, as does Martial, but just the once – nurse and mother forbid it becoming a habit: the bride is his *uxor*, not a *puer*; a wife, not a boy. Second-century AD Manetho describes 'breast relief' in his *Forecasts*.[70]

Dioscorides had twenty-four contraceptive potions, three of which were magic, including an amulet made of asparagus. Others involved the application of peppermint, honey, cedar gum, axe weed and alum in various concoctions to the genitals. Soranus is equally unromantic: his contraception of choice is old olive oil, honey or the sap from a balsam or cedar tree applied to the entrance of the vagina – on its own or (alarmingly) mixed with white lead and bunged up with wool. This has a coagulating and cooling effect which causes the vagina to close before sex, and acts as a barrier to the sperm. An alternative, just as inelegant, involved the woman holding her breath as her partner ejaculates, pulling away so that his semen does not penetrate too deeply, then getting up straightaway and squatting and sneezing before wiping her vulva. He also recommends the use of vinegar, olive oil, ground pomegranate peel and ground flesh of dried figs as vaginal suppositories. Things change slowly: olive oil was still being advocated by the Marie Stopes Clinic as recently as 1931 along with other effective spermicides like lemon, alum and vinegar. Douches made from vinegar, alum or lemon juice were still used by the working classes in New York in 1947 and lemons were in use in 1970s Glasgow.

Aetius vouches for the liver of a cat inserted inside a tube fitted to the woman's left foot, or a section from the womb of a lioness in an ivory tube. In the fourth century AD Oribasius advocated a cabbage pessary post-coitus. These methods were hardly discrete or convenient and they certainly demanded consummate foresight and pre-coital preparation. They all also indicate that it was up to the woman to organise contraception – although we do hear, from Pliny, of spermicides rubbed onto the penis and the use of goats' bladders as a primitive condom. The 'safe' period seems to be unknown; no one mentions *coitus interruptus* which may suggest that it was so common and obvious as to not merit comment. Withholding ejaculation was discouraged by Rufus of Ephesus because it damaged the kidneys and bladder;[71] surgical sterilisation only developed as far as experimentation on sows[72] while vasectomy seems to have been carried out just on gladiators.[73]

Soranus's advice is offered on the grounds that contraception is much safer than abortion. Inducing effective abortion involved the opposite to the advice given to avoid miscarriage. Taking brisk walks or horse rides, jumping high into the air, massage, or lifting weights that are too heavy; if this fails the patient should be immersed in a boiled mixture of linseed, fenugreek, marsh mallow, and wormwood, using poultices and fusions of the same. A less strenuous alternative involves taking long baths and eating spicy food; the woman is then bled aggressively and made to take a horse ride. A suppository may be inserted, made up from myrtle, snowdrop seeds and bitter lupines, so long as it is not too powerful, and care must always be taken not dislodge the embryo with sharp instruments which may nick neighbouring organs. Uterine sounds or dilators for probing the uterus through the cervix have been excavated at Hockwold in Norfolk and may well have been used to induce abortion.[74]

Two of Ovid's poems clearly show that he was passionately opposed to abortion, particularly when it exposed his mistress' vanity: 'The woman who first set about ripping out her foetus deserves to die midst the carnage she started.' Ovid, mindful of the risks, can scarcely believe that his woman wants an abortion to prevent developing stretch marks on her stomach; if the mothers in the good old days had done this, the human race would be extinct, he splutters. He questions how a woman can tear out her stomach with sharp instruments or administer *dira venena* to her unborn child. The passage is significant for a number of reasons: these evil poisons are reminiscent of the poisons used by witches described in the previous chapter and which conjure up an association between abortion and nefarious activity It highlights, as does the advice from Soranus nearly a century later, the prevalence of what we today call backstreet abortions; it demonstrates the obsession, a modern obsession Ovid would say, that some women had – as they do now – with self-image, even to the point of endangering their lives in the pursuit of perfection. To Ovid, the whole issue is unnatural and he ends his poem with a salutary warning to the *tenerae puellae* – they can have their abortions but not with impunity – all too often they will die along with the unborn child they have murdered. Crowds watching the funeral procession exclaim 'merito!' (serve you right!); Ovid is only thankful that his girl has got away with it this time – if she does it again, though, let her pay the price! In the second poem he seems too preoccupied with the dangers to be angry: Corinna's life was in the balance, *in dubio vitae,* and he does everything in his power to ensure her recovery.[75]

Ovid was not alone: Juvenal and Seneca both deplored abortion, as did Cicero – because it reduced the population and wiped out good families. Juvenal talks of the powerful *medicamina* and the women who have industrialised sterility, killing human life in the stomach. Pliny regarded *abortiva*, abortifacients, to be more evil than poison.[76] Domitian reputedly impregnated his niece, Julia, and arranged an abortion that killed her. Abortion was finally criminalised in the second century AD under Severus.

The exposure of disabled or simply unwanted children has already been mentioned; Juvenal describes the practice whereby discarded babies are left abandoned for adoption. Tacitus records that German tribes considered birth control and infanticide to be evil – all very different to prevailing Roman opinion.[77] The remains of babies have been found under the excavated floors of houses at Brough-on-Humber (Petuaria).

For normal childbirth, Soranus[78] recommends the following sympathetic, patient-centered procedures: oil for injections and cleansing, hot water for washing, hot compresses to relieve labour pains, woollens to cover the mother and bandages to swaddle the baby in, citruses to help the mother regain her strength. The midwife should wash her hands in oil and, when the mouth of the womb opens, she should insert the trimmed forefinger of her left hand and rearrange the opening so that the amniotic sac falls forward ... three women should be in attendance to reassure the mother, even if they have no experience of childbirth; the midwife should then sit lower down and opposite the mother holding her thighs apart; she should tell the woman behind to hold the mother's anus with a cloth lest it be pushed out with the straining. If the amniotic sac fails to open the midwife should break it with her nails, insert her finger and widen it gradually, taking care that the baby does not drop out. On delivery the midwife cuts the umbilical cord and the infant is placed on the floor, symbolising contact with Mother Earth; it is encouraged to cry, lifted up, then cleaned and wrapped up and presented to the mother. A grandmother or maternal aunt would then massage the baby's forehead and lips with a finger covered in lustral saliva, a gesture designed to ward off the evil eye.[79] It is at this point that the father would perform the heart-stopping ritual of lifting up the baby, and giving his decision as to whether it lives or dies. Those accepted into the family were named; girls on the eighth day, boys on the ninth – after the critical period for infant death had passed. Unwanted babies might be abandoned at the Temple of Pietas or the Columna Lactaria; those with serious abnormalities would be drowned or suffocated.[80]

Soranus was, in general, an enlightened advocate of mother–infant bonding in preference to the common practice of hiring wet-nurses; he did, though, advise new mothers to have a three-week period of rest during which they might employ a wet nurse. He was very clear in his belief that the well-being of the mother took precedence over the child's. Moreover, an expectant mother should be careful what she looks at during her term: contemplating a fine piece of statuary resulted in well-proportioned babies; observing monkeys, however, produced hirsute infants with long arms. A case of beauty, or otherwise, being literally in the eye of the beholder.[81]

Multiple births were generally ominous, although not in Egypt where the waters of the River Nile induced fertility. Pliny cites the quads delived to a lady called Fausta in Ostia on the day of Augustus's funeral; this presaged the food shortages which followed. He records the Peloponnesian woman who produced four sets of quintuplets, most of whom survived; he cites Trogus who reported seven children born at the same time in Egypt.

Soranus also covers the disposal of the placenta, hygienic cutting of the umbilical cord and sound post-natal care for both infant and mother. He deplores the German, Greek and Scythian practice of plunging the newborn into a vat of cold water in a sink or swim procedure – only the fittest survive.[82] Swaddling, the avoidance of ulceration, bedding, teething and a description of a babywalker are all covered.[83] Feeding and the inadvisable temptation to feed on demand, the weakness caused by excessive bathing and what to do when a baby persistently cries are all usefully dealt with.[84] He recommends that weaning should commence around eighteen months or two years – on the basis, no doubt, that breast milk was one of the most nutritious, and sterile, foods available and a valuable weapon in the battle against paediatric disease. Pliny includes breast milk in his list of medicines derived from women that are effective against a whole range of maladies.[85]

Today, hysteria as a diagnosis or disorder is no longer recognised and has been replaced by 'histrionic personality disorder' which is associated with conditions such as social anxiety and schizophrenia; women have always been particularly prone, hence 'female hysteria'.[86] Up until the late nineteenth century it was inextricably linked to movements of the womb, the *hystera*, presenting as a lack of self-control caused by intense fear or anxiety often related to the imagined disease of a particular body part. Treatment was, for nearly two centuries, pelvic massage – in which the doctor stimulated the genitals until the patient achieved hysterical paroxysm, or orgasm.[87] The condition was thought to have been first noted around the time of the early Hippocratic writings and persisted as a diagnosis right through the Roman era. The Hippocratics never used the term *hysteria*; to them it was *pnix* – suffocation. They taught that the womb became dry if a woman did not have frequent sexual intercourse; infrequency would cause the womb to gravitate towards moister organs such as the liver, heart, brain, diaphragm or bladder at which point the woman would faint, lose her voice and become 'hysterical'. The administration of sweet-smelling odours often restored the womb to its rightful place. Failing that, increasingly desperate measures involved binding the woman tightly beneath her breasts, palpating the affected organ, or hanging the woman upside down from a ladder. Plato believed that an animal living inside a woman's womb was responsible for driving the maternal instinct to have children; if deprived of sexual activity the animal became restless and wandered throughout the body causing apnea (difficulty in breathing) and other conditions and diseases. Sexual activity relieved the symptoms.[88]

Aretaeus later describes the symptoms of this erratic 'wandering womb'; it is attracted to pleasant smells but is repelled by foul odours which cause it to rise and suffocate the woman, squashing many of the vital organs into a confined space. In such an emergency the patient must be made to smell stale urine or have perfumed pessaries applied. Pliny thought that jet was efficacious here. Soranus, who rejected the wandering womb idea, adds that hysteria is preceded by a raft of gynaecological conditions or disorders, including repeated miscarriage, premature childbirth, widowhood, menopause, swelling of the womb and dysmenorrhea. Symptoms include fainting, speechlessness, difficulty in breathing, stridor (wheezing caused by an obstructed airway), grinding of the teeth, bloating of the abdomen, chill, sweating, spasms, and a weak pulse. Generally, the woman recovers if she is calmly laid down, slowly warmed up and refreshed with a sponge. Soranus refutes the efficacy of foul and pleasant smells and tends towards a diagnosis that is akin to today's hysterical conversion disorder.[89]

Galen came very close to establishing a psychological cause for hysteria when he diagnosed a patient demonstrating all the symptoms: he established, by deduction, that the cause of her illness was her obsessive infatuation with Pylades, a dancer, and more or less concluded that hysteria was a psychosomatic disorder.[90]

Hysteria was especially problematic in virgins and widows. Hippocrates warns that girls who delay marriage suffer nightmares from the time of their first period. This can result in them choking to death: the blood in their womb cannot escape because the cervix is still intact and so it flows back up to the heart and lungs, driving the woman mad. Fever ensues, accompanied by a tendency to suicide caused by the nightmares; these encourage the women to jump down wells or to hang themselves. Hippocrates' advice is for girls in such a condition to waste no time in losing their virginity; they will be cured if they fall pregnant.[91] Widows, similarly, are cured by sex, or just by climaxing, so that the retained female semen can be released. The inevitable conclusion was that, deprived of sex, a woman would go mad, and the best way to preserve one's sanity was to have sex, and often.

The only real cure, then, for the 'hysterical' woman, was to become pregnant – thus conveniently enabling the woman to fulfil her role as a wife, as well as satisfying the husband's need for sexual gratification. Hysteria, though, was really a cry for help. It is easy to see how the symptoms for what is termed histrionic personality disorder[92] might have presented in Roman women, given the pressures on them and their restricted circumstances, 'a need to be the center of attention; inappropriate, sexually seductive, or provocative behavior while interacting with others; rapidly changing emotions and superficial expression of emotions; vague and impressionistic speech (gives opinions without any supporting details); easily influenced by others; believes relationships are more intimate than they are'.

Hysteria was a naturally occurring outlet for them, a reaction to the *matrona* ideal, when they could cope no more; for some women it was a release from the tedium, the daily grind of being a good, compliant wife and a *matrona*. Hysterical behaviour, of course, was unseemly to the Greek male and to the conservative Roman, and so it was medicalised with the prognosis that it could only be cured through regular sexual intercourse and childbirth.[93] A vicious circle for the Roman woman.

Hippocrates gives us some intriguing gynaecological case studies: a woman from Pheres suffered from idiopathic headaches, which persisted even after her skull was drained; during her period the headache was less severe. The headaches stopped when she became pregnant, suggesting that the time-honoured excuse for declining sex is not always the best way to a good night's sleep. A woman from Larissa suffered pain during intercourse (dyspareunia); when she reached sixty she felt what she thought were severe labour pains after eating lots of leeks. She stood up and felt something in her vagina, and fainted; another woman pulled out what appeared to be the whorl of a spindle. Hippocrates records that the woman made a full recovery; one wonders if the other woman ever did.

For Celsus the softer bodies of women (*molliora*) made them prone to a number of ailments, including *lippitudo* (dry eye), *tormina* (colic) and fever in a dry winter with prevailing north winds or a wet spring with southerly winds. Pliny reports that women, slaves and the lower classes were immune from *lichena*, a kind of ringworm.[94]

An example of leprosy has been found at Poundbury while Pott's Disease or tuberculous spondylitis – extrapulmonary tuberculosis affecting the spine – was traced in skeletons found in York and Cirencester. Excavations of Roman sewers in York reveal that worms and bowel parasites were pandemic. For Pliny, jet was effective: when boiled with wine it relieved toothache, and mixed with wax it was effective against scrofulous tumours. Hyperactive children were calmed down by putting goat dung in their nappies – particularly effective with girls, according to Pliny.[95]

Ailments consistent with old age are evident from cemetery excavations. In Cirencester, for example, more than 80 per cent of the adult skeletons indicated osteoarthritis, with more women than men afflicted. This, and the existence of nodules on the vertebrae, lend support to the belief that women were routinely doing heavy, manual work; the frequency of arthritis of the neck in female skeletons further confirms this. Squatting facets – the remodelling of the bones at the front of the *talus*, or ankle – in women's bones found in York indicate that they spent a lot of time squatting: cooking and tending the fires. Arthritis and osteoporosis seem to have been common in the elderly in Pompeii, postmenopausal osteoporosis affecting the women.

Recent research has revealed that, contrary to the images conveyed by many of the frescoes found in Pompeii, around 10 per cent of the local women were obese, hirsute; furthermore they have been found to have suffered from headaches and diabetes. Skeletal examinations revealed a small bony growth on the inside of their skulls behind the forehead, indicative of a hormonal disorder, hyperostosis frontalis interna (HFI), which causes these signs and conditions.[96]

Uterine dropsy, or hydrometra, results in fever, weak periods, swelling in the abdomen and withered breasts: Hippocrates recommends a laxative and immersion in a vapour bath made from cow dung, followed by pessaries made from cantharid beetle and then bile; after three days insert a vinegar douche. If the fever subsides and the stomach softens then the woman should have intercourse. She should drink samphire bark and eat dark peony berries with as much mercury plant, raw and cooked garlic as possible, and begin a diet of squid. If she gives birth she is cured.

For uterine prolapse the *Hippocratic Corpus* advises garlic, undiluted sheep's milk, fumigation and a laxative, followed by another fumigation of fennel and absinthe and then two pessaries – one of squill, the other of opium poppies. If the woman's periods have stopped then she should drink four cantharid beetles (legs, wings, head removed), and eat four dark peony seeds, cuttlefish eggs, parsley and wine. If her womb nears her liver she will lose her voice, turn a dark colour and her teeth will chatter; a bandage should then be tied below her ribs and sweet wine poured into her mouth while bad-smelling vapours are burnt beneath her womb. This condition particularly affects old women and widows.[97] Soranus recommended surgery for a prolapse that had turned black.

What was hopefully a last resort in operations for scoliosis involved succussion (*katasteisis*): tying the patient to a ladder by his or her ankles, raising it to the gable or a tower, dropping it repeatedly and banging it, and the patient, hard against the ground in a bid to straighten the spine. To the best knowledge of the Hippocratic author describing this there was never a successful outcome but the procedure did attract large, vulgar crowds who applauded every time the ladder hit the ground.[98]

Uterine cancer is rarely mentioned, probably because the symptoms were difficult to differentiate from other conditions or diseases – vaginal bleeding and discharge, and periods stopping, for example. Plutarch mentions that cancer of the womb is particularly distressing. Philoxenus of Alexandria, in the mid-first century BC, was something of a cancer surgery specialist and was an exponent of surgical intervention in cervical cancer.[99]

Diseases of the breast receive comparatively little attention, possibly a result of the attention paid to the womb. Aetius describes various cancers and their surgical treatment or drug therapies. Hippocrates describes a case of breast cancer where the patient died after the bloody discharge from her nipple stopped. Soranus records in graphic detail a mastectomy performed around AD 100 by Leonides; as with all surgery it was without anaesthetic.[100] Galen tells of the crab-like (*karkinodeis*) swellings which form on a woman's breasts due to retained residues when menstruation is suspended. Dioscorides, Pliny and Celsus all describe various diseases of the breasts, for example swelling, induration, growths (*strumae*) and *carcinomata*.[101]

A case of clitoridectomy, female genital mutilation (FGM), is recorded by Aetius from sixth-century AD Egypt where, according to Strabo, such practice (*ektemein*) was common. The justification was to prevent masturbation or the desire for intercourse driven by an unnaturally enlarged clitoris. Paulus of Aegina, a seventh-century AD urologic surgeon, was something of an expert and describes the procedure in Book 6 of his *De Re Medica Libri Septem*. There is evidence that another form of FGM, female infibulation, was practised on prepubescent girls, if Strabo and Philo are to be believed. This is where the the labia are removed and the girl's legs are bound to allow the surgery to heal forming a skin over the vagina; a small hole is made to allow for urination and menstruation. Its purpose then, as now in some societies, was to reassure a husband that he is marrying a virgin.[102]

Malaria (*plasmodium falciparum*) was widespread in many parts of Italy and other parts of the Empire despite attempts to improve drainage of marshlands and river plains. In a fifth-century AD cemetery near Lugnano in Umbria almost all of the forty-seven graves contained either infants, neonates or foetuses. The foetuses were from miscarriages, particularly from *primigravidae* mothers, caused by the immune suppression common in women in the final two trimesters of pregnancy, brought on by malaria. The female anopheles mosquito is thought to be attracted to certain chemical receptors found in the placenta of pregnant women.

Empedocles blocked off a gorge in Acragas, Sicily, because it was found to be a funnel for a southerly wind bringing in mosquitoes, which introduced placental malaria. Pliny quotes Icatidas, a Greek doctor who taught that malaria in men is cured by having sex with a woman just starting her period.

On hygiene generally, Plutarch advises men against bathing with a woman: apart from being indecent, some effluvia and excretions from women's bodies are harmful to men. Pliny deplores the vogue for effeminate ointments among wrestlers, and hot baths, and depilation by women, especially in the pubic region. A graffiti writer from Pompeii shares Pliny's distaste, coming down on the side of non-depilation because 'it [the unshaven vulva] stays warm and excites the [male] organ.'

Sexually transmitted infections would of course have plagued both men and women alike, particularly in a society that freely endorsed men consorting with prostitutes. Discharges and ulcers are recorded but their is little on infection or contagion. The Campanians, apparently, had a predilection for oral sex, resulting in a high incidence of *campanus morbus* – a facial skin condition, probably a sexually transmitted infection. The Hippocratics, using findings from a dissected inflamed urethra, and Celsus and Galen all describe the symptoms of gonorrhoea, referring to it as 'strangury' (painful urination) caused by the 'pleasures of Venus'. Martial and Galen mention anal warts and piles (*ficus*), Celsus and Galen genital warts, and the Hippocratics and Galen oral sores that present during menstruation – possibly *herpes zoster*.[103]

Breastfeeding seems to have been a virtue if the epitaph to twenty-four-year-old Graxia Alexandria from Rome is anything to go by: she is praised for her chastity, and for the fact that she breastfed her sons. Whether this signifies a norm or whether it is exceptional practice, in the light of the middle-class tendency to hire wet nurses (*nutrices*), it is quite impossible to say. We do know, however, that Tacitus praised German women because they breastfed their own children, an implicit criticism of their Roman counterparts and an appreciation of the nutritional and psychological benefits to both mother and child. Interestingly, in the same paragraph, he deprecates the Roman practice of marrying off daughters at an early age: no German would do that.[104] The philosopher Favorinus from the second century AD outlines sound arguments as to why a mother should nurse her own baby, demanding to know why a woman is born with nipples if they are not for feeding her infants. A stranger's milk should be avoided – who knows, the nurse may be from a barbarian country, she may be dishonest, ugly, immodest, a drinker and promiscuous – everything a *matrona* should not be.[105] In the second half of the third century AD a petulant mother in Egypt complains that her daughter has been forced to breastfeed and offers to pay for a wet nurse.[106] Funerary evidence for the *nutrix* comes in the shape of Prima, a freedwoman in the service of Tiberius, and wet nurse to his granddaughter, Julia Livilla, and Severina from Cologne who is shown on her tombstone attending to the infant and then giving her the breast.[107]

Women's bodies were a vital source of medicine: a living medicine chest if Pliny and his sources are to be believed. Pliny himself considered such medicines to be the product of old wives' tales peddled by midwives and whores (thereby repudiating the skill, education and probity we have noted in the midwifery profession). The smell of a woman's burning hair was particularly efficacious: apart from deterring snakes, the fumes eased the breathing of women choking with hysteria; it cured dry and irritable eyes, as well as warts and sores on babies; mixed with honey it salved head wounds and ulcerative cavities; with honey and frankincense it mended abscesses and gout; with fat it cured cellulitis and staunched bleeding; it was effective against irritating rashes.[108]

Breast milk too had marvellous medicinal qualities: it was good for chronic fevers, coeliac disease and stomach-ache, and poured directly into the eye it repaired ophthalmic trauma. Some said that the milk of a woman who had borne a girl was only effective against spots on the face; the best milk came from a woman who had given birth to a boy; twin boys was better still, particularly if the mother abstained from wine. It worked well when a toad had squirted its fluid into the eye and against toad bites. Confusingly, we learn that eye problems were banished for life in patients massaged with the milk of a mother and her daughter together. Ear infections were successfully treated by milk mixed with oil, or warmed with goose grease where there had been a painful blow. Breast milk worked well as an antidote for the poison of the sea-hare, of the buprestis beetle and for insanity brought on by drinking poisonous henbane. With hemlock it could be prescribed as a liniment for gout and as an application for pains of the uterus; it was an effective emmenagogue. Lung infections were cured by women's milk; if Attic honey was mixed with it and the urine of a prepubescent child, it would expel worms through the ears. The mother of a boy produced milk which stopped dogs going mad.

Women's saliva made a good medicine for bloodshot eyes, all the more powerful if she had fasted from food and wine for twenty-four hours. A woman's breast-band tied around the head relieved headache.[109]

Controversy surrounded the menopause. Most writers agreed that it occurred between the ages of forty and fifty but Soranus extended it to sixty and Oribasius had it in the early thirties, particularly for obese women. The *Lex Julia* gives a useful indicator of what was thought officially to be the age when childbearing stopped: a woman over fifty was not expected to have any more children and so was exempt from this part of the law.[110]

Some doctors specialised in cosmetic dermatology: case loads included the eradication of tattoos branded onto the foreheads of manumitted slaves by cutting out the offending marks and burning the flesh so that scar tissue formed on the wound concealing the tattoos.[111]

In dentistry children were occasionally born with teeth *in situ*; in the early days of Rome, if it was a girl, this was considered to be bad luck. A girl called Valeria was born with her teeth in place; when consulted about this the soothsayers declared that wherever she went disaster would follow. Soon after, Valeria went to the ancient Latin city of Suessa Pometia – and disaster did indeed ensue – it was captured by Tarquinius Superbus. Pliny records that Agripinna the Younger was born with a double set of canines in her right jaw: a good omen. Cosmetic dentistry seems to have been popular: Messalina, Empress to Claudius, whitened her teeth and brightened her smile by applying antler horn mixed with resin and salt. Dentures would appear to have been common

– even witches wore them, as we saw when Canidia's fell out while fleeing Priapus. Laecania bought her white teeth while Thais still had her own, which were black; Laelia has false teeth and a wig: Martial muses on what prostheses she will resort to when her eyes fail. Aelia coughed her remaining four teeth out and, although now edentulous, can cough safely in future. The despised and pilloried old woman of Roman literature is characteristically toothless: Priapus describes an old hag with two teeth, Martial's Vetustilla has but four. Pliny tells us that a woman can banish pain in her groin if she wears in an amulet containing the first tooth of a child, so long as it has not touched the ground.[112]

Generally, dental health appears to have been comparatively good, with oral disease affecting 11.3 per cent of the population in Britannia after the invasion (up, though, from 7.5 per cent pre-invasion), while skeletons reveal a lower incidence of dental caries than exists in the West today; diet was obviously a factor and in some cases the teeth of women were somewhat better than men's – indicating that women perhaps had a less sugary diet, and drank less sweetened wine than men. Lead poisoning was a problem for both sexes from lead water pipes and utensils, exacerbated by its use in some potions. Interestingly, our word for a plumber is derived from the Latin word for lead, *plumbum*. A popular method of preserving wine was to produce a syrup called *sapa* from must and store it in lead containers: this would give a drinker 20mg of lead per litre of wine consumed – forty times the chronic toxicity level.

Evidence of how women fared in terms of mental health is uncommon, an indication that psychiatry as we understand it was not routinely practised or studied as a speciality and did not exist until the nineteenth century; 'psychiaterie' was coined in 1808. Work was done, however, on mental illness: Hippocrates ascribed it to an imbalance of the humours; erotic dreams were an indicator of madness and very ill patients without pain were deemed mad. Rufus of Ephesus wrote a treatise on melancholia, now lost, and Aretaeus gave us the first clinical description of manic depressive psychosis. Manetho believed that the moon (*luna*) was to blame, hence lunacy. More rationally Celsus divided mental illness into three distinct categories: phrenitis, melancholia and mania.

Melancholia in women was considered serious, and presented with insomnia, withdrawal, paranoia, depression, tearfulness and suicidal thoughts; treatments included purgation, bleeding and vomiting. So far this exhibits similarities to what we today call bipolar depression; Hippocrates and Rufus add delusions and hallucinations to the symptoms, thus associating it with our schizophrenia. Mania, or insanity, according to the Hippocratics, was common in girls and presented with hallucinations and fear; Soranus disagreed saying it rarely occurred in women. However, Soranus treated it with characteristic empathy offering therapeutic vomiting and blood-letting but, more importantly, visionary and enlightened calming techniques such as quiet conversation, music therapy, story-telling and trips to the theatre.

That women were under considerable social and dometic stress is not in doubt. The early marriage, the pressure to produce an heir, managing the household, dealing with slaves, the endless subordination to the husband or father, caring for the children and, in some cases, coping with their husbands' affairs and the abuse they sometimes handed out, the frustration of not being able to express independence or artisitic ability – all of these factors would have caused levels of stress in the Roman woman, presenting perhaps in hysteria. As we have noted, the stress is probably consistent with what we today label as social phobias – and contributed, in some cases, to an early death. A particularly anxious time would have been that one month post-partum period when mother and baby were both extremely vulnerable and, for some, when the father was deciding the baby's fate – a decision often influenced by the judgment of another woman in the house, the midwife.

Artemidorus Ephesius was a second-century AD oneiromancer (diviner of dreams) and author of the five volume *Oneirocritica*. He gives us a rather extreme and terrible example of the potential outcome of such stresses on Roman women: a woman dreamt that stalks of wheat sprouted from her breast extending back through her vagina; this occurred after an incestuous episode with her child. She later committed suicide.[113]

Women with mental health problems would have been treated in much the same way as men: they were shunned, taunted and often spat at in public. Spitting was thought to prevent the spread of disease and madness;[114] Pliny records how it was customary to spit at epileptics when they are fitting in a bid to throw back the contagion. Spitting was a weapon against witches, spitting at anyone lame in their right leg dispelled bad luck.[115]

Alexander of Tralles leaves us the case of the woman who always bandaged up her finger; she believed that if she bent it then the world would end. From Galen we know the man who thought he was a pot and was terrified in case he shattered, the man who thought he was a chicken and men who thought they were carrying the world on their shoulders, just like Atlas all typical of cases which could have been and probably were non-gender specific.[116]

Epilepsy is marginally more common in men than in women but it has implications for women in reproductive health – fertility, puberty, menstruation, for example – so would have had potentially serious social as well as medical consequences when diagnosed in premenopausal women. Caelius is scathing of those practitioners who prescribe for epileptics the binding of limbs or a diet of weasel, smoked brain of camel or the testicles of a beaver – even the tickling of the patient while a flame is placed close to his or her eyes.

According to Caelius the causes of mental illness were many and various, and included persistent inebriation, excess of love, grief, anxiety, the removal of haemorrhoids or amenhorrea. His therapies were empathetic: he recommended massage and rest in a calm environment. For the woman who believed she had swallowed a snake and was in pain if she did not eat lots of food, he prescribed an emetic, surreptitiously placing a snake in her bowl for her to see. He recommended the depressed go and watch a comedy, the manic a tragedy – signs of an early attempt at understanding bipolar disorder, perhaps. He was also quite pragmatic, recommending that phrenitis (acute inflammation of the brain and body) sufferers be kept in rooms with high windows as they were inclined to jump out of them to their deaths. On the other hand, Celsius advocated the use of torture and shackles in what was routine bestial treatment of the mentally ill, a practice which persisted in Europe right up to the nineteenth century when Philippe Pinel introduced humane reforms at Bicêtre in Paris in 1792 and the Quaker Tuke family did likewise at the Retreat in York in 1796.

Hypersexuality – classified today in *ICD-10* as satyriasis in men and as nymphomania in women – appears frequently in the medical authors. Aretaeus denies its existence in women, saying that others believe that it manifests, as in men, as a desire for sex; Soranus adds the 'itching' felt in the genitals which makes women touch themselves: this, naturally, increases their sexual urge and causes 'mental derangement' and an immodest desire for a man. His treatment involved bleeding, a liquid diet, refreshing poultices applied to the genitals and avoiding anything which caused flatulence or sexual desire. Mustio and Aretaeus's translator, Caelius Aurelianus, both agree on the clinical signs. Theodorus Priscianus termed it *metromania*. The therapy recommended by Rufus of Ephesus included blood-letting, taking honeysuckle seed and the root of the water lilly, hot baths and the avoidance of all things erotic. For the same reason Caelius discouraged young visitors of either sex. Rufus compares the treatment of female satyriasis with the therapy for spermatorrhea – an involuntary ejaculation of sperm which was thought to occur in both men and women.[117]

Skeletal excavations at York show the average height of women to be very much as today at around 5.2 feet. Scurvy (vitamin C deficiency) and osteomalacia (vitamin D deficiency) are absent, indicating a relatively healthy diet. The smallest recorded woman was Andromeda, one of Julia Augusta's freedwomen. Unfortunately Pliny omits to give her height but we may assume that she was about the same – or even shorter – than the inappropriately named Manius Maximus, and Marcus Tullius, who were around 3 feet tall. No information is available from him on the tallest woman, although he records the tallest man, Gabbara in the reign of Claudius, as being 10 feet tall.

Pliny adds as a footnote that the Greeks call such people *ektrapeloi*, 'freaks', but that the Romans have no name for them. Hermaphrodites (*androgyni*) used to be thought of as prodigies but Pompey changed all that when he made them figures of entertainment, putting them on the stage in his theatre. They were joined in the limelight by such exceptional people as Eutyche, who was later led to her funeral pyre by twenty children – to celebrate the thirty individual babies she had given to the world; by Alcippe who had given birth to an elephant; by the slave girl who was delivered of a snake. Sightings of centaurs were not uncommon, it seems: Pliny saw one immersed in honey. A baby was born in Saguntum soon after it was sacked by Hannibal: it took one look around, was not impressed by what it saw, and immediately returned to its mother's womb.

Diodorus (in the late first century BC) described hermaphrodites as marvellous creatures (*terata*), who announce the future, for good and bad. Around AD 500 Isidore of Seville described hermaphrodites as having the right breast of a man and the left of a woman, and after sex can both sire and bear children. In Roman law, a hermaphrodite was classed as either male or female. After Pompey made celebrities out of them they had, by Pliny's time, become objects of delight and fascination (*deliciae*) highly sought after in the slave markets.

Pliny is equally insistent on the phenomenon of instantaneous transgender transgression or gender reassignment. No dream, *non est speculum*: in 171 BC a girl from Casinum instantaneously changed into a boy before her parents' eyes; the augurs banished her to an island. Licinius Mucianus records the case of Arescon, a 'man' from Argos who married a man as Arescusa; 'she' then developed a beard and other male features and got married to a woman; there was a similar sighting in Smyrna. Pliny himself saw a bride turn into a man on his-her wedding day. The mother of a boxer, Nicaeus of Byzantium, was born from her mother's adulterous affair with an Ethiopian: the mother was born white but Nicaeus, one generation later, was born black. Perhaps another Ethiopian was involved, or was it the same one? Pliny goes on to assert that certain Indian tribes bear children from the age of seven and are old by the time they reach forty, while others conceive aged five and die three years later; the children of others go grey immediately after birth. Women who want a black-eyed baby must eat a shrew during their pregnancy.[118]

Equally mawkish and irrational were the observances of Phlegon of Tralles, a freedman of Hadrian's. Phlegon's chief work was the

Olympiads, a sixteen-book history of Rome from 776 BC to AD 137. Other publications included *On Long Lived Persons*, a riveting list of Italian and Roman centenarians culled from the censuses; but it is his paradoxographical *Marvels* that interests us here – a half-serious compilation of ghost stories, congenital abnormalites, strange hybrid creatures, hermaphrodites, giant skeletons and prophesising heads. He records, for example, a hermaphrodite from 125 BC who caused such a stir that the *Sibylline Oracles* were consulted; a highly-thought-of slave woman who in AD 49 gave birth to an ape; a four-headed child who was presented to Nero; and a child born with its head protruding from its shoulder.[119]

Pliny suggests that women were just as capable of prodigious physical endurance as men: the prostitute Leaena apparently endured unspeakable torture but would not betray Harmodius and Aristogiton in 514 BC. She did not go as far as Anaxarchus, a philosopher in the court of Alexander the Great who, under torture, bit off his own tongue to prevent it being used as a potential instrument of treachery, and spat it in the face of his torturer, Nicocreon of Salamis in Cyprus. There are no reported cases of women dying from over-exertion during sex but Pliny reports that both Cornelius Gallus, the first century BC poet, and Titus Hetereius died in the throes of sexual ecstasy – with women, he primly adds.

8

SEX & SEXUALITY

This chapter will cover aspects of female sexuality, men's attitudes to it, and the role of women in the Roman sex industry; in doing so we take in lesbianism, sexual pleasure and sexual variations, erotica, 'pornography', prostitution and brothels.

It is important here to see sex and sexuality as the Roman man and woman might have seen it, rather than from a modern twenty-first-century perspective with all the baggage that it has accumulated over the centuries. The ubiquity of the erotic in wall paintings and mosaics, in sex manuals, poetry and plays, in phalluses, on coins and in ceramics would clearly suggest that Romans were accustomed to and even liked looking at sex. The shame, embarrassment and secrecy which accompanies erotica or 'pornography' (itself a nineteenth-century term) in many societies today would probably have been quite alien to the Roman, for whom it was all probably quite normal. There were, of course, limits – particularly the stigma attached to oral sex and male penetration as the receiving partner – but, by and large, sex and sexuality seem to have been relatively unremarkable facets of everyday life. Importantly, these images would have been seen by as many women as men; the love poetry, the plays and the satires were read and watched by literate women as well as literate men, indicating that women were probably just as relaxed about it and unphased by it as Roman men.

An important aspect of the sexual images depicted in mosaics and wall paintings, and the sex described in graffiti is that they constitute evidence that for once was not necessarily produced by elite men. The wall painters, mosaic makers and scribblers were just as likely to be men, or women, from the lower orders – as

such they give a unique perspective into women's sexuality that is
absent from literature or from much of the inscriptional evidence.

There is frequent mention of female homosexuality in the
literature. Caelius seems to be alone among Greeks and Romans
in describing homosexuality as a psychiatric illness. As Toner
points out, his categorisation survived for around two centuries:
DSM I and *II*, the gold-standard work in the classification of
mental disorders, published in 1952 and 1968 respectively, classed
it likewise.[1]

Caelius called lesbians *tribades* – women who are 'more eager
to lie with women than men and in fact pursue women with
almost masculine jealousy ... they rejoice in the abuse of their
sexual powers' – probably reflecting a general male antipathy
to lesbianism. Caelius is helpless to help: to him the condition
is quite incurable; these *disgraceful vices* are an affliction of the
mind, which must be controlled. The situation was hopeless: he
believed that homosexuality intensified with age, resulting in 'a
hideous and ever increasing lust'.

Tribas derives from the Greek *tribo* (I rub), and was a perjorative
term, defined as 'a woman who practises unnatural vice with
herself or with other women', and in Latin: 'a woman who
practices lewdness with women'.[2] Other Latin words are *frictrix*
(she who rubs), and *virago*. The revulsion towards *tribades* stems
from the assumption that tribadism entailed penetration (by a
dildo, for example); but penetration was very much an exclusively
male function. Martial calls Philaenis a *tribas* in the obscene
diatribe in which she buggers the boys as vigorously as any man,
and performs cunnilingus on the girls. As far as insults go this was
extreme and double-edged: Philaenis was not only penetrating
like a man, she was licking too – cunnilingus, be it homo- or
heterosexual was seen by Roman men as degrading. Bassa is a
similar case; on first sight she appears as chaste as a Lucretia,
because she in never implicated with a man, but she is really a
fututor – a fucker – bringing together two *cunni*, pretending to
be a man.[3] Catullus asserts that any woman who has sex with
the odious Aemilius[4] would be just as likely to lick the anus of a
hangman with diarrhoea.

Martial seems almost obsessed with the act, with twelve

epigrams referring to it. He excoriates Nanneius, an inveterate cunnilinguist suffering from lingual dysfunction after contracting a disease of the tongue. So prolific was he that whores preferred to perform fellatio on him rather than kiss him – his penis being much cleaner than his mouth.[5] Cunnilingus, like fellatio, assumed questionable oral hygiene, anathema to many Romans who held the purity of the mouth in high esteem, not least because the mouth was the vehicle for oratory and declamation, it was also the custom to kiss on meeting so bad breath was an extreme embarrassment. Wall paintings in the Suburban Baths in Pompeii depict cunnilingus; here the beautiful, naked prostitute is in a dominant role while her fawning, fully clothed male client is something of a comedic figure – another indication of the scorn oral sex attracted and the opportunity it gives for parody.

Pliny rubbished the *magis'* belief that wearing an amulet of hyena's genitals smeared with honey excited homosexual tendencies.[6] The contrivances of such charlatans did not end with and were not restricted to ancient *magi*: as recently as 1920 John Romulus Brinkley (1885–1942) set up a clinic in Kansas; here he performed hundreds of operations implanting goats' testicles in men's scrotums and in the ovaries of women to restore fertility, and as a cure for twenty-seven other ailments ranging from flatulence to cancer of the spine. His clientele included judges, an alderman, a society matron and the chancellor of the University of Chicago Law School.

A graffito from Pompeii describes lesbian love: 'I wish I could hold to my neck and embrace the little arms, and bear kisses on the tender lips. Go on, doll, and trust your joys to the winds; believe me, light is the nature of men.'

Two of Lucian's *hetairae*, Clonarium and Leaena, discuss the pros and cons of lesbian sex, indicating that such services were readily available on the streets and in the brothels.[7] They tell of Megilla, a rich woman, who went for Leaena like a man; both courtesans agree that this was unnatural (*allokoton*), commenting that in Sparta they have tribadists just like Megilla who look like men. Notwithstanding, Leaena coyly reveals the details of her seduction by Megilla and her friend Demonassa at a *symposium*. After playing her cithara Leaena is invited into their bed where they kiss with tongues and squeeze her breasts. Megilla throws off her wig to reveal a bald head and assumes the identity of an athletic Megill*us*, 'husband' to Demonassa. Leaena enquires of Megilla-us if she is a hermaphrodite and possesses a penis; she is not and does not, reassuring Leaena that, although she is in fact a woman, she has the desires of a man; she can, therefore, penetrate her (with a dildo, *olisbos*), although Leaena is coyly reticent on further detail here. After a necklace and fine dress have exchanged hands, Leaena is duly penetrated – accompanied by kissing, heavy breathing and obvious enjoyment.

In the story of Iphis in the *Metamorphoses* Ovid describes the prospective lesbian union of Iphis (the girl who had to masquerade as a boy to avoid being exposed) and Ianthe as monstrous, an act unprecedented in nature. She has to be changed into a boy to avoid the calamity. Stoic Seneca the Younger generalises that women 'satisfy the strangest of sexual tastes, acting as men among men', alluding to their use of dildos for penetration. He believed that homosexuality was *contra naturam*. Seneca the Elder shows that lesbianism was not confined to the brothel; he cites a case where a man murdered his wife and her lover *in flagrante delicto*, having thoughtfully checked first to establish whether the lover was 'natural' or 'artificial' (*proserraptai*) – a woman wearing a dildo. Juvenal assails Tullia, a *matrona*, and her lover Maura who take it in turns to ride each other: 'in ... vices equitant'.

In Juvenal's second Satire we get a rare chance to hear what appears to be a woman's voice when Laronia joins the poet to criticise a hypocritical male homosexual, Hispo. To Juvenal nothing is as it first seems: *frontis nulla fides*; he opens his homophobic attack on these pathics (*cinaedi*), these sad perverts (*tristes obsceni*) in grand style, calling them stupid (*indocti*), and noting their buggery-induced haemorrhoids. Enter Laronia to lend support, grinning at having found a third conservative, censorious Cato in Hispo (Cato the Younger was the second). She ridicules his effeminacy, invoking the *Lex Scantinia* to parry his reference to the *Lex Julia de Adulteriis Coercendis*: look at the men first, they do the worst things, she argues: women don't tongue each other yet Hispo submits to young boys; women don't involve themselves in men's matters – litigation, wrestling and the like.

On the other hand, men do women's things – they work the wool (that badge of good wifely behaviour), *lanam faciunt!* Laronia's advice to Hispo's *puella* (still a virgin?) is to keep quiet about her husband's proclivities and keep taking the jewels. To Juvenal this was all *vera manifesta* – the blinding truth, and Laronia provided powerful support to his invective.

It is obviously difficult to reconcile this with Juvenal's excoriating attack on women in Satire 6, where he savagely contradicts much of what he has Laronia say here. The important point is that Laronia's eloquent and reasoned arguments constitute a point of view that Juvenal obviously realised was the sort of thing a woman might say in a situation like this: a woman like Laronia might well be indignant about the hypocrisy and duplicity of men like Hispo, and she, as a *docta puella* perhaps, would be quite capable of expressing those views in such a clever way. There is no need to marginalise or even erase Larona (as Susan Braund has done): Laronia is indeed used by Juvenal, but her opinion would seem to be quite plausible and possibly representative among certain women of Juvenal's day.

What Laronia also shows us is that when it came to men, women had competition. Lucretius could see the attraction of boys. Ovid, though, was unequivocal: women make better sexual partners than men; sex with a woman was preferable because of the possibility of mutual pleasure. Plutarch was equally unequivocal: sex with boys is highly preferable – heterosexual sex smacked of effeminacy.[8] In the first century AD, Strato in the *Greek Anthology* expresses a preference for boys because girls derive little enjoyment from anal sex and are frigid when sodomised. Martial says as much when he rebukes his wife for describing her *culus* as a sphincter when, according to him, she really has two vaginas (*cunni*).

There is plenty of evidence in the literature for women taking the initiative in sex and assuming the dominant role. In his description of the sexual frenzy generated by the Bona Dea rites Juvenal describes two aristocratic women vying with each other, and with the whores, in the torrent of lust (*torrens Veneris*) that overcomes them: Saufeia and Medullina gyrate lasciviously together. The second century BC satirist Gaius Lucilius has an image of a woman grinding corn with her buttocks, while Martial describes the famous Gaditanian dancing girl as bumping and grinding so sexily that she could make Hippolytus masturbate. For Lucretius, a woman writhing on top was also practising a method of contraception, Apuleius too describes the lubricious movements of the dominant woman, as does Petronius (*pygisiaca sacra*). Horace compares the *meretricula* on top with a horse rider. Martial describes a wife mounting the horse of Hector as the slaves masturbate behind the bedroom door, while Ovid recommends the position for the shorter woman.[9]

The *Hippocratic Corpus* says that heterosexual female sexual pleasure is induced by the rubbing on the vulva during intercourse and lasts throughout the act until the man ejaculates. If she is in the mood, as it were, the woman orgasms first; if she is not, then the couple climax together. A woman's orgasm is less intense than a man's, but it lasts longer; sexual intercourse is generally good for a woman's health. The aim of sexual intercourse was conception rather than any pleasure on the woman's part; she was to be consensual at all times. Masturbation was pointless because it could not lead to conception. Phalluses, such as cucumbers, were used by women to prepare themselves for penetration by their husbands, not for any enjoyment; women suffer less frequently with bladder stones because women do not masturbate. An example of a masturbating woman – *cunnum tibi fricabo* – is described in an inscription. Somewhat later, Martial, fantasising in a poem where he whinges about a wife's coolness towards his sexual advances, alludes to a long tradition of female masturbators, beginning with Penelope and Andromache; in the same epigram he moans about the woman's refusal to indulge in anal sex, scandalously claiming that the traditionally virtuous Cornelia, Pompey's wife Julia and Brutus's wife Porcia have been willing participants in the act. We have seen how sodomy was not unknown on the wedding night for some brides.

Oro-genital sex was much in evidence. The Campanians, as we have noted, apparently had a predilection for oral sex resulting in a high incidence of *campanus morbus* – a facial skin condition which was probably a sexually transmitted infection. Fellatio is privileged with two precise nouns in Latin – *irrumatio* is the action of the penis; *fellatio* the action of the mouth: it was obviously a popular alternative to coitus for the clientele of prostitutes. It may also represent an intention to avoid pregnancy, not just in extramarital relationships but also within marriage in a bid to break the cycle of childbearing. Martial, of course, in his frequent references to the act, tends towards the extramarital: we hear of Vetustina's warm mouth (*calda bucca*) and how Thais sucks. In his poem about Galla and Aeschylus he acknowledges that you can do it but you should keep your mouth shut about it, as it were; he accuses Aeschylus of paying over the odds to ensure his fellatio goes no further; he was no doubt mindful of the disgust which attended this sexual proclivity. Suetonius deplores Quintus Remmius Palaemon's predilection for cunnilingus.[10] Galen believed that orogenital sex was unnatural.

The soldiers of Octavian's army were only too aware of the deep insult tied up in the salvoes they sent towards Antony and Fulvia Flacca Bambula. For men the shame implicit in penetration by another male goes some way to explain the disgust commonly felt towards lesbians who perform penetrative sex. Penetration was what men do; men could penetrate but they should not be penetrated. The *Lex Scantinia* of 216 BC had criminalised *stuprum* against a freeborn male minor and penalised adult male citizens who took a passive role in sex with other men: allowing one's body to be used for pleasure by others in sodomy and oral sex was a sign of weakness, a deficiency of *virtus*. It was fine, however, for a man to indulge with males lower down the social ladder, male prostitutes or slaves, so long as he assumed the penetrative role.

Most of the highly imaginative sexual graffiti found in Pompeii is embellished and exaggerated, as presumably anywhere else in the Roman world, by male fantasy, bragging, insult and vindictiveness. It portrays women in every conceivable erotic position, indulging even in bestiality, all with compliant submissiveness. Graffiti proclaims that all the women of Pompeii were 'up for it'. For the ladies 'Glyco does cunnilingus for 2 asses'; Martimus, however, is not such a good deal: he does it for 4, but will entertain virgins for free – all suggesting a lively trade in male prostitution for the bored housewives of Pompeii.

Group sex (*koine cupris*) was an occupational hazard, or rather a business opportunity, for prostitutes: Gallus describes three men penetrating Lyde, while Nicarchus, in the first century AD describes another foursome where the three men draw lots for the orifice.[11] One of the scenes at the Suburban Baths in Pompeii shows one man taking a woman from behind while he receives a man standing behind him. Catullus, in *Carmen* 56, re-enacts it, considering it hilarious. Another scene shows a foursome in which a man sodomises another man on whom a woman performs fellatio; another woman performs cunnilingus on her.

The *cinaedus*, a bisexual, effeminate male, was also attractive to some women. The middle man in the troilism at the Suburban Baths may well have been a *cinaedus*. The *pathicus*, similar to the cinaedus but more of a submissive masochist, may have held similar appeal: with *pathici* the woman assumes the role of *domina* and receives cunnilingus.

The Hippocratics contended that when a woman became pregnant, she had enjoyed the sex during which she conceived; Soranus believed that a woman could only conceive if she was sexually excited – which led him into a corner where he was forced to say that if a woman became pregnant after being raped then she had subconsciously enjoyed the violation. Lucretius contended that sex provided mutual pleasure for man and woman – *est communis voluptas* – and that any conceived children would take after the mother when the woman took the dominant role during sex. Women, he says, do not always fake sexual excitement – sometimes it is for real. Ovid, in his turn of the millennium *The Joy of Sex*, the *Ars Amatoria*, methodically runs through the various sexual positions a woman should adopt to achieve mutual orgasm with her partner, or, if she wants to show off her looks and body to best effect, he gives handy tips on how to conceal stretchmarks. Women who cannot climax are encouraged to fake it – convincingly though – with much flailing about, gasping and rolling of eyes.[12]

There is a long tradition of bestiality in classical mythology and literature although there is little to suggest that it was any more common in Rome than in any other society. It starts with Europa's rape by Zeus masquerading as a bull, as described by Moschus and then by Ovid in the *Metamorphoses* (7, 681ff). The Minotaur was born from the union between a bull and the wife of King Minos, Pasiphae, as described by Virgil in *Eclogue* 6: 'virgo infelix, quae te dementia cepit' (crazy, sad girl!). Zeus's rape of Leda in the guise of a swan is another famous mythological example (Ovid, *Met.* 6, 109). Martial in his *De Spectaculis* 6 (5) suggests that bestiality was reenacted on stage at the inaugural games of the Flavian Amphitheatre in AD 80. Pliny records that Semiramis, the ninth century Assyrian queen, had sex with a horse (*NH* 8, 64). Juvenal, as we have seen, says that women are so sexed up at the Bona Dea that they will fornicate with a donkey, as a last resort. Apuleius, in the *Metamorphoses* (16; 17), describes how Lucius, as the donkey, has vigorous, and consensual, intercourse with an insatiable woman who pays Thiasus, his master, for the pleasure of it. Thiasus sees an opportunity here and Lucius's next engagement is in an amphitheatre, caged up with a woman condemned to be fed to wild animals; before the spectacle can begin, however, he escapes.

Dancing girls were considered by many to be one step removed from the prostitute – indeed many dancers probably were prostitutes. As noted in our chapter on the fine arts, dancing attracted the derision of men, Sempronia and Sallust being a good example. Ovid, though, loves the lubricity of it all, while the proud, grieving father of the deceased Eucharis – a celebrated dancer – has no reservations about his late daughter's talent. Juvenal, though, is with Sallust: in his eleventh Satire he deprecates the Spanish dancers' movements, calling them worse than a prostitute, making women wet themselves with excitement. On a par with the dancers were the girls who worked in the baths: Martial describes the *tractatrix* – the masseuse who spreads her practised (*manus docta*) hand over every limb, the *unctores* (perfumers), *fricatores* (rubbers), *alipilarii* (depilators) and the *picatrices* – the girls who trimmed the pubic hair.

Countless girls and women resorted to prostitution in one form or another, be they a *hetaera, meretrix, lupa, scortum,* or *fornicatrix* plying their trade, literally, under Juvenal's stinking arches, or those urbane courtesans who were so appealing to the love poets. Latin, like other languages, has many words and euphemisms for prostitute, around fifty at least. There is a certain irony in the fact that the legendary founders of Rome, Romulus and Remus, were suckled by a she-wolf, a *lupa*, and that recourse to prostitution, or the intention to sell a baby girl into prostitution, undoubtedly saved many from exposure or abandonment.

Propertius tells us that many prostitutes came from Syria (around the Rivers Euphrates and Orontes) and that they frequent parks and porticos and the Via Sacra; to that we can add the Subura, the Esquiline-Viminal, the Caelian Hill, Juvenal's arches (particularly around the Colisseum) and the Circus Maximus;[13] a house nearby displays the graffito: 'hic bene futui' (I had a good shag here). Some whores were peripatetic, *scorta erratica*; the lowest were the *diobolariae,* worth two obols, and those who entertained clients among the tombstones. Sex was cheap: the cheapest girls cost the equivalent of a loaf of bread, and something more exotic was around two hours' pay for an average worker.

Prostitutes were distinguishable by their dress: they did not wear the traditional long *stola* of the *matrona* but a short *tunica* and an often garish toga – also the badge of an adulteress. Prostitutes were regulated by the aediles and, from Caligula's reign, paid tax on their earnings equivalent to one client's charge in any given day, even after retirement from the profession. How this was effectively collected remains a mystery.[14] Tacitus records that Vistilia, a lady of praetorian rank, confessed to being a prostitute and was charged under the *Lex Julia* which banned prostitution amongs the wives, daughters and granddaughters of Roman *equites*; she was exiled to the island of Seriphos in AD 19.

Visiting brothels – *stabuli* or *lupanares* – was acceptable behaviour to and by men, highlighting the double standards relating to adultery and infidelity. Horace condones the stinking brothel if it stops men committing adultery with respectable married women.[15] He cites Cato the Censor who congratulated a man coming out of a brothel; when Cato saw him coming out a few more times he protested that he had not intended he live there. Cicero agreed that men buying sex was good for the nation: anyone who thought it wrong was being a bit harsh and out of step with modern ways. How long has it been wrong to do what is lawful? he demands.[16]

Stink, no doubt, many brothels did. There were, however,

efforts to provide a modicum of hygiene with relays of water collected from fountains for washing down after each client. Some brothels were even connected to nearby aqueducts.

According to Suetonius, Horace himelf preferred sex at home to visiting brothels, inviting escorts back to his place where the mirrors in his bedroom literally reflected his sexual activity: *coitus* from every angle.[17] Martial knows exactly what he wants from a prostitute: low prices and a willingness to take three clients at a time, and the older the whore, the less he pays.[18] Juvenal and Strabo describe temple prostitution: sex that was rife in temples such as Eryx in Sicily and at Corinth. Prostitutes also provided a lucrative sideline for low-rent hotels (*tabernae cauponiae*), bars and inns, offering their services as *noctilucae*, night-lights, in the tiny cubicles out the back with their stone beds and straw mattresses. One amusing inscription from Aesernia describes a client paying his hotel bill; the extras included the services of a girl costing eight asses and hay for the mule costing two. The guest protests that it is the mule that is the likely cause of his financial ruin.[19]

Wall painting and graffiti in Pompeii may suggest that the work of bar maids elided easily from serving drinks to serving clients with sexual services. The unimaginative graffito proclaiming that 'I fucked the landlady' and the highly imaginative nineteenth-century version of a painting from the Via di Mercurio, now sadly lost, which depicts a well-endowed man taking a bar maid from behind in what looks like a drinking competition, may suggest as much. On the other hand, the former may indicate quite the opposite: perhaps it was scrawled out of spite from hurt male pride, while the latter may just be good advertising. The bronze pygmy with the huge regenerating phallus outside a bar in the Via dell' Abbondanza would indicate that girls (and boys) were available inside. The local baths were another popular venue for sex as well as for bathing and general socialising: in Pompeii the Suburban Baths have a series of paintings depicting a range of erotic scenes which, again, is probably an advertisement for the services offered by the slave girls working there.

The ubiquity of phalluses around Pompeii reminds us of two things: first that Roman society, in every way, was dominated by men; second that the phallus was also a good luck token against evil spirits. It was a defence against the 'evil eye' and was exhibited to ward off the pernicious, largely devoid of much of the shame or embarrassment it evokes in later societies. Hence the phallus could be seen, sometimes personified as Priapus, in fields, vineyards and gardens – as a crop enhancer or a bird scarer – and on chariots as a type of modern 'go faster' sticker, as wind chimes (*tintinnabula*) as well as on street signs or buildings, in the shape of loaves, as wine flasks – all to secure good health and good fortune.[20]

In Rome, prostitutes were first among the female providers of sexual services, followed by female slaves. Both groups of women were fair game for men, married or otherwise, who needed to satisfy their sexual appetite or demonstrate their virility and prowess over women: the prostitute allowed the client to assert his manhood and virility through serial penetration. Paradoxically, though, this provided the whore or slave girl with a degree of vicarious sexual power: as Mary Beard points out, the obsession with the public phallus indicated a disturbing weakness and anxiety as well as a strength among Roman men. Just as it was a mark of potency, so it was an indicator of *another man's* potency – a man who may be consorting with your wife, a man who may even be the father of 'your' children – *horribile dictu!*[21]

Juvenal recalls Horace's squalid brothel in his description of the bizarre, incognito nocturnal visits made by Messalina (*meretrix Augusta*) to a whorehouse (*lupanar*). Here she habitually prostituted herself, naked and nipples gilded; at the end of the night she was the last to leave, reluctantly, 'with her clitoris still on fire and full of lust'.[22] Elsewhere, in his description of a dissolute dinner party and the entertainment offered by those lascivious Spanish dancing girls, Juvenal compares the scene to a stinking brothel, a world apart from the cerebral evening he prefers with recitations of Homer and Virgil.[23]

In Pompeii there were seven brothels (some say as many as thirty-five), one of them sharing premises with a hairdressers. Not surprisingly then, the town is a rich source of graffiti celebrating prostitutes, and offers all sorts of advice, prices and recommendations: 'thrust slowly'; Candida (no doubt a white girl) hates black girls but can still 'love' them willingly; Myris is good at fellatio; Sabina is not so good; Veneria got a mouth full of semen (*mucus*); Euplia is too slack, but she does have a large clitoris; the price for Attice is 16 asses. Rome had at least forty-five brothels; one is known (in fiction at least) at Puteoli, or Cumae, depending on where Petronius sets the start of his *Satyricon*; here the hapless Encolpius finds himself among *nudae meretrices* wearing just their price tags. It is impossible to estimate how many women were active in the sex trade at any one time or in any one place: we can assume, though, that grinding poverty and the vulnerability of slavery will have left many women with little or no choice. Candida may reflect a degree of racial discrimination against black women: Ovid includes them in his *Remedia* 'fifty ways to leave your lover' *Amoris*: think of her as a black woman if she's *fusca*, dusky.[24]

Rich women could afford the services of male prostitutes: Martial describes Chloe, who extravagantly rewards her Lupercus with an endless supply of lavish clothing, jewels and coins; Martial advises caution, however, lest she end up fleeced and exposed (*glabraria* and *nuda*) by him. He is less charitable towards Thais: she stinks like urine from a smashed jar, like a randy goat, a putrefied chicken, rancid fish sauce.[25] He also describes how the squalid whore, the *moecha bustuaria*, conducts business among the tombs in a cemetery – a place, as we have seen, that she would have shared with others from the lowest rungs of society, including witches and other nefarious practitioners of the dark arts.[26]

At the other end of the spectrum were the Lesbias, Cynthias, Delias and Corinnas who fascinated and frustrated their lovers with their sophistication, erudition, aloofness and unobtainability. Whether they were all high-class, educated prostitutes or simply high-class, educated and liberated women it is impossible to know. What we can say is that they were the antithesis of the Roman *matrona* – they exuded excitement, they were obtrusive, extrovert and often exasperatingly wilful.

In our discussion of Plautus's and Terence's stock female comedy characters we concluded that the New Comedy prototypes were imbued with characteristics and behaviour redolent of Roman society that would be familiar to the audiences. The *meretrix* is no exception. The whole gamut of prostitute types show up in Plautus's plays: the naive, the novice, the one-man *meretrix*, as exemplified by Philaenium in the *Asinaria*, Pasicompsa in the *Mercator* and Philematium in the *Mostellaria*. The busy, sophisticated prostitute who spent her day working, or working at working, with her make-up, fine clothes, dinner parties, bathing and clever conversation, is represented by Gymnasium in the *Cistellaria*, Erotium in the *Menaechmi*, Acropolis in the *Epidicus* – all are the closest to the frustrating and exasperating women who excited the lives of the love poets. Finally, there were the whores who were way past their best, the *lenae*, procuresses, who further corrupted their already corrupted charges, much to the disgust of Propertius and the like.

Petronius in his *Satyricon* has Chryseis describe how some well-to-do women 'love a bit of rough', 'quaedam enim feminae sordibus calent'; how they are aroused even by slaves, donkey drivers, gladiators and actors, even going so far as to lick the wounds of the flogged. Juvenal echoes this *libido* for gladiators in his tirade against women.[27] Ovid teaches that women like rough sex (*vis*): they like being forced against their will and they love their violators; rape is a blessing for the victim, while the woman who is unmolested remains dejected. In Ovid's *Ars Amatoria* when women say no, they really mean yes.[28]

Some of the most extreme disgust aimed at women is reserved for older women, where the vitriol is inextricably associated with sex. Lucilius is repelled by the thought of sexual intercourse during a woman's period;[29] Horace, in a poem reminiscent of those in which he deprecates witches,[30] blames his impotence on his woman's repellent appearance: she smells like a goat, she sweats, and her genitals are shrivelled up. Martial's aged Vetustilla endures a verbal onslaught that is punctuated with references to her sexuality.[31] She too smells like a goat, her breasts sag like a spider's web and her vagina is bone-hard, good only for a funeral torch. On the other hand, Ovid's erectile dysfunction persists despite his girl's obvious beauty and culture.[32] In the *Greek Anthology* Rufinus typifies the *schadenfreude* when he delights in his *hetaira*'s fall from grace, and beauty: her proud breasts, fine stature and divine tresses are but shadows of what they once were; ravaged by old age, she now resembles an ape.[33] The god Priapus, in a homily addressed to his uncooperative, flaccid penis, threatens it with the vagina of a hag, old enough to have known Romulus: concealed by a sagging belly it is depressingly cold and cavernous, dirty and covered in cobwebs, a veritable swamp.[34] Publilius Syrus, that first-century composer of maxims, said that old men pursuing affairs was criminal; to Ovid sex and old people was a repellent notion: *turpe senilis amor*. Age or beauty, though, were no guarantees of good sexual hygiene: one resident of Pompeii found that his beautiful whore was still full of the semen deposited by a previous client, and was sufficiently annoyed by this to record the fact on a wall.[35]

Risible it all may have been to writers of love and invective, but the long-lasting loving relationship – usually, but not always, within marriage – was held in high regard and was something to be emulated. We have seen how the marriage that ended in the death of one of the partners had become a regrettable rarity in the wake of increasing divorce. Both Pliny and Martial extol the extended marriage: Pliny hopes that his happy marriage to Calpurnia will go on forever (4, 19) while Martial wishes that Claudia Peregrina and her husband will love each other well into old age (4, 13). This is supported by the epigraphical evidence: we see longevity in marriage from Carthage where the husband reaches 102 and the wife 80 (*CIL* 8, 12613), and from Hispania Baetica where the couple are 100 and 99 (*CIL* 2, 5464).

Lucretius describes the blindness caused by love (*cupido*) when men simply cannot see the truth before their eyes: repulsive women become *deliciae*, sheer delights, and there follows a whole catalogue of false perceptions where the dusky become honey-brown, the stunted a Grace, the buxom a Ceres, the lank a gazelle, the bulky divine. He concludes by deriding the use of perfumes to conceal the truth, by ridiculing the locked-out lover – the *paraclausithyron* – and by recommending that men accept that women are imperfect and should just make do with a bad lot. Lucretius elaborates on this later in the poem: despite physical imperfections a little woman, *muliercula*, can still be lovable; she can win love by her pleasantness and her *cultus*; the sheer habit of life (*consuetudo*) together with her husband can develop into love. Ovid agreed; he too turns the myopia to good advantage: he recommends that a woman's imperfections be disregarded and that the lover replaces them with positive, euphemistic attributes. The skinny are to be told they are slender, the stunted trim, the cross-eyed are heavenly.[36]

Propertius is concerned about the effect of the erotic wall decoration in public budings and private homes on impressionable young girls. He deplores the *obscaenae* and the corrupting effect they have on the innocent eyes of girls. He has an agenda, though: his only concern is that the pictures will engender in them a promiscuity which will not always be to his benefit. Ovid writes to Augustus from exile in Tomis describing quite casually the *tabella* he has seen there which depict *concubitus varii* (different ways of having sex) and *figurae veneris* (sexual positions). It is impossible to know how women reacted to such *obscaenae;* Propertius and Ovid seem oblivious to any prudishness or of any offence taken. But Propertius and Ovid probably would. Nevertheless, in the Pompeiian wall paintings at least, women are frequently shown playing an equal or dominant role; this may be to invalidate connotations of impropriety or female exploitation; obscenity was still obscenity but its reception by the Roman man and woman was very different to the reception of the Victorians and later societies, for example, who hid the paintings away from us for many years.[37]

It was not just men who taught the *artes amatoriae*. Women too contributed to the supply of sex manuals. Martial alludes to books by Elephantis in his review of the work of Sabellus. We saw in the chapter on the *docta puella* how he recommends the books written by Sulpicia to women and men alike if they want guidance on how to achieve the perfect marriage – on both sides of the bedroom door. Elsewhere women lend a helping hand when he recommends that Istantius Rufus has his girl masturbate him as he reads the salacious books, *pathicissimi libelli,* of Musaeus.[38]

Propertius is working to an agenda again in his poem praising the natural beauty of women. He deplores the fine clothes, perfumes and hairstyle worn by his girl, recommending instead that her natural beauty be allowed to shine through. As with his *obscaenae* poem, Propertius is being somewhat disingenuous, anxious as he is lest his 'done up' girl attract undue attention from other men.[39] Ovid had no such qualms: indeed, so important did he consider *cultus*, good grooming, and a woman's use of cosmetics that he wrote a book on it, the *Medicamina Faciei*. Advice for the many girls who are less than beautiful is handed out in the *Ars Amatoria* where Ovid shows how to make the most of shortcomings. He covers dress, make-up, halitosis, how to conceal bad dentition, even how to laugh discreetly.[40]

What emerges from this brief survey is first the ubiquity of erotic images, symbols and literature visible to all – women and men alike – and presumably admired by both sexes: sex for the Roman was much more of a pleasure than a sin or something to feel ashamed or embarrassed about. Sex was a public affair for Roman men and women, indicative of pleasure. It is only later societies that hid it away and associated it with shame and guilt. In Rome, when a sexual act is dispayed on a house wall, on a lamp or on a wine jug it becomes part of the domestic wallpaper, accepted as normal by normal people.

Second, the casualness with which men describe and enjoy female sexuality and the assumption that a range of female sexual services are there for the taking, be they with a wife, slave girl or prostitute. It reflects, of course, Roman male dominance and male promiscuity – acceptable in Roman society, so long as it did not expose adultery. Despite the obvious pleasures men derived from their own permissiveness, elite men in the form of poets – didactic and invective – and not so elite men in the shape of graffiti writers are all quick to deride and denigrate the objects of their desires, complaining when they are snubbed by a well dressed *docta puella*, paranoid that a wall painting will impell their mistress into the bed of another lover, whingeing when denied what some then, and now, might call deviant sex, indignant that a whore smells or that a procuress trains her girls to be meretricious. Lesbians, low-rent prostitutes, even women generally, are vilified in books and and on walls – but not on all walls – the graffiti may be fantasist and insulting but the interior decoration we are now allowed to see shows the sexual woman in a better light, on equal, or superior terms even, with her male partner. The fruits, perhaps, of a less privileged, less conservative, more populist and artisanal type of artist who, like the love poets, was not particularly bothered about a *cursus honorum, virtus, stuprum* or chauvinism?

In literature, women working in the sex trade were, with the exception of the objects of desire put on pedestals by the love poets (if they indeed ever did commercialise their talents), marginalised, second-class citizens in the eyes of most men. In Rome, as anywhere, sex has always been another means by which men exert power and control over women – not least in invective literature, some interior decoration and in some graffiti. But there is evidence that women, as wives, mistresses and prostitutes, were themselves increasingly able to exert a degree of independence, influence and power themselves, in and out of bed. This is particularly obvious among the Lesbias, Cynthias and Corinnas who are the *dominae* in the *servitium amoris* – unyielding to to the *exclusus amator,* vanquishing the *miles amoris* – but it also manifests in the graffiti and in the wall paintings and other depictions where they are represented as active, sometimes dominant, participants in consensual sexual activity.[41] It shows too in the way in which women were able to assume more responsibility within the *familia,* how they occasionally and defiantly took the stand publicly and how, as *matronae,* they displayed loyalty and devotion to their husbands and children in the tradition of a Lucretia or a Cornelia.

EPILOGUE

This, then, is the history of the woman in Ancient Rome as it relates specifically to her role in the family, as a wife and a mother, and to her performance on the public stage, both as an individual and in a group, protesting her rights. We have seen too how she was educated, and how she behaved as an intelligent and talented woman. We have defined her function in state and unofficial religions and we have adumbrated her role in prophecy, and in the murkier side of life as a witch or ghost. We have examined her role as a health professional and the diseases to which she was prone. Finally, we have surveyed her sexuality as a lesbian and as a heterosexual, and the essential part she played in the Roman sex industry.

The picture is, of course, far from complete and it is hoped that a further volume will cover the involvement of Roman women in such areas such as slavery, fashion and beauty, work and leisure and death, powerful women in the Empire, their treatment in mythology, tragedy and epic, Christian women, the reappearance and reception of Roman women in later European literature, art and music, and their role in the cinema.

However, from what we have covered, a number of things about the lives of women in ancient Rome are very clear. She had no place in public life, despite occasional demonstrations: politically, juridically and militarily she was insignificant; in religion she was much the same until she started to carve out a viable role in the exciting, dangerous religions spilling in from the East. However, in the home she was influential, managing the day to day work of the household, educating the children and keeping things on the rails, a veritable *hausfrau*. She may well have been subservient and exploited to some extent but she was admired and loved for her loyalty, fidelity and for her fecundity. Her ancestors, Lucretia, Verginia and Cornelia, were held up as paragons by conservative and more liberal men alike. The constraints on her lifestyle relaxed over time, with a freer form of marriage and the loosening of control by her father, husband or guardian; this allowed her to act more independently as she assumed more responsibility within and without the family as war, widowhood or extended separation from absent husbands increased. As Rome became wealthier through territorial expansion, so the middle and upper classes benefited; women had a share in this wealth which enabled some to pursue a *rouée* lifestyle, worlds away from the *matrona*. Such permissiveness was particularly at odds with what we assume to be the traditional submissive role of Roman women in sex. Certainly, a wife was under extreme pressure, domestically and officially, to produce as many children as possible – a dangerous and wearing responsibility – but there is no reason to believe that she was not a consensual, happy partner most of the time. Morally, she was at a disadvantage in that her husband could philander all he wanted so long as he did not bother other *matronae*; she, however had no such liberty and was stigmatised if found to be complicit in adulterous affairs. Her education was cut short by early marriage, but gifted and accomplished women shone through; most men probably appreciated this, and some certainly encouraged it, but it is the cynical, suspicious and misogynist comments we tend to remember most. To many men, the obtrusive, extrovert, clever woman was equated with the sexually permissive woman: the docile, modest and inconspicuous baby factory was what they believed was needed to keep Rome on top of the world, although some, of course, like the love poets and Martial, wanted the best of both worlds. Superstition was rife, and here too women were excluded from the top jobs – in conventional religion, typically, as in other societies, they were consigned the more nefarious roles as witches and child-frightening bogeywomen. The all-important Sibyl, legendary reader of the national future, however, was always a woman – although the officials who read her oracles were always men. Women shone in medicine, as doctors and as midwives – virtual doctors themselves – and we hear of medical families where women are considered the equal of their fathers or husbands. Gynaecology gets appropriate coverage by the medical writers, men and women, and probably gives a rare, indirect voice to women, assuming that much of the medicine expounded is derived from patient history taking and examination. Women were central and crucial to the sex industry, providing the services required by men, married and single. As anywhere, they attract abuse and ridicule in invective literature and graffiti scrawled on the walls; lesbians and old women are similarly lampooned and excoriated. No more, though, than effeminate, sexually submissive men. Some relief comes from wall paintings which turn the tables, depicting women to be in the dominant role with their men comedic and compliant.

Roman women then, while never emancipated, enjoyed a limited and qualified freedom, some more than most others. They could choose to be a Cornelia or a Lesbia, or somewhere in between; they had a social life and could go out to dinner with their husbands or to the theatre or the games with their friends; they could stand up for their rights and they could exercise increasing independence in freer marriages, which eventually allowed them their say in divorce, inheritance and property. To some degree, they could help and influence their husbands politically and they were important, though probably not always willingly so, in the merry-go-round of divorces and re-marriages. They were educated and could demonstrate erudition and talent. Early marriage, exclusion from public office and male chauvinism were undoubted and defining constraints but the Roman women, though largely silent and kept that way by some husbands, do speak to us of a degree of increasing individuality, freedom and independence.

KEY DATES

BC

753	The founding of Rome by Romulus, establishing Rome as a kingdom.
750	Rape of the Sabine women.
642	Horatia killed by her brother.
509	Lucretia commits suicide. Tarquins expelled; beginning of the Roman Republic.
450	The Twelve Tables posted.
449	Verginia killed by her husband to avoid *stuprum*.
445	*Lex Canuleia*: marriage between patricians and plebeians permitted.
440	Hippocratic school of medicine founded on Cos.
293	Asclepius arrives in Rome.
272	Bona Dea brought to Rome.
264–241	First Punic War.
261	Carvilius Ruga successfully sues his wife for divorce on the grounds of her infertility; Rome's first divorce.
239	Ennius born.
234	Cato the Elder born.
219	Archagathos, the first Greek physician to come to Rome arrives.
218–201	Second Punic War.
216	Rome defeated at Cannae.
215	*Lex Oppia* sumptuary law passed.
204	Magna Mater brought to Rome from Pergamum. Plautus writing.
195	Repeal of *Lex Oppia*, championed by women.
186	Bacchanalians suppressed.
169	*Lex Voconia* passed.
167	Polybius arrives in Rome.
166	Terence writing plays.

154	Publilia and Licinia strangled by their families for poisoning their husbands.
150	Cornelia, mother of the Gracchi brothers, active.
149	Third Punic War.
146	Roman victory over Corinth and Carthage; Greece becomes a Roman territory.
116	Varro born.
86	Sallust born.
70	Cicero's *Verrine* orations.
64	Strabo the geographer born.
63	Catiline conspiracy.
62	Publius Clodius Pulcher gatecrashes the Bona Dea at Caesar's house.
60	Diodorus Siculus and Dionysius of Halicarnassus writing their histories.
59	Catullus and Lucretius writing.
49	Civil war between Caesar and Pompey.
48	Caesar dictator.
44	Caesar assassinated.
42	Octavian and Antony defeat Brutus and Cassius at Philippi. Hortensia's famous speech to the triumvirs.
41	Fulvia, wife of Antony, leads resistance in Italy; Antony consorts with Cleopatra VII.
40	Virgil writing *Eclogues*; Horace composing *Satires* and *Epodes*.
39	Octavian and Scribonia have Julia; Octavian divorces Scribonia to marry Livia.
38	Velleius Paterculus born.
31	Antony and Cleopatra defeated by Octavian at Actium.
29	Livy begins his *History of Rome*.
27	Beginning of the Roman Empire: Octavian becomes Augustus Caesar.
26	Sulpicia, Propertius and Tibullus composing their elegies.
25	Ovid starts his *Amores*.
18	*Lex Julia de Adulteriis Coercendi; Lex Julia de Maritandis Ordinibus* moral and family laws passed.
2	Julia, daughter of Augustus, exiled.

AD

| 4 | Seneca the Younger born. |
| 9 | *Lex Papia Poppaea.* |

14	Death of Augustus; Tiberius becomes emperor; Celsus writing on medicine.
23	Pliny the Elder born. Valerius Maximus writing his history.
30	Musonius Rufus born.
37	Tiberius dies; Caligula becomes emperor.
40	Agricola born.
41	Caligula assassinated; Claudius becomes emperor; Seneca exiled. Martial born.
45	Statius born.
54	Claudius poisoned by Agrippinilla. Her son Nero becomes emperor.
53	Lucan, Persius and Petronius all writing.
60	Columella writing his *De Re Rustica*.
69	Year of the four emperors; Vespasian emerges as emperor. Suetonius born.
79	Titus emperor. Destruction of Pompeii and Herculaneum.
81	Domitian emperor.
90	Quintilian writing.
95	Appian born.
96	Pliny writing his letters; Plutarch writing. Nerva emperor.
98	Trajan emperor.
110	Tacitus writing. Juvenal satirising.
117	Hadrian emperor. Florus writing his history.
120	Lucian writing.
130	Soranus writing on gynaecology; Julia Balbilla inscribes Memnon colossus.
131	Aulus Gellius born; author of *Noctes Atticae*.
138	Antoninus Pius emperor.
150	Dio Cassius the historian born.
155	Apuleius accused of witchcraft. Writing *Metamorphoses*.
161	Marcus Aurelius emperor.
160	Galen writing on medicine.
211	Ulpian the jurist writing.
363	*Sibylline Books* last consulted.
370	*Ius vitae necisque* abolished.
374	Newborn exposure outlawed.
394	Vestal Virgins disbanded.
400	Macrobius writing his *Saturnalia*.

GLOSSARY OF GREEK & LATIN TERMS

adulterium	Adultery – made illegal by Augustus's *Lex Julia de Adulteriis Coercendis* of 18 BC.
affectio maritalis	The intention of a betrothed couple to marry.
archiatrus	Physician.
atrium	The central area of a Roman house where the household gods were installed.
coemptio	A form of marriage which involved the notional purchase of the wife.
cognomen	A man's third name; a woman's second.
collegium	A club or guild; priesthoods were organised into *collegia*.
confarreatio	An old form of marriage used by the flaminica dialis priesthood.
contubernium	Literally ' tenting up' or 'shacking up together'. Common-law marriage.
conubium	The legal right to marry.
cultus	Sophistication.
cursus honorum	The sequence of public offices held by men of senatorial class.
deductio in domum mariti	The procession that leads a newly married woman to her husband's home.
defixionum	Curse tablet.
deliciae	Darling, delight.
dextrarum iunctio	Symbolic joining of right hands at the Roman wedding ceremony.
divinatio	Divination.
docta puella	An educated, clever woman.

domina	Mistress, mistress of the household.
domus	The Roman house or household.
dos	Dowry.
equites	The equestrian order ranked below senators; the equites were often middle-class businessmen and farmers.
familia	The family.
fascinum	Phallus.
filiafamilias	Daughter, under *paterfamilias.*
freedman/woman	A slave who had been emancipated; many were tradesmen and women.
Hellenism	The culture of classical Greece, which percolated into Rome.
hetaira	Prostitute, concubine.
hippomanes	An aphrodisiac
hysterike pnix	Uterine suffocation.
iatraliptes	Medical assistant.
iatros	Doctor.
incestum	Unchastity, particularly in Vestal Virgins; incest.
infamia	Ill repute.
ius patrium, ius vitae necisque	A father's right to decide whether a newborn lives or dies.
katabasis	A going down; a journey through hell.
lena	Bawd, procuress.
lex	Law.
libertina/liberta	Freedwoman.
magus	Magician.
maia	Midwife.
manus	An early form of marriage which consigned the woman to the *potestas* of her husband, or his father.
materfamilias	Mother, female head of the family.
matrona	A respectable Roman woman.
medica	Female doctor.
medicamentum	Drug, poison, love potion.
meretrix	A prostitute.
mola salsa	Salt cakes made by the Vestal Virgins to accompany sacrifices.
morbus comitialis	Epilepsy.
necromanteia	Necromancy, a rite which involved calling up ghosts for questioning.
nekuia	Necromancy.

obstetrix	Midwife.
otium	A lifestyle of ease and commercial, political or military inactivity.
paelex	Concubine, mistress.
paterfamilias	Father, male head of the family.
patria potestas	The father's power over his household.
patrician	The dominant political class.
pharmaka	Pharmaceutical drugs; spell; poison.
pharmakis	Witch, sorceress.
philtrum	Love potion.
pietas	Dutifulness – in all aspects of life.
pontifex maximus	Chief priest.
probosae	Women working in disreputable occupations.
pudicitia	Chastity, fidelity – one of the badges of a good *matrona*.
pudor	Modesty, propriety.
puellae Faustinianae	Girls who benefited from a welfare programme set up by Antoninus Pius.
res gestae	Political and military achievements.
rhizotomos	Root-cutter; quack.
sacerdos	Priestess.
scortum	A prostitute.
sponsa	An engaged girl.
sponsalia	The engagement party; betrothal.
stipulatio	Informal agreement to marry.
stola	Worn by *matronae* over their tunics.
stuprum	Sexual depravity.
sui iuris	Independence from a legal guardian.
tabellae defixionum	Curse tablets.
tribas	Lesbian; a sexual act between lesbians.
tutela	Guardianship for women who were without husbands or fathers; guardians administered their legal and financial affairs.
unicuba	A woman who had slept with only one man.
univira	Another badge of the good matron – a one-man woman.
usus	De facto *manus* marriage.
vates	Soothsayer, prophetess, priestess.
venefica	Witch, sorceress.
veneficium	Poisoning.

venenum	Drug, poison, potion.
vidua	A single woman.
virtus	Manliness, courage, virtue.
vis	Force, rape.
vulva	Womb, uterus.

ABBREVIATIONS

AC	*L'Antiquité Classique*
ACD	*Acta Classica Debrecen*
AE	*L'Année Epigraphique*
AJAH	*Americal Journal of Ancient History*
AJPh	*American Journal of Philology*
Anc Soc	*Ancient Society* (Louvain)
ANRW	*Aufstieg und Niedergang der Römischen Welt*
APA	*American Psychiatric Association*
BGU	*Berliner Griechische Urkunden*
BHM	*Bulletin of the History of Medicine*
C&M	*Classica et Mediaevalia*
CB	*Classical Bulletin*
CEG	P. A. Hansen, *Carmina Epigraphica Graeca,* Berlin 1983
CIG	*Corpus Inscriptionum Graecarum,* Berlin 1825–77
CJ	*Classical Journal*
CIL	*Corpus Inscriptionum Latinarum,* Berlin 1863
Cl. Ant	*Classical Antiquity*
CP	*Classical Philology*
CQ	*Classical Quarterly*
CW	*Classical World*
FHG	*Fragmenta Historicorum Graecorum,* ed. C. Muller, 1841–1870
FIRA	*Fontes Iuris Romani Anteiustiniani*
FOS	Raepsaet-Charlier, M. Th., *Prosopography de l'ordre Senatoriel,* Louvain 1987
G&R	*Greece and Rome*
HN	*Historia Naturalis,* Pliny the Elder
IG	*Inscriptiones Graecae,* Berlin 1873

ILA	R. Cagnat, *Inscriptions Latines d'Afrique*, Paris 1923
ILS	*Inscriptiones Latinae Selectae*, ed. H. Dessau
Inscr. Eph.	*Inschriften von Ephesus*, ed. H. Engelmann, Bonn 1980
JRS	*Journal of Roman Studies*
LCM	*Liverpool Classical Monthly*
NH	*Natural History*, Pliny
P. Bour	*Les Papyrus Bouriant*
PCPhS	*Proceedings of the Cambridge Philosophical Society*
Peek	*Griechische Verse- Inschriften*, Berlin 1955
PGM	K. Preisendanz, *Papyri Graecae Magicae*, Leipzig 1928
Pleket	H. W. Pleket, *Epigraphica II*, Leiden 1969
P. Lond	*London Papyrus*
P. Oxy	*The Oxyrhynchus Papyrus*
PVS	*Proceedings of the Virgil Society*
P. Wisc	*The Wisconsin Papyri*
RBPH	*Revue Belge de Philologie et d'Histoire*
RE	Pauly-Wissowa, *Real Encyclopedia der Classischen Altertumswissenschaft*
REL	*Revue des Etudes Latines*
RhM	*Rheinisches Museum fur Philologie*
Sammelbuch	*Sammelbuch Griechischer Urkunden aus Aegypten*
SEG	*Supplementum Epigraphicum Graecum*, Leiden 1923
SO	*Symbolae Osloensis*
SHPBBS	*Studies in History & Philosophy of Biological & Biomedical Sciences*
TAPhA	*Transactions of the Proceedings of the American Philological Asscn*
Thesleff	H. Thesleff (ed.), *The Pythagorean Texts of the Hellenistic Period* (1965)
WHO	World Health Organisation
WS	*Wiener Studien*

NOTES

Introduction

1. Livy 34, 7.
2. Notably, Finley, 'The Silent Women of Rome'; Fraschetti, *Roman Women*, 'Introduction'.
3. Martial 8, 12.

1 Women in the *Familia*

1. *CIL* 6, 11602.
2. *CIL* 1, 1007.
3. In *Rari Exempli Femina*, p. 493.
4. Allia Potestas *CIL* 6, 37965. Ulpia Epigone, Museo Gregoriano Profano, Vatican 9856.
5. *CIL* 6, 29580.
6. *CIL* 6, 18817; 6, 29436; *L'Année Epigraphique* 1922, 48.
7. *CIL* 6, 9499.
8. *CIL* 13, 1983; 13, 2182.
9. Seneca *de Matrimonio* 72–7.
10. *CIL* 8, 11294 found in Algeria. *CIL* 3, 3572.
11. Seneca, *op. cit.* (frag. 58 Haase 1872); Tacitus *Annals* 15, 63.
12. This is explored at length in Dixon, *Reading Roman Women*, p. x.
13. Martial 5, 34; 5, 37; 10, 61.
14. For infanticide see Brunt, *Roman Manpower*, pp. 148–154.
15. 2, 15.
16. Philo, *De Specialibus Legibus* 3, 114–115.
17. Livy 27, 37.
18. Suetonius, *Augustus* 94, 3; Musonius Rufus, *Reliquae*, 80f.
19. Soranus, *Gynaecology*.
20. *P. Oxy* 744. *The Gnomon of the Ideologue* (41 and 107) provides

for male foundlings – 'children of the dung heap', but there is nothing for females.

21. Ovid, *Metamorphoses* 9, 669–684; 704–706. *The Codex Theodosianus* 11.27.1 in AD 315 makes provision for state assistance for families who are driven to expose or give away their children on account of poverty.

22. *P. Oxy* 1895. Private charity, or alms, existed too, as shown on a monument from around AD 175 in Sicca, North Africa (*CIL* 8, 1641). It bequeaths the interest on a 1.3 million sesterces donation for the feeding and upkeep of 300 boys and 300 girls, in perpetuity (replaced when girls reached the age of thirteen and boys fifteen).

23. See the plangent papyrus letter from a young girl, Tare, from Apamea in Syria, to her aunt, appealing for someone to take her in, 'all alone in a strange land'. *P. Bour.* 25.

24. Pomeroy, *Goddesses*, pp. 164–165 points out the short-sightedness of these policies, delimiting as they do the supply of child bearers and their male offspring, much needed for the army; the comparison with Spartan policy is stark. See Golden, *Did the Ancients Care?*, p. 155. Cicero, *Tusculanae Disputationes* 1, 39, 93; *IG* 5, 2, 43.

25. Livy 1, 26.

26. *Ibid.* 3, 44–58

27. Cicero, *Atticus* 12, 15 and 12, 46; 1, 8 for *deliciolae*. For a reply see Servius Sulpicius Rufus's at *Ad Familiares* 4, 5, 1, 4–6. Dolabella: *Att.* 7, 2.

28. *CIL* 1, 1214. See also the gifted Menophilia from Sardis from the same time (*Peek*, 1881) and five-year-old Politta from Memphis at the end of the second century AD (*Peek* 1243) – blameless and without fault in her parents' eyes.

29. *CIL* 6, 38605 and *CEG* 153.

30. *CIL* 6, 8517.

31. Valerius Maximus 2, 4, 5.

32. Pliny the Younger 5, 16, 1–7. Other instances of the deaths of young daughters recorded on tombstones are Lutatia Secundina aged four years, six months and nine days (*CIL* 6, 21738); Magnilla, aged eight – 'a positive delight' (*CIL* 6, 21846); and Heteria Superba who died aged one year, six months and twenty-five days. Sosias Isas, the twelve-year-old daughter of a 'desolate' father from Bologna in the second century AD (*AE* 1976, 202) and eighteen-month-old Irene from Ariminum (*CIL* 11, 466); Minicia's epitaph can be seen on the family tomb now in the Terme Museum in Rome. See also thirteen-year-old

Corellia Optata whose headstone was uncovered in 2011 at the
Hungate dig in York. For Julia, Revocata and Murra see *CIL* 3,
2399; 3, 3017; 13, 2219.

33.   Catullus 62, 63–70.

34.   *CIL* 6, 10230.

35.   *CIL* 1, 2, 1211. See also *CIL* 1, 2, 1221 where Lucius Aurelius
Hermia similarly praises his faithful, devoted, happy, dutiful
wife – for better or for worse. See also *CIL* 6, 6593 from the
tomb of the Statilii in Rome and the epitaph to Urbana in third-
century AD Rome (*CIL* 6, 29580). Other similar inscriptions
include *CIL* 6, 29149; 11, 1491 – to Scribonia Hedone, with whom
her husband had lived for eighteen years without a quarrel! *ILA*
175, p. 54; *CIL* 5, 7453.

36.   *CIL* 6, 1527, 31670. Valerius Maximus, *Facta et Dicta
Memorabilia* 6, 7, 1–3.

37.   Tacitus, *Agricola* 4, 2–4. Translation H. Mattingley, *Tacitus, The
Agricola and the Germania.*

38.   Tacitus, *Dialogus de Oratoribus* 28.

39.   Quintilian, *Institutiones Oratoriae* 1, 1, 6–8, 15–17, 20; Nepos,
Fragmenta 1–2 de Viris Illustribus.

40.   Pliny, *Historia Naturalis* 7, 69. We will hear much more from
Pliny throughout the book; it is as well to bear in mind his
caveat that he has no responsibility for the veracity of anything
he writes; this is down to his sources, the original authors (*op.
cit.* 7, 8).

41.   4, 3; 19, 1–3. Translation Ian Scott-Kilvert, *Plutarch, Makers of
Rome.*

42.   1, 2–5. Translation Ian Scott-Kilvert, *op. cit.*

43.   Propertius 4, 11. Paullus was consul in 34 BC and Censor in 22
BC. The quotation is at lines 45–46, translation G. Lee, *Propertius
– The Poems.*

44.   So Hallett, *Role of Women*, p. 119.

45.   Livy 10, 2, 7–8.

46.   *Ad Helviam* 16, 5. *Ad Marciam* 16, 1.

47.   Pliny, *Epistulae* 7, 24.

48.   *CIL* 10, 6009.

49.   *CIL* 6, 37965.

50.   Martial 11, 53.

51.   Seneca the Younger, *De Providentia* 2, 5.

52.   Marcus Aurelius, *M. Cornelius Fronto: Epistulae ad M.Aurelium* 4,
6.

53.   *BGU* 380.

54.   Valerius Maximus, *op. cit.* 4, 4.

55. Dio Cassius, *Historia Romanae* 78, 2.
56. *CIL* 1, 2, 1837. See also *CIL* 8, 8123 where a twenty-five-year-old mother's last wish is that her daughter is chaste.
57. Pliny, *Ep.* 7, 24.
58. Statius, *Silvae* 3, 5.
59. *ILS* 1046a.
60. *Sammelbuch* 6263.
61. Tacitus, *Agricola* 7.
62. Seneca the Younger, *Ad Helviam* 2, 4; 19, 6.
63. *Ibid.* 19, 1–3.
64. Martial 9, 30.
65. Quintilian, *op. cit.* 6, *Preface* 4 and 5.
66. Pliny, *op. cit.* 6, 7; see also a similar refrain in 7, 5 and Pliny's concern about his wife's illness in 6, 4.
67. *Idem* 4, 19.
68. Pliny, *op. cit.* 8, 5, 1–2; 3, 3.
69. 'Mother's breast is best' seems to be another badge of the good matron, *CIL* 6, 19128; presumably preferable to the use of wet nurses.
70. Ovid, *Ars Amatoria* 1, 31–32; Martial 1, 35, 8–9; Valerius Maximus, *op. cit.* 8, 3.
71. Livy 1, 57–60.
72. *Ibid.* 1, 58, 7.
73. See Edwards, *Death*, pp. 180ff.
74. Ovid, *Fasti* 2, 720–58.
75. Pliny, *op. cit.* 3, 16, 3–6.
76. Martial 1, 13.
77. Pliny *ibid.* 7, 19.
78. *Idem*, 6, 24.
79. Plutarch, *Brutus* 13 and Dio 44, 13–14. See also Valerius Maximus *op. cit.* 4, 6 and 6, 7 on brave and faithful wives; Appian *BC* 4, 39–40 and Tacitus, *Annals*, on wives in civil wars.
80. Pliny, *op. cit.* 6, 29.
81. See also Tacitus, *Annals* 6, 29; 16, 10.
82. *Ibid.* 6, 40.
83. *Ibid.* 6, 29.
84. *Ibid.* 15, 63, 2–4.
85. *Ibid.* 16, 34.
86. Pliny, *op. cit.* 3, 16, 7–9.
87. Tacitus, *op. cit.* 14, 21
88. See above p. 20.
89. Valerius Maximus, *op. cit.*, 6, 7, 1–3.
90. Augustine, *Confessions* 9, 9.

91.   See Grmek, *Les Maladies*, pp. 214–225.
92.   Appian, *Bella Civilia* 4, 39–40.
93.   Dio Cassius, *op. cit.* 62, 13, 4.
94.   Sallust, *Catilina* 25. See Balsdon, *Roman Women*, pp. 47–49 for
      the controversy surrounding Sallust's description of her.
95.   Seneca, *Ad Marciam* 1, 1; *Ad Helviam* 16, 5.
96.   Plutarch, Cato *Maior* 8, 4; *Life of Themistocles* 18.
97.   Livy, 34, 2, 1, 2; 8–11, 14.
98.   *Aulularia* 498–550.
99.   Valerius Maximus 9, 1, 3.
100. Cicero, *Att.* 15, 11.
101. Cicero, *Ad Familiares* 14, 4–6.
102. Cicero, *Att.* 3, 19.
103. Plutarch, *Cicero* 20. Ovid, *Tristia* 4, 10, 69ff.
104. Suetonius, *Augustus* 73, 1; 64, 2
105. Balsdon, *Roman Women*, p. 270 and n. 59.
106. Ovid, *op. cit.* 3, 817–820.
107. Columella, *Praef.* 1–3; 7–9.
108. Aelius Aristeides, *Roman Oration* 71b.
109. Petronius, *Satyricon* 37, 67.
110. Cornelius Nepos, *De Viris Illustribus Praef.* 6.
111. Columella 12, 3.
112. See Gardner, *Women in Roman Law*, pp. 14ff.
113. Ulpian, *Regulae* 11, 1, 21, 27, 28. Also Cicero, *Pro Murena* 12, 27,
      where he asserts that women require guardians because of their
      inferior intellect.
114. Translation by Lewis, *Roman Civilization Vol. II*, p. 339.
115. Gaius, *Institutiones* 145, 154. See Gardner, *Family*, pp. 241ff.
116. Justinian, *Institutes* 1, 9.
117. Cf. Chalmers, pp. 24–25; 30ff.
118. *Poenulus* 32–35, 28–31.
119. *Women's Roles*.
120. See Arnott, *Menander*, pp. 33–34: 'it was obvious ... that Plautus
      ... had larded in a whole host of purely Roman features'.
121. See Moore, *The Theater of Plautus*, pp. 53f.
122. *Truculentus* 13–17.
123. *Ibid* 448–452; 654–470.
124. See Arnott, *op. cit.*, p. 44.
125. See Radice, *The Plays of Terence*, pp. 20–21.
126. See above p. 28.

2 Betrothal, Marriage, the Wedding

1. Livy 34, 7, 12.
2. See Hopkins, *Age of Roman Girls,* and Amunsden, *Age of Menarche.*
3. *FIRA* 3, 13.
4. Paul, *Opinions* 2, 19, 2–2, 6–9; 2, 20, 1; *Edict* 35, 1.
5. Dio 54, 6, 7.
6. Aulus Gellius 10, 10; Egyptian post-mortems provided the evidence, apparently.
7. Gifts of a substantial nature between married couples were illegal.
8. Livy 39, 19, 5.
9. Theodosius 3, 17, 4. See Gardner, *Women in Roman Law*, p. 150 for limited ability to be a tutor before this time.
10. Gardner, *Family and* Familia, pp. 209ff.
11. *Digest*, 23, 2, 28 (Marcianus).
12. See Cornell, *Beginnings of Rome*, p. 285 and n. 46.
13. Gaius 1, 112; Servius on Virgil, *Aeneid* 4, 374.
14. Plutarch, *Questiones Romanae* 50.
15. Gaius, *Institutiones* 1, 108–19; Servius on Virgil, *Georgics* 1, 31; Aulus Gellius, *Noctes Attica* 3, 2, 12f.
16. *Digest* 25, 7, 4 (Paul).
17. *Ibid.* 22, 3, 1.
18. Ulpian, *On the Edict* 35.
19. Pomponius, *On Sabinus* 5.
20. Balsdon, *Roman Women*, p. 183 and n. 40; for the wedding dress see La Follette, *Roman Bride*, 54–64.
21. For dolls see Persius, 2, 70. See Balsdon, *op. cit.*, pp. 183–4 and nn. 42, 43.
22. On the origin of this see Livy, 1, 9.
23. Balsdon *op. cit.*, pp. 184–185 and nn. 44–53.
24. Statius *Silvae*, 1, 2.
25. Tacitus, *Annals* 15, 37, 8f.; Suetonius, *Nero* 28, 1. Juvenal 2, 117ff.
26. Martial 12, 42; see also 1, 24. Cicero, *Philippics* 2, 44.
27. Varro, *De Lingua Latina* 6, 29 and Macrobius 1, 21.
28. See Balsdon, *op. cit.*, p. 181 and n. 34.
29. Ulpian, *Reg.* 5, 2–6.
30. *Idem, Digest* 23, 1, 12.
31. For a woman's responsibility for invitations see Cicero, *Att.* 5, 1; 2, 3, 4. Dio records (57, 12, 5; also 55, 2, 4 and 8, 2) that Tiberius prevented Livia from hosting a mixed dinner party and

entertained the men himself while she looked after the women.
For accompanied postings see Marshall, *Roman Women* and
Marshall, *Tacitus.*

32. Plutarch, *Moralia* 139D, F; 140A.
33. Cicero, *Att.* 1, 5, 1 and 5, 1, 3–4; 14, 13, 5. See Johnson,
    Sister-in-Law.
34. Plutarch, *Moralia* 141A and *Aemilius Paullus* 5, 2ff.
35. Juvenal 6, 300.
36. Pliny, *Natural History* 14, 89; Polybius 6, 11a; Plutarch,
    Questiones Romanae 6.
37. Valerius Maximus 2, 1, 6.
38. Dio 54, 16, 7.
39. *CIL* 1, 1221. See above p. 15.
40. See above p. 25.
41. See above p. 19.
42. *AE*, 1971, 534.
43. See Harkness, *Age at Marriage.*
44. Pliny, *Epistles* 1, 14; see also 1, 10; 6, 26; 6, 32.
45. Cicero *Att.* 6, 6, 1 and *Fam.* 8, 6, 2 for his sanguine resignation.
46. Cicero *Att.* 1, 3, 3 and 6, 6, 1; *Ad Q. Fratrem* 2, 4, 2; 2, 6, 2;
    See also Collins, *Tullia's Engagement*; Treggiari, *Roman Social
    History*, pp. 49ff.
47. Livy 38, 57, 5–8.
48. Plutarch, *Tiberius Gracchus* 4, 3ff. For a more accurate account
    see Polybius 31, 27.
49. Ulpian, *Digest* 23, 2, 19.
50. On love, emotion and sex in Roman marriages, see Hemelrijk,
    Matrona Docta, p. 63 and n. 63.
51. *BGU* 1052.
52. Plutarch, *Cato Maior* 17.
53. 4, 10.
54. Polybius 31, 27.
55. Cicero, *Att.* 11, 2, 2; 11, 23, 3.
56. *Ibid.* 16, 15, 5.
57. Pliny, *HN* 7, 48, 158.
58. Plutarch, *Aemilius Paullus.*
59. Pliny, *Ep.* 2, 4; 6, 32.
60. Aulus Gellius, *Noctes Atticae* 4, 3, 2.
61. *Ibid.* 10, 23, 5. For an exception see Cicero, *Fam.* 8, 7, 2.
62. Plautus, *Mercator* 823–9.
63. Ovid, *Amores* 3, 4, 37.
64. Plutarch, *Moralia* 145A.
65. Martial 6, 7.

66. Rapsaet-Charlier, M. -Th., *Ordre Senatorial.*
67. Pliny, *HN* 7, 5.
68. Plutarch, *Romulus* 22.
69. Dionysius of Halicarnassus 2, 25, 7.
70. *BGU* 1103.
71. Valerius Maximus 8, 2, 3.
72. Catullus 61, 71–73; Propertius 2, 7, 13f.
73. Soranus, *Gynaecology* 1, 34, 1.
74. *CIL* 6, 10320.
75. Plutarch, *Sulla* 3, 2.
76. Petronius, *Satyricon* 74.
77. Plutarch, *Cato Minor* 25, 52; Lucan, *De Bello Civili* 326–371.
78. Tacitus, *Agricola* 6.
79. Plutarch, *Sulla* 35.
80. Suetonius, *Augustus* 62, 63, 69.
81. Plautus, *Captivi* 889: 'liberorum quaerundorum causa ei, credo, uxor data est'.
82. *CIL* 6. 1527: 'rara sunt tam diuturna matrimonia, finita morte, non divertio in nobis'.
83. Paul, *Sent. Recept* 2, 26, 4; *Digest* 48, 5, 30.
84. Valerius Maximus, *Facta* 6, 1, 3 and 6.
85. Aulus Gellius, *op. cit.* 1, 6, 2; 1, 17, 4.
86. Malcovati, fr 6.
87. Tacitus, *Annals* 3.25.
88. Ovid, *Fasti* 1, 33–36.
89. Paul, *Sent.* 1, 21, 13.
90. Seneca, *Ep.* 63, 13.
91. Plutach, *Numa* 12; Livy, 22, 56, 4–5.
92. Pliny, *Ep.* 2, 20.

3 Women in the Public Eye

1. Juvenal 6, 242–245.
2. See Leen, Clodia Oppugnatrix for more on this. On the identity of Clodia see 'Lesbia and Her Children' in Wiseman, *Cinna the Poet*, pp. 104–118.
3. Asconius, *Pro Milone* 28 and 35.
4. Pliny, *Ep.* 6, 33.
5. See above p. 29; Valerius Maximus, *Facta* 8, 3.
6. *Fasti* 2, 721–852.
7. 6, 1, 1.
8. Virgil, *Aeneid* 1, 364; Tacitus, *Agricola* 16, 1; 31, 4.

9. Plutarch, *Marius* 17.

10. *In Verrem* 2, 1, 137.

11. *Life of Lucullus* 6 and Cicero. *Paradoxa Stoicorum* 5, 3.

12. Cicero, *Philippics* 3, 16.

13. Velleius Paterculus, *Histories* 2, 74.

14. Dio, Cassius, *Roman History* 47, 8, 4.

15. Plutarch, *Cicero* 49.

16. *Phil.* 13, 18.

17. Appian, *B. Civ.* 3, 8, 51.

18. Dio 48, 4, 1–6.

19. Appian 5, 3, 19.

20. *Ibid.* 5, 4, 32–3.

21. Velleius Paterculus 2, 74, 3.

22. See Hallet, *Perusinae Glandes.*

23. 11, 20.

24. Sallust, *Bellum Catilinae* 27, 3–28, 3.

25. *Annals* 15, 57.

26. Twelve Tables 4, 2; Aulus Gellius, *Noctes Atticae* 5, 19, 9.

27. Livy 39, 14; 18.

28. *Ibid* 48, 12–13.

29. See Gaughan, *Murder*, p. 83.

30. Tacitus, *Annals* 13, 32. Translation by Grant.

31. Plutarch, *Gaius Gracchus* 4, 3–4; Tacitus, *op. cit.* 59, 3; Dio 58, 11, 5.

32. See Hoffsten, *Roman Women*, pp. 88–89.

33. Pomeroy, *Goddesses,* pp. 202–203.

34. Suetonius, *Augustus* 41; Pliny, *Pan* 26, 28, 1–3.

35. Livy 3, 45–50.

36. *Ibid* 22, 57.

37. *Historia Augusta Elagabalus* 4, 4.

38. Appian 4, 32–4.

39. *Ibid.*

40. 8, 3.

41. *CIL* 14, 2120; 5, 2072.

42. Livy 27, 37, 8–9.

43. Suetonius, *Galba* 5, 1.

44. Livy 10, 23, 10; 2, 7, 4; 2, 16, 7; 5, 25, 8–9. Valerius Maximus 5, 2, 1; 8, 3.

45. Cicero, *De Orat.* 2, 11.

46. Propertius 4, 3; see above p. 21.

47. *Silvae* 5, 1.

48. See Phang, *Marriage.*

49. *Bowman and Thomas* No 5, 1987.

50. See *CIL* 4, 207; 171; 913; 3291; 1083; 6610; 3678; 3684; 3527; Savunen, *Women and Elections*. For Tatia see Thonemann, *The Women of Akmoneia*; the translation of the inscription is by Thonemann.
51. *CIL* 10, 810.
52. *Pleket* 8G.
53. *Pleket* 19G.
54. *CIL* 8, 23888.
55. See Finley, *Silent*, pp. 125–126.
56. See Matthews, *Some Puns*.

4 Educated Women, the *Puella Docta* & the Fine Arts

1. Plutarch, *Gaius Gracchus* 19, 2–3; 4, 3, 19; *Tiberius Gracchus* 1, 2, 5; *Pompey* 55, 2. Sallust, *Catilina* 25. Tacitus, *Agricola*, 6. Quintilian, *Institutiones Oratoriae* 1, 1, 6; Cicero, *Brutus* 2, 11.
2. Tacitus, *Dialogus de Oratoribus* 28; Quintilian *loc. cit.*, 15–17, 20; Nepos, *Fragmenta 1–2 de Viris Illustribus*. See above p. 25.
3. Appian, *Civil Wars* 4, 136–146; Valerius Maximus 8, 3, 3; Quintilian 1, 1, 6. See above p. 61.
4. Cicero, *Brutus* 58, 211.
5. Tacitus, *Annals* 4, 53. Pliny, *NH* 7, 46.
6. *Pleket* 30; *CIL* 6, 33898.
7. *FHG* 3, 520ff. Pornography, of course, is a nineteenth-century term, but examples of material of what we would now define as pornographic go back to time immemorial. See Hyde, *A History of Pornography*.
8. Martial 10, 35.
9. Musonius Rufus 3, 4, 13a.
10. Arrian, *Discourses of Epictetus* fr. 15.
11. Pliny, *Ep.* 4, 19; 5, 16.
12. Plutarch, *Moralia* 138a – 146a.
13. All originally by Cicero: *Orator* 161; *Att.* 7, 2, 21; *Tusculanae Disputationes* 3, 45. See Chrystal, *Investigation*, pp. 15ff; Ross, *Backgrounds*; Tuplin, *Cantores Euphorionis*; *idem, Cantores Euphorionis, Again*; Luck, *Latin Love Elegy*, pp. 49ff; Crowther, *Valerius Cato*; see Lyne, *Latin Love Poets*, pp. 169–174. For *otium* see Andre, *L'*Otium.
14. Plutarch 8, 1; 18; Polybius 31.
15. Plutarch, *loc. cit.*; Livy 24, 2–4; Aulus Gellius 7, 6–8. Cf. Arkins, *Aspects of Sexuality*, pp. 8ff.
16. See G. Colin, *Rome et la Grèce*; J. Griffin *Augustan Poetry*, pp.

88ff and the Appendix, 'Some Imperial Servants'. Various suggestions for the start and or cause of the decline have been made: Polybius, 31, 25 ascribes it to the victory over Macedonia; L. Calpurnius Piso (Pliny, *NH* 17, 38, 244) goes with 154 BC; Appian, *Bellum Civili* 1, 7 for the end of the war in Italy; Livy 39, 6, 7 prefers 186 BC; Valleius Paterculus, *Historiae Romanae*, and Sallust, *Catilina* 10 opt for the end of the Third Punic War. See also Putnam, *The Roman Lady*; Reinhold, *The Generation Gap*, pp. 52ff.

17. See Pomeroy, *Relationship*, pp. 222ff; del Castillo, *Position*, p. 171; and Villers, *Statut*, pp. 184f.

18. Kiefer, *Sexual Life*, p. 24.

19. See Horace, *Odes* 3, 6; Kajanto, *On Divorce*; Hamilton, *Society Women*. Pomeroy, *op. cit.*, argues that in Catullus's day women were enjoying a kind of *de facto* freedom on account of the disinterest shown by many *propinqui*. Decline in *patria potestas* is covered by Reinhold, *op. cit.* p. 49; see also Fau p. 30 and del Castillo, *op. cit.* pp. 167–170; Richlin, *Approaches.*

20. On educated women generally, see Best, *Cicero*; Griffin, *op. cit.*, p. 103, and Fau, *op. cit.*, p. 12. Eucharis: *CIL* 1, 1214; Cytheris: Cicero, *Fam.* 9, 26; *Phil.* 2, 69. See also Hallet, *The Role of Women,* and Lyne, *op. cit.*, p. 7.

21. Cornelius Nepos, *Praefatio* 8; Friedlander, *Roman Life* Vol. 1, pp. 238ff; Mohler, *Feminism*; Will, *Women in Pompeii*; Sullivan, *Propertius*, pp. 82–83; Fau, *op. cit.*, p. 13; del Castillo, *op. cit.*, pp. 168–169.

22. See Griffin, *op. cit.*, p. 96; Mohler, *op. cit.* p. 155. Griffin, on page 103 lists the types of independent women circulating in Rome in the early Empire.

23. Morel, *Fragmenta* 275B, 274B and 179B.

24. See Ross, *op. cit.*, pp. 1–17, and Hus, Doctus. Other 'in' words we could add are *dicax* and *doctus*. Ross, *Style*, p. 106 points out 'such words did not form part of a neoteric program; but their avoidance by later poets only emphasises the singular use Catullus made of them'.

25. Catullus 10, 4, 17; 33–34; 6, 1–2; 32, 1–2.

26. *Ibid* 86, 3–4; 43, 4; 35, 16–17.

27. Cicero, *Pro Caelio* 13, 32. On the identification issue see Dixon, *Reading Roman*, pp. 137ff.

28. So Rankin, *Clodia II*, p. 505, 'it would be possible to claim Clodia (Lesbia) as an intellectual on the grounds of poem 36 alone'. Gallus's wife (78, 2) is *lepidissima coniunx*; Laodamia, = Lesbia, is *docta* (68, 80).

29. Servian commentary on Virgil, *Eclogues* 10; for an appraisal of Gallus's output see Boucher, *Gallus*, pp. 69ff.

30. Propertius 2, 3, 9; 17–21; 1, 2, 27–30; 2, 1, 3–4; 9–10. *Docta* at 1, 7, 11; 2, 11, 6 and 2, 13, 11. Helicon 2, 30, 25–30. Acanthis 4, 5, 54.

31. *Ibid.* 3, 20, 7–8.

32. *Ibid.* 1, 2, 29; 2, 15, 3. As a poetess: 2, 3, 31–32.

33. Tracy, *The Poet Lover*, p. 576; King, *Sophistication*, p. 69.

34. Tibullus 1, 5, 25–28; 1, 3, 85–88.

35. *Ibid* 3, 12, 2. For Sulpicia, see Pearcy, *Erasing Cerinthus*; Santirocco, *Sulpicia Reconsidered*; Keith, 'Critical Trends'; Hubbard, *The Invention of Sulpicia*; Holzberg, *Four Poets*; Hallett, *The Eleven Elegies*; Churchill, *Women Writing*.

36. Horace, *Odes* 1, 36, 13–13, 17–20; 2, 11, 22–24; 3, 14, 21–22.

37. *Ibid.* 2, 12, 17–20; 3, 9, 10; 2, 11, 22; 3, 28, 11; 4, 11, 35–37; 3, 14, 21; 1, 17, 10f.

38. Horace, *Odes* 3, 6, 21–25. The quotation is from Balsdon, *Roman Women* p. 275.

39. Scipio: Macrobius *Sat.* 3, 14. Cornelius Nepos, *Epam* 1f.

40. Ovid, *Amores* 2, 4, 9–10; 47–48. See also 2, 10, 5–6. *Ars Amatoria* 3, 311–28; 3, 349–52.

41. Ovid, *Ars Amatoria* 1, 97–98; *ibid.* 1, 462; *Amores* 2, 4, 22; *ibid.* 3, 8, 5–7; *Ars* 2, 107–112.

42. Ovid, *op. cit.* 281ff.

43. *Ibid.* 3, 771ff.

44. Propertius 4, 5.

45. For Sulpicia, see Pearcy, *op. cit.*; Santirocco, *op. cit.*; Keith, *op. cit.*; Hubbard, *op. cit.*; Holzberg, *Four Poets*; Hallett, *The Eleven Elegies*; Churchill, *Women Writing Latin*.

46. Martial 10, 35; see also 10, 38.

47. *CIG* 3, 4725–30. Catullus 68, 149–50; Horace, *Odes* 3, 11, 51–52; Ovid, *Heroides* 14, 128.

48. Statilia: according to the scholiast on Juvenal 6, 434 (*FOS* 730). Dio Cassius, 78, 18.

49. Valerius Maximus 8, 3. See Hermann, *Le Rôle Judicaire*, pp. 100ff.

50. Pliny, *Ep.* 1, 4; 2, 4; 3, 3; 4, 19; 6, 4; 6, 6; 7, 5.

51. Suetonius, *Gramm.* 16.

52. Horace, *Ep.* 2, 1, 70–71; *Saturae* 1, 1, 25–26. Cicero, *De Leg.* 2, 59.

53. Martial 9, 68; Seneca, *On Anger* 2, 21, 1–6.

54. Horace, *Ars Poetica* 325–30. Cicero, *Tusc.* 1, 5.

55. Pompeia: Strabo 14, 1, 48; Plutarch, *Quaest Conv.* 9, 1, 3. The quotation is from Homer, *Iliad* 3, 428. Augustus: Suetonius, *Augustus*, 64, 2. Julia: Macrobius, *Sat.*, 2, 5, 2; Agrippina,

Suetonius, *op. cit.* 86. For Aufidianus's daughter see above p. 52. For Claudia Severa see Bowman, *Life and Letters.*

56. Plutarch, *Romulus* 6; Livy 3, 44, 6; Cicero, *Att.* 12, 23.

57. Horace, *Sat.* 1, 10, 91; Ovid, *Tristia* 2, 369–370; Juvenal 14, 209.

58. Martial 1, 35; 3, 69; 8, 3; 3, 69, 8; 9, 68, 2.

59. Pliny, *op. cit.* 8, 14, 6f; Tacitus, *Dialogus* 28; 14. For a glimpse into school life see Dickey, *The Colloquia.*

60. Cicero, *Brutus* 305–16. Suetonius, *op. cit.* 3; Quintilian 1, 2.

61. Petronius, *Satyricon* 58, 7.

62. See Joshel, *Work, Identity and Legal Status.*

63. Pliny, *op. cit.* 1, 16, 6; 4, 19; 6, 7.

64. Plutarch, *Praecepta Coniugalia* 48.

65. See Hemelrijk, Matrona Docta pp. 35–36.

66. Suetonius, *De Grammatias* 16.

67. Lucian, *De Mercede Conductis* 36; translation is by A. M. Harmon, adapted by Hemelrijk, *op. cit.* p. 37.

68. Seneca, *Cons. Helv.* 17, 3–4.

69. See above p. 32; Virgil and Homer: Juvenal 11, 179–182; Menander: Plutarch *Mor.* 712B. Pliny, *op. cit.* 3, 1, 9; 1, 15, 2; 9, 17; 5, 19; 9, 36, 4. Nepos, *Attic Nights* 14, 1.

70. Ovid, *Ars Amatoria* 1, 31–34; Martial 11, 2, 2; 3, 69, 7–8; 5, 2; 11, 15, 1–2.

71. Women reading philosophy: Cicero *Att.* 13, 21a 4–5; 13, 22, 3; Horace *Epodes* 8. Epic: Propertius 2, 1, 49–50; Juvenal 6, 434ff. Comedy: Martial, 8, 3, 15–16; 10, 35, 1.

72. Statius, *Silvae* 3, 5, 33–36.

73. Horace *Epodes* 8; Cicero, *Att.* 13. 21a 4–5.

74. Sidonius Apollinaris, *Ep.* 2, 9, 4.

75. Ovid, *Ars Amatoria* 1, 67–262; 3, 387–396; *Tristia* 2, 279–300.

76. Juvenal, 6, 184ff; 242ff; 319ff; 434ff.

77. Cicero, *Pro Caelio*, 64.

78. Persius, *Prol.* 13. Male poets, it should be said, do not escape his criticism either.

5 Sibyls & the Dark Arts

1. Homer, *Odyssey 10, 203–47.*

2. *Ibid* 19, 562–9; 10, 504ff; 19, 562–9; 9, 62–66; 24, 1ff; for Circe see 569–74 as well. Helen: *ibid.* 4, 219–319. *Idem Iliad* 23, 62–76.

3. *Hesiod Works & Days* 121ff; *Theogony,* 720ff; Pindar *Olympian* 2, 56–80; *Fragment* 114 OCT; *Fragment* 127 OCT; F534–6 *TrGF; Oedipus* 530–526; *Persae* 607–99.

4. Antiphon 1, 14–20. Herodotus 5.92; Empedocles F101 Wright, *Empedocles*; F111 DK (Diogenes Laertius 8.59); Plato *Phaedo* 81B–D; 111Cff.; *Gorgias* 493A; 526C; *Cratylus* 400C; *Phaedrus* 250C. See also *Timaeus* 30ff. *Republic* 613E–621D.

5. For Lycophron see Horsfall, *Virgil and the Poetry of Explanations*, p. 206. Theocritus, *Idyll* 2. Appollodorus Rhodius, *Argonautica* 3, 475–80; 533; 1026–62; 1191–1224; 1246–67; 4, 123–66; 445–81; 1636–91. Diodorus Siculus 4, 36, 38.

6. Pliny the Elder, *NH* 7, 16; 30, 7–8. Plautus, *Mostellaria* 446–531. See Foster, *Aeneidea* on how Virgil alludes to this at *Aeneid* 1, 349ff.

7. Apollodorus *Bibliotheca* 2, 5, 1; 1, 9, 26.

8. Cicero, *De Republica* 6; see also *Natura Deorum* 2.30 and *Tusculanae Disputationes* 1, 166 for example.

9. *Idem, ND* 1.57; *In Vatinium* 14C244–6, including Ephorus, *FGH* 70 F134a.

10. Varro, *Antiquitates Rerum Humanarum et Divinarum* 41. Quintilian 10, 1, 98. Ovid, *Heroides* 12; *Metamorphoses* 7, 1–403.

11. Death, Elysium and Tartarus, *Elegies* I, 3; witch I, 2, 42–66; *nefanda* I, 5, 39–59; 2, 5: divination. See below p. 93f.

12. Life after death: *Odes* 4, 7, 16; Augustus's life after death, *ibid.* 3, 3, 11–12; Archytas's ghost, *ibid.* 1, 28; a glimpse of Hades, *ibid.* 2, 13; *Satires* 1, 8, 18ff., necromancy and witches; Canidia the witch, *ibid.* 2, 1, 48 and 2, 8, 95; Odysseus and Tiresias in the underworld, *ibid.* 2, 5; *Epodes* 5; Canidia, Sagana, Veia and Folia; *ibid.* 17.

13. Features a *katabasis*.

14. Cynthia's ghost, death and the underworld 4, 7; Propertius's curse and the afterlife he wishes on a prostitute 4, 5, 1–18; Gallus's ghost 1, 21.

15. Pythagoreanism, *Metamorphoses* 15, 75ff.; Orpheus's *katabasis*, *ibid.* 10; Medea's witchcraft *ibid* 7, 159–351 and *Heroides* 6, 83–94; *Fasti* 2, 572–583: the rites of Tacita; *Amores* 3, 7, 27–36, 73–84: Circean witchcraft; Dipsas the witch *ibid.* 1, 8, 1–20, 105–14. Quintilian (10, 1, 98) praises his lost tragedy, *Medea;* see also Tacitus, *Dial* 12.

16. *Satyricon* 63: witches. Seneca, *Epistulae* 102 deals with the soul after death. *Medea*: witchcraft. *Hercules Furens* has a description of Hercules crossing the Styx at 775ff.; the *Agamemnon* features the trance and possession of Cassandra (710–778). Pliny, *NH* 7, 16. Reputation for fear: *op. cit.* 28, 4.

17. Plutarch, *Moralia* 138a – 146a; *idem, De Superstitione*. Pliny, *NH* 28, 47 and 104; Plato, *Laws* 7, 808d. Translation is by T.

J. Saunders. Mormo: Plato, *Crito* 46c; Lucian, *Vera Hist.* 139; Empusa: Aristophanes, *Frogs* 285–295; Gello: Sappho *frag.* 178; Lamia: Horace, *Ars Poetica* 340 warns poets not to 'draw a living boy from the belly of Lamia that dined with him'. Diodorus Siculus 20, 41.

18. Flavius Philostratus, *Life of Apollonius of Tyana* 2, 4; 4, 25. Lucretius, 1, 132; 4, 722; Horace, *Epistles* 2, 2, 209.

19. Persius 2, 34; Juvenal 10, 289; Dio 49, 43, 5; 52, 36, 2–3. Livy 8, 18.

20. Terence, *Phormio* 705.

21. Cicero, *De Div.* 1, 34, 74.

22. Livy 31, 17, 12; 21, 62, 3; 3, 10, 6.

23. See also Suetonius, *Divus Julius* 81; *Caligula* 57.

24. Petronius, *Satyricon* 104; Pliny, *NH* 28, 26–29.

25. Pliny, *op. cit.* 28, 25. See above p. 48–9 and Silius Italicus 7, 172. Orwell, *Coming Up for Air*, pp. 51–52.

26. Cassius Dio, *Roman History* 49, 43, 5; 52, 36, 3. Livy 39, 8–19; 39, 41; 40, 43. Suetonius, *Tiberius* 63, 1; *idem, Life of Claudius* 25. Pliny, op. cit. 30, 4. Suetonius, *Augustus* 31. Sulla: Paulus, *Sententiae* 5, 23, 14–19. *Digest of Justinian* 48, 8, 2. Cicero, *Pro Cluentia* 148. Libo: Tacitus, *Annals* 2, 27–32.

27. Ammianus Marcellinus, *History* 29, 1–2.

28. Ziebarth 24, 1–4, pp. 1042ff.

29. *CIL* 6, 20905; translation R. Lattimore.

30. *ILS* 8751; *IG* 3, 3, 97, 34–41; *CIL* 10, 8249; *IG*, 3, 3, 78; *SEG* 27, 1717.

31. *CIL* 8, 12507; *PGM* 36, 283–294; 1, 83–87; 1, 167–168; 32.

32. Hyenas: Pliny, *op. cit.* 28, 106. Virgil, *Aeneid* 6, 71–74. Dionysius of Halicarnassus, *Roman Antiquities* 4, 62, 5–6. Virgil, *Eclogue* 4, 6, 24, 31.

33. Heraclitus *fr.* 92. Varro = Lactantius, *Divine Institutions* 1, 6. Virgil, *Aeneid* 6, 78–102; 3, 444. Tibullus 2, 5.

34. Portents: Lucan *de Bello Civili* 1, 522ff.; *Arruns:* 584f.; 673f. Delphi, 5, 67–235.

35. Seneca, *Agamemnon* 710–778; cf. Virgil, *op. cit.* 77–82; 98–102.

36. Silius Italicus, *Punica* 13, 400ff.

37. *Idem* 93–138.

38. Statius, *Thebaid* 4, 406–603. Plutarch, *On the E at Delphi*, 396–397.

39. Virgil, *Eclogues*, 8, 69. Martial 12, 57, 16–17; cf. Tacitus, *Annals* 1, 28. Pliny, *NH* 28, 157; Horace, *Saturae* 1, 8, 42; Horace, *Epodes* 17, 7.

40. Horace, *Saturae* 1, 9, 28–34. *Epodes* 5.

41. *CIL* 6, 19747. LIvilla: Suetonius, *Tiberius* 62ff. Horace, *Saturae* 1, 8; *Epodes* 3; *Saturae*, 2, 1, 48 and 2, 8, 95.

42. Ovid, *Fasti* 2, 571–582; *Heroides* 6, 83–94.

43. *Idem, Amores* 3, 7, 27–36, 73–84; 1, 8, 1–20.

44. Virgil *Aeneid* 4, 300–301; 384–387; 450–473; 483ff.

45. Propertius 3, 6; 4, 5. Tibullus 1, 5, 37–56; 1, 2, 42–66.

46. Juvenal 6, 610–626.

47. Tacitus, *Annals* 2, 69; 2, 74; 3, 7.

48. Seneca, *Heracles on Mount Oeta* 449–472.

49. *Idem, Medea* 6–23; 670–843.

50. Valerius Flaccus, *Argonautica* 5, 238f., 329f.; 7, 309ff., 347ff., 631ff.; 8, 20ff.

51. Petronius, *Satyricon* 131–138; 63ff.

52. Lucan, *De Bello Civili* 6, 419ff.

53. Apuleius, *De Magia* 25–43.

54. *Idem, Metamorphoses*, 1, 21; 2, 21; 4, 10 ; 5.

55. Lucian, *De Mercede Conductis* 4. The translation is by C. D. N. Costa.

56. Heliodorus, *Aethiopica* 6, 14–15.

57. Pliny, *NH* 28, 256. Marcus Aurelius 19.

58. Plato, *Phaedo* 81c–d; see above pp. 86 for bogeywomen; Pliny, *Ep.* 7, 27, 4ff. Lucian, *Philopseudes* 30–31.

59. Virgil, *Aeneid* 2, 736–40; 771–795. *Idem.* 6, 405–476.

60. Propertius 4, 7.

61. Lucan, *op. cit.* 1, 111–120; 3, 10ff.

62. Suetonius, *Nero* 34.

63. Apuleius, *op. cit.* 9, 29–31.

64. *Bibliotheca* (3, 8, 1) and Ovid, *Metamorphoses* I.219–239; Virgil, *Eclogues* 8; Pliny the Elder, *NH* 22; 34.

65. Petronius 62.

6 Women & Religion

1. *Cicero, De Deorum Natura* 2, 70–72; Virgil, *Georgics* 4, 221ff.

2. Cf., however, Beard, *Rome*, pp. 25ff who argues against this view.

3. Cato, *De Ag.* 143.

4. Plutarch, *Romulus* 15, 4; 19, 9.

5. Gellius 10, 23, 1–2.

6. See Holland, *Women and Religion* and Schulz, *Women's Religious Activity*.

7. Ovid, *Fasti* 3, 269–72; see also Propertius 2, 32, 9–10.

8. This can be seen, for example, in the Altar of Aelia Procula in the Louvre. *CIL* 6, 10958.

9. Lactantius 1, 20, 36.

10. *De Civ Dei* 6, 9.

11. The ancients believed that women too ejaculated during intercourse. There is much controversy today surrounding female ejaculation and whether it actually exists or not.

12. Dionysius 4.1, 2; Ovid *Fasti.* vi, 625; Pliny *NH* 36, 27, s. 70; Festus, *s.v. Nothum*; Plutarch, *De Fort. Rom.* 10.

13. *Fasti* 6, 473–568.

14. Livy 10, 23; see also Propertius 2, 6, 25.

15. Livy 10, 31, 9; 2, 39f. See above p. 60.

16. Ovid, *Fasti* 4, 133–16.

17. Juvenal 6, 306–310.

18. *Caesar* 9.

19. Juvenal 6, 314–334.

20. Cicero, *De Domo Sua* 53, 136.

21. See Brouwer, *Bona Dea.*

22. *De Haruspicum Responsis* 17, 37–18, 38.

23. *Roman Questions* 104; *Moralia* 288–289; translation F. C. Babbitt, 1936, Vol 4.

24. *Op. cit.* 56, 278.

25. *Op. cit.* 57, 278.

26. Pomeroy, *Goddesses*, p. 211.

27. Tacitus, *Annals* 2, 86, 2.

28. Aulus Gellius, *Attic Nights* 1, 12.

29. Tacitus, *Annals* 2, 86, 1; 3, 69, 9; *ILS* 4923. For details, see Ryberg, *Rites of the State Religion*, p. 41.

30. See Ovid, *Fasti.*

31. Suetonius, *Caesar* 83; Dio 61, 30.

32. *Roman Questions* 96, *Moralia* 286–287.

33. Plutarch, *Numa* 10.

34. Livy 22, 57, 2.

35. Tacitus, *Annals* 11, 32, 5; *Histories* 3, 81.

36. Dionysius 2, 68; *RE* vii A 768–770; Valerius Maximus 8, 1, 5; see also Richlin, *Carrying Water.*

37. Suetonius, *Domitian* 8, 3–5; Pliny, *Ep.* 4, 11, 6.

38. Valerius Maximus 3, 7, 9; 6, 8, 1.

39. Cicero, *Cat.* 3, 9.

40. *Sat.* 3, 13.

41. Dio 777, 16, 1–3; 79, 9.

42. Macrobius, *Saturnalia* 3, 13, 11. Pliny, *NH* 28, 13.

43. Dio 55, 22, 5.

44. Aulus Gellius, 1, 12, 9.
45. Macrobius, *op. cit.* 1, 16, 30; 1, 15, 18.
46. Festus, 439, citing Aelius Stilo and Cincius.
47. Livy 39, 15, 6; 39, 8.
48. *De Legibus* 2, 9, 21.
49. Livy 39, 17.
50. See above p. 58.
51. Livy 39, 19–22.
52. *CIL* 10, 816, 998; *Inscr. Eph.* 1063–1064; *ILS* 4144 (*CIL* 6, 1779).
53. 4, 223ff.
54. Livy 29, 10; 29, 14, 10–14.
55. Varro, *De Lingua Latina* 6, 15.
56. Lucretius 2, 594–601; 606–614; 618–632.
57. *CIL* 10, 3800.
58. *P. Oxy* 11, 1380, 214–216.
59. I, 3, 23–34.
60. 2, 33, 1.
61. *Ars Amatoria* 635f.
62. *Amores* 1, 8, 73.
63. Juvenal 6, 511–541.
64. 11, 9–10.
65. *CIL* 6, 224.
66. Tacitus, *Annals* 2, 85; Suetonius, *Tiberius* 36.
67. Josephus, *Jewish Antiquities* 18, 81–84.
68. Tacitus, *op. cit.*, 12, 32 and 13, 32.

7 Women's Medicine & Women's Health

1. Greek doctors: see Flemming, *Medicine*, p. 50. Pliny, *NH* 29, 21; 29, 8, 16–18; 29, 6. Martial 8, 74; 1, 47. Aristaeus, *Deipnosophistae* 666A. Galen, *On the Divisions of the Medical Art* 2.
2. Galen, *On Anatomical Procedures* 1, 2.
3. See Bursztajn, *Who Killed Julius Caesar?*
4. Suetonius, *Julius Caesar* 42.
5. *Idem, Augustus* 59, 81.
6. Tacitus, *Annals* 12, 67, 2.
7. Pliny, *Natural History* 25, 6, 17–18.
8. *Ibid*, 23, 28, 21. *Greek Anthology* 4, 129.
9. Plutarch, *Moralia* 134b; 125a.
10. Martial 1, 47; 8, 74.
11. Seneca, *Epistulae Morales* 95, 16ff.
12. Seneca, *On Benefits* 6, 15, 4.

13. Soranus, *Gynaecology* 1, 45 (*CMG* 4, 31, 26ff.) and Hippocrates, *Aphorisms* V.
14. *CIL* 6, 9720; 9723.
15. *CIL 6,* 6647.
16. *Thesleff,* pp. 123–124.
17. *CEG* 571.
18. *Compositiones* 5; 16 and 22.
19. Galen, *On the Usefulness of Parts of the Body,* 14, 6–7ff.; hair: *idem,* 11, 14.
20. Martial 5, 9.
21. Pliny, *Ep.* 6, 3.
22. *Elements of Oratory* 1, 1, 4–5.
23. See Jackson, *Doctors,* p. 106.
24. Pliny, *NH* 13, 250. On female doctors and the issues surrounding them, see Flemming, *op. cit.,* pp. 35ff.
25. *CIL* 13, 2019.
26. *CIL* 2, 497.
27. *Euporista* 3, 1, 13.
28. Baader, *Spezialärzte,* p. 233, fn. 62.
29. *Tiberius* 43, 2; Martial 43, 1–4.
30. Aelius Aristides, *Hieroi Logoi* 1, 61–68.
31. See Jackson, *op. cit.,* pp. 140ff.
32. *Places in Man* 47.
33. *Diseases of Women* 1, 1.
34. *Glands* 16.
35. Larson p. 153.
36. *Superf.* 31.
37. *Frag.* A81, B65, B67.
38. For Herophilus: Soranus 3, 3; 1, 29; Galen, *On the Seed* 2, 1. Soranus, *op. cit.* 1, 2–4. Pliny, *op. cit.* 7, 67.
39. Pliny *NH,* 26, 90; Soranus, *op. cit.* 4, 14–150.
40. Celsus, *De Med* 5, 21, 1; Pliny *op. cit.* 26, 90, 152–158.
41. Soranus, *op. cit.* 4, 38.
42. *Op. cit.* 3, 41.
43. *De Med* 7, 28, 2; *Mul* 230.
44. Pliny, *op. cit.* 7, 33; 24, 27; 117–118; 27, 4; 27, 262; 34, 169. Celsus, *De Medica* 4, 27; 5, 21; Pliny, *op. cit.* 30, 41.
45. See Jackson, *op. cit.,* pp. 92–93 for details, including a technical description from a contemporary of Soranus, Archigenes of Apamea, via Paul of Aegina, 6, 73.
46. Lucretius 4, 1290.
47. Aulus Gellius, *Noctes Atticae* 3, 10, 8; 3, 16; Pliny the Elder, *op. cit.* 7, 38–43, 48–49.

48. Pliny, *Ep.* 4, 21.
49. *Population Reference Bureau* 2006 and Bliss: bliss.org.uk.
50. Soranus, *op. cit.* 4, 7; 8.
51. See Suetonius, *Nero.*
52. Celsus, *De Med* 7, 29, 7.
53. Soranus, *op. cit.* 4, 2.
54. Celsus, *op. cit.* 7, 29, 4–5; Soranus, *Gyn* 4, 12.
55. 3, 14, 17.
56. Pliny, *NH* 28, 9, 42.
57. Soren, *Excavations*, p. 482.
58. See Jackson, *op. cit.*, 103–104. Treggiari, *Roman Social History*, pp. 45–46.
59. Celsus, *De Med* 2, 8, 30–31.
60. Julia: Macrobius 2, 5, 9 (trans. A. Richlin). Juvenal 6, 366–348.
61. Pliny, *Ep.* 8, 10.
62. Pliny *NH* 28, 99. Hippocrates, *op. cit.* 1, 1, 25.
63. Celsus, *De Med* 2, 7, 7; 6, 6, 38; 2, 8, 7 and 25.
64. Soranus, *op. cit.* 1, 33; 1, 29–30
65. Soranus, *op. cit.* 1, 24. Pliny, *NH* 28, 23. On menstrual cloths, see Croom, *Running the Roman Home*, pp. 96–97.
66. Pliny, *op. cit.* 27, 23, 85.
67. *NH* 20, 99, 263; 25, 54, 97; 30, 43, 123; 25, 18, 39.
68. Aristotle, *Historia Animalium* 583A; Hippocrates, *Natura Mulierum* 98; *Muliebria* 1, 76. Dioscorides, *De Materia Medica* 3, 34; 1, 77, 2; 3, 130; 5, 106, 6. Lucretius, 4, 1269–1278. Pliny, *op. cit.* 29, 27, 85. Soranus, *op. cit.* 1, 60, 4; 1, 61, 1–3; 1, 64, 1–2, 1, 65, 1–7. Aetius 16, 17. See Hopkins, *Contraception.*
69. *CIL* 4, 107.
70. *CIL* 4, 4185; Seneca, *Controversies* 1, 2, 22. Manetho, *Forecasts* 4, 312.
71. Martial 11, 78.
72. In Oribasius 68.
73. Pliny, *NH* 8, 209.
74. See Rouselle, *Body Politics*, p. 308 and Kapparis, *Abortion.*
75. Ovid, *Amores* 2, 14, 5–10, 19, 20, 27–28, 35–40; 2, 13.
76. Juvenal 6, 595–597; Seneca, *Helv.* 16, 1. See also Ovid, *Fasti* 621–624; *Heroides* 37–42; Cicero, *Pro Cluentio*, 2–4. Pliny, *op. cit.* 25, 7, 24–25. See Gardner, *Law and Society* 158–159 for the legal implications.
77. Juvenal 6, 602–608. Tacitus, *Germania* 19. Soranus, *op. cit.* 1, 67–69; 17, 4, 9. For infant burials in Roman Britain, see Allason-Jones, *Women in Roman Britain* (1989) 42ff. Monkeys etc: Soranus, *op. cit.* 1, 55; 1, 49, 1, 54, 1, 39.

78. Soranus *op. cit.* 2, 5–6.
79. Persius 2, 31–34.
80. Seneca, *De Ira* 1, 15, 2.
81. Soranus, *op. cit.* 1, 89.
82. *Ibid* 2, 6.
83. *Ibid* 2, 45.
84. *Ibid* 2, 38; 30; 40.
85. *Ibid* 2, 47; Pliny, *NH* 28, 21. *Peek* 1233; *CIL* 8, *Supplement* 20288; *CIL* 8, 24734; *Peek* 1871; *CIL* 14, 2737; *ILS* 8451. Soranus, *op. cit.* 2, 18–20; 11, 19 (translation adapted from Temkin); Plutarch, *Moralia* 3C-D, also recommended maternal breast feeding. Tacitus, *op. cit.* 20.
86. See King, *Once upon a Text.*
87. See Maines, *The Technology of Orgasm.*
88. *Tim.* 91a–c.
89. *Gyn* 3, 29. See DSM-IV and ICD-10 for definitions.
90. Galen, *On Prognosis* 6.
91. Hippocrates, *On Virgins* 8, 466–70.
92. APA *Diagnostic and Statistical Manual of Mental Disorders IV.*
93. See Jackson, *op. cit.* pp. 89–90.
94. *NH* 26, 3, 3.
95. Hyperactivity: Pliny, *op. cit.* 28, 259.
96. For a summary of health care in Roman Britain see Summerton, *Medicine.* For HFL see Dayton, *The Fat, Hairy Women of Pompeii.*
97. See Jackson, *op. cit.*, pp. 89–94 for uterine disorders.
98. *Gyn* 1, 15; 4, 39. See Phillips, *Doctor and Patient*, pp. 77–78.
99. *Mor.* 518d. Galen 13, 539.
100. Hippocrates, *Epidemics* 5, 101; Soranus, *Leonidas* quoted by Aetius 16, 44. Aetius 16, 115.
101. See Jackson, *op. cit.*, pp. 90–91.
102. See Bryk, *Circumcision*, p. 271. Strabo 17, 25. Philo, *Questions on Genesis* 3, 47.
103. Celsus 4, 28; Galen *Nat. Mul.* 109; *Epid.* 3, 7. Martial 1, 65, 4; 7, 71. See Fenton, *The Late Roman Infant Cemetery.* Grmek, *Les Maladies;* Younger, *Sex,* p. 184. Horace, *Satires* 1, 5, 62.
104. *CIL* 6, 19128. Tacitus, *Germania* 20.
105. Aulus Gellius, *Attic Nights* 12, 1.
106. *P. Lond* 951 *verso.*
107. *CIL* 4352.
108. *NH* 28, 20.
109. *Ibid.* 28, 21–22.
110. Oribasius, *Ecloga Medicamentorum* 132, 1.
111. See Jones, *Stigma.*

112. Pliny, *NH* 7, 68–69; 71. Horace, *Saturae* 1, 8; see above p. 94. Martial 1, 19; 5, 43; 12, 23. Vetustilla: 3, 93; *Priapea,* Virgilian Appendix 83, 26–37. Pliny, *op. cit.* 28, 9.

113. Artemidorus 5, 63.

114. On spitting see Pliny, *op. cit.* 28, 36; Plautus, *Captivi* 547–555; and Apuleius *Metamorphoses* 44 where an epileptic is spat at and ostracised from his family. Caelius, *On Chronic Diseases* 1, 4, 116–119; 4, 9, 131–137; *On Acute Diseases* 1, 9, 58. Celsius, *De Med* 3, 18, 21.

115. Pliny *NH* 28, 7, 35.

116. Alexander of Tralles, *Twelve Books on Medicine* Vol. 1, pp. 605, 607 (ed. Puschmann). Galen K8 190. See Toner, *op. cit.* Chapter 4: 'Mental Illness' for a fascinating discussion of the subject.

117. See Chrystal, *The Rowntree Family* pp. 34–37. For nymphomania see WHO *ICD-10;* Gourevitch, *Women Who Suffer.*

118. Diodorus Siculus 4, 6, 5. Isidore of Seville, *Eytmologiae* 11, 3, 11. Pliny, *NH* 7, 33; 36; 51; 30; 23. Shrew: *NH* 30, 134.

119. Phlegon, *Marvels* 10, 28.

8 Sex & Sexuality

1. Caelius, *On Chronic Diseases* 4, 9, 131–137. Translations of Caelius are as in Toner, *Popular Culture,* p. 77. *DSM = The Diagnostic and Statistical Manual of Mental Disorders.* After protests by the gay rights movement the references to homosexuality were replaced with a category labelled 'sexual orientation disturbance' for the 1974 edition.

2. *Tribas:* Liddell & Scott, *A Greek–English Lexicon, ad loc.;* Lewis & Short, *A Latin Dictionary, ad loc.*

3. Martial 7, 67; 1, 90. See also 7, 70.

4. Catullus 97.

5. Martial 11, 61. See Younger, *Sex, ad loc.*

6. Pliny *NH* 28, 99.

7. *CIL* 4.5296; translation is by Richlin, *Sexuality in the Roman Empire,* p. 347. Lucian, *Dialogues of the Courtesans,* 5.

8. Seneca *Ep.* 122. Seneca the Elder, *Controversiae* 1, 2, 23. Juvenal, 6, 306ff. Ovid, *Ars Amatoria* 2, 683–684. Lucretius, *De Rerum Natura* 4, 1052–1056. Ovid, *Metamorphoses* 9, 727, 733–4. See Braund, *A Woman's Voice?*

9. Strato, *Greek Anthology* 12, 7. Martial, 11, 43. Juvenal 6 314–326; Lucilius, *Satires* 7; Petronius 140; Lucretius, see above p. 137; Horace, *Satires* 2, 7, 46–56; Martial 11, 104. *Lewis & Short*

defines *pygisiacus* as 'belonging to secret buttock worship, i.e. copulation'.

10. Masturbation *CIL* 10, 4483. Martial 2, 28, 4; 9, 27, 14; 4, 84, 1–4; 4, 71, 5–6. Cf. Clarke, *Looking at Lovemaking*, p. 220 who says that no Roman of the elite class would ask his wife to perform fellatio. Suetonius *Ad Gramm.* 23.

11. *Greek Anthology* 5, 49; 11, 328.

12. Ovid, *Ars Amatoria* 3, 769ff.

13. Juvenal 11, 162ff.; Martial 3, 82, 13. Tacitus, *Annals* 2, 85. Propertius 2, 23, 5–6; 21.

14. Suetonius, *Caligula* 40.

15. Horace, *Satires* 1, 2, 28–36.

16. Cicero, *Pro Caelio*, 48–50.

17. Suetonius, *Life of Horace.*

18. Martial 9, 32; 10, 75.

19. Juvenal 9, 24; Strabo 6, 2, 6; 8, 6, 20. *CIL* 9, 2689.

20. *CIL* 4, 794; 9847; 1391; 2273; 4185; 10004; 1751.

21. See Beard, *Pompeii*, p. 233.

22. 6, 114ff.

23. 11, 162–174.

24. Candida, *CIL* 4, 1512–4. Ovid, *Remedia Amoris* 327. Petronius, *Satyricon* 7.

25. Martial 4, 28; 6, 93.

26. *Idem* 1, 34, 8.

27. Petronius, *Satyricon* 126; Juvenal 6, 103–112.

28. Ovid, *Ars Amatoria* 1, 663–668.

29. Lucilius, *Fragment* 1182W.

30. Horace, *Epodes* 12, 1, 1–20.

31. Martial 3, 93.

32. Ovid, *Amores* 3, 7, 1.

33. *Greek Anthology* 5, 76.

34. *Priapea*, Virgilian Appendix 83, 26–37.

35. *CIL* 4, 1516.

36. Lucretius 4, 1153ff.; 1278–1287. Ovid, *Ars Amatoria* 2, 657–666.

37. Propertius 2, 6, 27–34; Ovid, *Tristia* 2, 521–28.

38. *Priapea* 4. Martial 12, 43; 10, 35; see above pp. 69, 74. Martial 12, 95.

39. Propertius 1, 2, 1–8.

40. Ovid, *Ars Amatoria* 3, 255–286.

41. See Clarke, *op. cit.* pp. 275ff. For female sexual dominance see, for example, Apodyterium 7, Scene 1 Pompeii Suburban Baths; Pompeii House of the Centenary IX, 8, 6 room 43.

BIBLIOGRAPHY

Primary Sources

Aelius Aristides, *Hieroi Logoi.*
Aelius Aristides, *Roman Oration.*
Alexander of Tralles, *Letter on Intestinal Worms.*
Alexander of Tralles, *Twelve Books on Medicine.*
Ammianus Marcellinus, *Res Gestae.*
Appian, *Bellum Civili.*
Apollodurus, *Bibliotheca.*
Apollonius Rhodius, *Argonautica.*
Apuleius, *De Magia.*
Apuleius, *Metamorphoses.*
Aristaeus, *Deipnosophistae.*
Aristotle, *Historia Animalium.*
Aristophanes, *Frogs.*
Arrian, *Discourses of Epictetus.*
Asconius, *Pro Milone.*
Augustine, *Confessions.*
Aulus Gellius, *Noctes Atticae.*
Caelius, *On Acute and Chronic Diseases.*
Cato, *De Agricultura.*
Catullus.
Celsus, *De Medicina.*
Cicero, *Actio in Verrem.*
Cicero, *Ad Atticum.*
Cicero, *Ad Familiares.*
Cicero, *Ad Q. Fratrem.*
Cicero, *Brutus.*
Cicero, *De Deorum Natura.*
Cicero, *De Haruspicum Responsis.*
Cicero, *De Legibus.*
Cicero, *De Oratore.*

Cicero, *De Re Publica.*
Cicero, *In Catilinam.*
Cicero, *Oratio de Doma Sua.*
Cicero, *Oratio in Vatinium.*
Cicero, *Paradoxa Stoicorum.*
Cicero, *Philippics.*
Cicero, *Pro Caelio.*
Cicero, *Pro Cluentia.*
Cicero, *Pro Murena.*
Cicero, *Tusculanae Disputationes.*
Columella, *De Re Rustica.*
Dio Cassius, *Historia Romanae.*
Diodorus Siculus, *Bibliotheca Historica.*
Diogenes Laertius, *Lives of the Eminent Philosophers.*
Dionysisus of Halicarnassus.
Dioscorides, *De Materia Medica.*
Fronto, M. Cornelius, *Epistulae ad M. Aurelium.*
Gaius, *Institutiones.*
Galen, *Elements According to Hippocrates On Anatomical Procedures.*
Galen, *Glossary of Hippocratic Terms.*
Galen, *On Bones for Beginners.*
Galen, *On the Dissection of the Muscles.*
Galen, *On the Divisions of the Medical Art.*
Galen, *On Prognosis.*
Galen, *On Pulses for Beginners.*
Galen, *On the Seed.*
Galen, *On the Usefulness of Parts of the Body.*
Galen, *Opinions of Hippocrates and Plato.*
Greek Anthology.
Heliodorus, *Aethiopica.*
Herodotus, *Histories.*
Hesiod, *Theogeny.*
Hesiod, *Works and Days.*
Hippocrates, *Aphorisms.*
Hippocrates, *De Super Foetatione.*
Hippocrates, *Disease of Women.*
Hippocrates, *Epidemics.*
Hippocrates, *Glands.*
Hippocrates, Natura Mulierum.
Hippocrates, On Virgins.
Hippocrates, *Places in Man.*
Historia Augusta Elegabalus.
Homer, *Iliad.*

Homer, *Odyssey*.
Horace, *Ars Poetica*.
Horace, *Epodes*.
Horace, *Odes*.
Horace, *Satires*.
Isodore of Seville, *Etymologia*.
Josephus, *Jewish Antiquities*.
Justinian, *Institutiones*.
Juvenal, *Satires*.
Lactantius, *Divine Institutions*.
Livy, *History of Rome*.
Lucan, *De Bello Civili*.
Lucian, *De Mercede Conductis*.
Lucian, *Philopseudes*.
Lucian, *Vera Historia*.
Lucilius.
Lucretius, *De Rerum Natura*.
Macrobius, *Saturnalia*.
Marcellus Empiricus, *De Medicamentis Empiricis, Physicis, et Rationabilibus*.
Martial, *Epigrams*.
Musonius, Rufus, *Reliqua*.
Nepos, *De Viris Illustribus*.
Nepos, *Epaminondas*.
Oribasius, *Collectionum Medicarum Reliquiae*.
Oribasius, *Ecloga Medicamentorum*.
Ovid, *Amores*.
Ovid, *Ars Amatoria*.
Ovid, *Fasti*.
Ovid, *Heroides*.
Ovid, *Metamorphoses*.
Ovid, *Remedia Amoris*.
Ovid, *Tristia*.
Paul, *Opinions*.
Pedonius Dioscorides, *De Materia Medica*.
Pedonius Dioscorides, *Euporista*.
Persius, *Satires*.
Petronius, *Satyricon*.
Philo, *Questions and Answers on* Genesis.
Philo, *De Specialibus Legibus*.
Philostratus, *Life of Apollonius of Tyana*.
Phlegon, *Marvels*.
Pindar, *Olympian*.

Plato, *Cratylus.*
Plato, *Crito.*
Plato, *Gorgia.*
Plato, *Laws.*
Plato, *Phaedo.*
Plato, *Phaedrus.*
Plato, *Republic.*
Plato, *Timaeus.*
Plautus, *Aulularia.*
Plautus, *Captivi.*
Plautus, *Mercator.*
Plautus, *Mostellaria.*
Plautus, *Poenulus.*
Plautus, *Truculentus.*
Pliny the Elder, *Historia Naturalis.*
Pliny the Younger, *Letters.*
Pliny the Younger, *Panegyrius.*
Plutarch, *Appius Claudius.*
Plutarch, *Brutus.*
Plutarch, *Cato Maior.*
Plutarch, *Cato Minor.*
Plutarch, *Cicero.*
Plutarch, *De Fortuna Romanorum.*
Plutarch, *De Superstitione.*
Plutarch, *Gaius Gracchus.*
Plutarch, *Life of Themistocles.*
Plutarch, *On the E at Delphi.*
Plutarch, *Marius.*
Plutarch, *Moralia.*
Plutarch, *Numa.*
Plutarch, *Praecepta Coniugalia.*
Plutarch, *Quaestiones Convivales.*
Plutarch, *Quaestiones Romanae.*
Plutarch, *Romulus.*
Plutarch, *Sulla.*
Plutarch, *Tiberius Gracchus.*
Polybius.
Propertius, *Elegies.*
Quintilian, *Institutiones Oratoriae.*
Sallust, *Bellum Catilinae.*
Sappho.
Scribonius Largus, *Compositiones Medicamentorum.*
Seneca, L., *Ad Helviam.*

Seneca, L., *Ad Marciam.*
Seneca, L., *Agamemnon.*
Seneca, L., *De Ira.*
Seneca, L., *De Matrimonia.*
Seneca, L., *De Providentia.*
Seneca, L., *Epistulae Morales.*
Seneca, L., *Hercules Furens.*
Seneca, L., *Hercules on Mount Oeta.*
Seneca, L., *Medea.*
Seneca, L., *On Benefits.*
Seneca, M., *Controversiae.*
Servius, *On Virgil.*
Sidonius Apollinaris, *Epistulae.*
Silius Italicus, *Punica.*
Soranus, *Gynaecology.*
Statius, *Silvae.*
Statius, *Thebaid.*
Strabo.
Strato, *Greek Anthology.*
Suetonius, *Augustus.*
Suetonius, *Caligula.*
Suetonius, *Claudius.*
Suetonius, *De Grammaticis.*
Suetonius, *Domitian.*
Suetonius, *Galba.*
Suetonius, *Julius Caesar.*
Suetonius, *Life of Horace.*
Suetonius, *Nero.*
Suetonius, *Tiberius.*
Tacitus, *Agricola.*
Tacitus, *Annals.*
Tacitus, *Dialogus de Oratoribus.*
Tacitus, *Germania.*
Tacitus, *Histories.*
Terence, *Andrea.*
Terence, *Hecyra.*
Terence, *Phormio.*
Theocritus, *Idyll.*
Theodosius.
Tibullus, *Elegies.*
Ulpian, *Digest.*
Ulpian, *On the Edict.*
Ulpian, *Regulae.*

Valerius Flaccus, *Argonautica.*
Valerius Maximus, *Memorable Deeds and Sayings.*
Varro, *Antiquitates Rerum Humanarum et Divinarum.*
Varro, *De Lingua Latina.*
Velleius Paterculus, *Historiae Romanae.*
Virgil, *Aeneid.*
Virgil, *Eclogues.*
Virgilian Appendix, *Priapea.*

Secondary Sources

Adams, J. N., 'Latin Words for Woman and Wife', *Glotta* 50 (1972), 234–255.
Adams, J. N., *The Latin Sexual Vocabulary* (London, 1982).
Adams, J. N., 'Words for Prostitute in Latin', *RhM* 126 (1983), 321–358.
Allason-Jones, L., *Women in Roman Britain* (London, 1989).
Allason-Jones, L., 'Women in Roman Britain' in James, *Companion* (2012), 467–477.
American Psychiatric Association, *Diagnostic and Statistical Manual of Mental Disorders IV* (Arlington, 1994).
Amunsden, D. W., 'The Age of Menarche in Classical Greece and Rome', *Human Biology* 42 (1970), 79–86.
Andre, J. M., *L'Otium dans la Vie Morale et Intellectuelle Romaine des Origins à la Epoque Augusteenne* (Paris, 1966).
Ankerloo, B., *Witchcraft and Magic in Europe Vol 2: Ancient Greece and Rome* (London, 1998).
Archer, L. J. (ed.), *Women in Ancient Societies* (London, 1994).
Arkins, B. A., *Aspects of Sexuality in Catullus*, (diss. NUI, 1974).
Arnott, W. G., *Menander, Plautus and Terence* (Oxford, 1975).
Ash, R., 'Women in Imperial Roman Literature' in James, *Companion* (2012), 442–452.
Baader, G., 'Spezialärzte in der Spatantike', *Medizinhistorisches Journal* 2 (1967), 231–238.
Babcock, C., 'The Early Career of Fulvia', *AJP* 86, (1965), 1–32.
Baird, J., *Ancient Graffiti in Context* (London, 2010).
Baldwin, B., 'Horace on Sex', *AJPh* 91 (1970), 460–465.
Baldwin, B., 'Women in Tacitus', *Prudentia* 4 (1972), 83–101.
Balsdon, J. P. V. D., *Roman Women* (London, 1962).
Balsdon, J. P. V. D., *Life and Leisure in Ancient Rome* (London, 1969).
Barnard, S., 'Cornelia and the Women of her Family', *Latomus* 49 (1990), 383–392.
Barras, V., 'Galen's Psychiatry' in Hamanaka, pp. 3–8.

Bauman, R. A., *Women and Politics in Ancient Rome* (London, 1992).

Bauman, R. A., *Crime and Punishment in Ancient Rome* (London, 1996).

Beard, M., 'The Sexual Status of the Vestal Virgins', *JRS* 70 (1980), 12–27.

Beard, M., *Rome in the Late Republic* (London, 1985).

Beard, M., *Literacy in the Roman World* (Ann Arbor, 1991).

Beard, M., 'Re-Reading (Vestal) Virginity' in Hawley, *Women* (1995), 166–177.

Beard, M., *Religions of Rome: A Sourcebook* (Cambridge, 1998).

Beard, M., *Pompeii: The Life of a Roman Town* (London, 2008).

Bernstein, F., 'Pompeian Women' in Dobbins, *The World of Pompeii* (2007).

Bertman, S., *The Conflict of Generations in Ancient Greece and Rome* (Amsterdam, 1976).

Best, E. E., 'Cicero, Livy and Educated Roman Women', *CJ* 65 (1970), 199–204.

Betz, H. D., *Greek Magical Papyri in Translation 2/e* (Chicago, 1997).

Bevan, E., 'Classical Ghosts', *Quarterly Review* 246 (1926), 60–74.

Blandford, D., 'Virgil's Vicar of Dibley', *Virgil Society Newsletter* (2009).

Blayney, J., 'Theories of Conception in the Ancient Roman World' in Rawson, *Family*, 230–236.

Blok, J. (ed.), *Sexual Asymmetry: Studies in Ancient Society* (Amsterdam, 1987).

Bloomer, W. M., 'Schooling in Persona: Imagination and Subordination in Roman Education', *Cl. Ant* 16 (1997), 57–78.

Boatwright, M. T., 'Women and Gender in the Forum Romanum', *TAPhA* 141 (2011), 107–143.

Bodel, J., *Epigraphic Evidence: Ancient History from Inscriptions* (London, 2001).

Bonner, S. F., *Education in Ancient Rome: From Cato the Elder to the Younger Pliny* (London, 1977).

Bosman, P. (ed.), *Mania: Madness in the Greco-Roman World* (Pretoria, 2009).

Boucher, J. P., *Caius Cornelius Gallus* (Paris, 1966).

Bourgery, A., 'Lucain et la Magie', *REL* 6 (1928), 299ff.

Bouvrie, S., 'Des Augustus' Legislation on Morals', *SO* 59 (1984), 93–113.

Bowman, A. K., *Life and Letters on the Roman Frontier: Vindolandia and its People* (London, 1994).

Bradley, K. R., 'Wet Nursing in Rome' in Rawson, *The Family* (1986).

Bradley, K. R., *Discovering the Roman Family: Studies in Roman Social History* (New York, 1991).

Bradley, K. R., 'The Roman Child in Sickness and in Health' in George, *The Roman Family* (2005) 68–92.

Braund, S., 'Juvenal: Misogynist or Misogamist?', *JRS* 82 (1992), 61–76.

Braund, S., 'A Woman's Voice? Laronia's Role in Juvenal 2' in Hawley, *Women* (1995), 207–219.

Brennan, T. C., 'Perception of Women's Power in the Late Republic: Terentia, Fulvia and the Generation of 63 BC' in James, *Companion* (2012), 354–366.

Brouwer, H. H. J., 'Bona Dea', *The Sources and a Description of the Cult* (Leiden, 1989).

Brown, R., 'Livy's Sabine Women and the Ideal of *concordia*', *TAPhA* 125 (1995), 291–319.

Brunt, P. A., *Roman Manpower 225 BC–AD 14* (Oxford, 1971).

Burns, J., *Great Women of Imperial Rome* (London, 2007).

Bryk, F., *Circumcision in Man and Woman: Its History, Psychology and Ethnology* (Honolulu, 2001).

Burriss, E. E., *Taboo, Magic, Spirits: A Study of Primitive Elements in Roman Religion* (Oxford, 1931).

Bursztajn, H. J., 'Who Killed Julius Caesar? Psychoforensic Analysis of Decision Making under Stress', *American Psychoanalyst* 37 (2003).

Butler, R. M. (ed.), *Soldier and Civilian in Roman Yorkshire* (Leicester, 1971).

Butterworth, A., *Pompeii: The Living City* (London, 2005).

Cairns, F. (ed.), *Papers of the Liverpool Latin Seminar V 1985* (1986).

Cameron, A. (ed.), *Images of Women in Antiquity* (London, 1983).

Cantarella, E., *Pandora's Daughters: The Role and Status of Women in Greek and Roman Antiquity* (London, 1987).

Carlon, J. M., *Pliny's Women: Constructing Virtue and Creating Identity in the Roman World* (Cambridge, 2009).

Carp, T., 'Two Matrons of the Late Republic', *Women's Studies* 8 (1981), 189–200 in Foley, *Reflections*, 343–353.

Catelli, G., *Behind Lesbia's Door: Her Slave-Girls' Shocking Revelations* (New York, 2012).

Chalmers, W. A., 'Plautus and His Audience' in Dorey, *Roman Drama*, 1965.

Chrystal, P., *Differences in Attitude to Women as Reflected in the Work of Catullus, Propertius, the Corpus Tibullianum, Horace and Ovid* (MPhil thesis, University of Southampton, 1982).

Chrystal, P., *The Rowntree Family of York* (Pickering, 2013).

Churchill, L. J., *Women Writing Latin Vol. 1: From Roman Antiquity to Early Modern Europe* (New York, 2002).

Cilliers, L., 'Mental Illness in the Greco-Roman Era' in Bosman (2009), 130–140.

Clark, A. J., *Divine Qualities: Cult and Community in Republican Rome* (Oxford, 2007).

Clark, G., *Women in the Ancient World* (Oxford, 1989).

Clark, R. J., *Catabasis: Vergil and the Wisdom Tradition* (Amsterdam, 1979)

Clarke, J. R., *Looking at Lovemaking: Constructions of Sexuality in Roman Art 100 BC – AD 250* (Berkeley, 1998).

Clarke, J. R., *Roman Sex 100 BC to AD 250* (London, 2003).

Clarke, M. L., Cicero at School, *G&R* 15 (1968), 18–21.

Clarke, M. L., *Higher Education in the Roman World* (London, 1971).

Cohen, D., 'Seclusion, Separation and the Status of Women' in McAuslan, *Women in Antiquity*, pp. 134–145.

Colin, G., *Rome et la Grèce de 200 a 146 BC avant JC* (Paris, 1905).

Colin, G., 'Luxe Oriental et Parfums Masculins dans la Rome Alexandrine', *RBPH* 33 (1935), 5–19.

Collins, D. (ed.), *Magic in the Ancient Greek World* (Oxford, 2008).

Collins, J. H., 'Tullia's Engagement and Marriage to Dolabella', *CJ* 1952, 164–168.

Colton, R. E., 'Juvenal and Martial on Women who Ape Greek Ways', *CB* 50 (1973), 42–44.

Cornell, T. J., *The Beginnings of Rome* (London, 1995).

Corte, M. D., *Loves and Lovers in Ancient Pompeii* (Salerno, 1976).

Costa, C. D. N. (ed.), *Lucian Selected Dialogues* (Oxford, 2005).

Crook, J. A., 'Patria Potestas', *CQ* 17 (1967) 113.

Croom, A., *Roman Clothing and Fashion* (Stroud, 2010).

Crowther, N. B., 'Valerius Cato, Furius Bibaculus and Ticidas', *CPh* 66 (1971), 108–109.

Cruse, A., *Roman Medicine* (Stroud, 2004).

Currie, H. Mac, 'The Poems of Sulpicia', *ANRW II*, 30.3, 1751–1764.

Daehner, J. (ed.), *The Herculaneum Women: History, Context, Identities* (Los Angeles, 2007).

Daehner, J. (ed.), *The Herculaneum Women and the Origins of Archaeology* (New York, 2008).

D'Ambra, E., 'The Cult of Virtues and the Funerary Relief of Ulpia Epigone', *Latomus* 48 (1989), pp. 392–400.

D'Ambra, E., *Roman Women* (Cambridge, 2007).

D'Ambra, E., 'Women in the Bay of Naples' in James, *Companion* (2012), 400–413.

D'Ambrosio, A., *Women and Beauty in Pompeii* (New York, 2002).

D'Avino, M., *The Women of Pompeii* (Naples, 1967).

Davies, C., 'Poetry in the "Circle" of Messalla', *G&R* 20 (1973), 25–35

Dayton, L., 'The Fat, Hairy Women of Pompeii', *New Scientist* (1944) 24 September 1994.

Deacy, S. (ed.), *Rape in Antiquity* (London, 1997).

Dean-Jones, L., 'The Politics of Pleasure: Female Sexual Appetite in the *Hippocratic Corpus*' in Stanton 1992, *Discourses* 48–77.

Dean-Jones, L., 'Medicine: The "Proof" of Anatomy' in Fantham, *Women in the Classical World* (1994) 183–215.

Del Castillo, A., 'The Position of Women in the Augustan Age', *LCM* 2 (1977), 167–173.

Delia, D., 'Fulvia Reconsidered' in Pomeroy, *Women's History and Ancient History* (1991), 197–217

Demand, N., 'Women and Slaves as Hippocratic Patients' in Joshel, *Women* (1998), 69–84.

Deslauriers, M., 'Women, Education and Philosophy' in James, *Companion* (2012), 343–353.

Deutsch, M., 'The Women of Caesar's Family', *CJ* 13 (1918), 502–514.

Dick, B., 'The Technique of Prophecy in Lucan', *TAPhA* 94 (1963), 37 ff.

Dickey, E. (ed.), *The Colloquia of the Hermeneumata Pseudodositheana: Volume 1* (Cambridge, 2012).

Dickie, M. W., *Magic and Magicians in the Graeco-Roman World* (London, 2001).

Dickinson, S. 'Abortion in Antiquity', *Arethusa* 6 (1973), 158–166.

Dixon, S., 'The Family Business: Women and Politics in the Late Republic', *C&M* 34 (1983), 91–112.

Dixon, S., 'Family Finances: Tullia and Terentia', *Antichthon* 18 (1984), 78–101.

Dixon, S., 'Polybius on Roman Women and Property', *AJPh* 106 (1985), 147–170.

Dixon, S., *The Roman Mother* (London, 1988).

Dixon, S., *The Roman Family* (Baltimore, 1992).

Dixon, S., *Reading Roman Women* (London, 2001).

Dixon, S., 'Exemplary Housewife or Luxurious Slut: Cultural Representations of Women in the Roman Economy' in McHardy, *Women's Influence* (2004).

Dixon, S., *Cornelia: Mother of the Gracchi* (London, 2007).

Dobbins, J. J. (ed.), *The World of Pompeii* (London, 2007).

Dobbins, J. J., 'A Roman Funerary Relief of a Potter and His Wife', *Arts in Virginia* 25 (1985), 24–33.

DSM IV, *Diagnostic and Statistical Manual of Mental Disorders IV* (Arlington, 1994) see American Psychiatric Association.

Dudley, D., *Roman Society* (London, 1975).

Dudley, D. (ed.), *Neronians and Flavians: Silver Latin I* (London, 1972).

Dupont, F., *Daily Life in Ancient Rome* (Oxford, 1992).

Durry, M., 'Le Mariage des Filles Impubères dans la Rome Antique', *REL* 47 (1970), 17–25.

Edwards, C., *The Politics of Immorality in Ancient Rome* (Cambridge, 1993).

Edwards, C., 'Unspeakable Professions: Public Performance and Prostitution in Rome' in Hallett, *Roman Sexualities* (1998), 66–95.

Edwards, C., *Death in Ancient Rome* (London, 2007).

Edwards, C., 'Putting Agrippina in her Place: Tacitus and Imperial Women', *Omnibus* 63 (2012), 22–24.

Elia, O., *Pitture Murali e Mosaici nel Musea Nazionale di Napoli* (Rome, 1932).

Engels, D., 'The Problem of Female Infanticide in the Greco-Roman World', *CPh* 75 (1980), 112–120.

Evans, J. K., *War, Women and Children in Ancient Rome* (London, 1991).

Eyben, E., 'Antiquity's View of Puberty', *Latomus* 31 (1972), 677–697.

Eyben, E., 'Family Planning in Graeco-Roman Antiquity', *Anc Soc* 11–12 (1980), 5–82.

Fantham, E., 'Virgil's Dido and Seneca's Tragic Heroines', *G&R* 22 (1975) 1–9.

Fantham, E., '*Stuprum:* Public Attitudes and Penalties for Sexual Offences in Republican Rome', *EMC* 35 (1991), 267–291.

Fantham, E., *Women in the Classical World: Image and Text* (New York, 1994).

Fantham, E., 'Amelia Pudentilla or the Wealthy Widow's Choice' in Hawley R., *Women in Antiquity* (1995), 220–232

Faraone, C., *Ancient Greek Love Magic* (Harvard, 2001).

Fau, G., *L'Emancipation Feminine à Rome* (Paris, 1978).

Fenton, T., 'The Late Roman Infant Cemetery Near Lugnano', *Journal of Paleopathology* (1995), 13–42.

Ferguson, J., *The Religions of the Roman Empire* (London, 1970).

Ferrill, A., 'Augustus and his Daughter: A Modern Myth', *Latomus* 168 (1980), 332–346.

Filbee, M., *A Woman's Place* (London, 1980).

Fildes, V., *Breasts, Bottles and Babies: A History of Infant Feeding* (Edinburgh, 1987).

Fildes, V., *Wet Nursing: A History from Antiquity to the Present* (Oxford, 1998).

Finley, M. I., *Aspects of Antiquity* (Harmondsworth, 1972).

Finley, M. I., 'The Etruscans and Early Rome' in Finley, *Aspects*, pp. 110–123.

Finley, M. I., 'The Silent Women of Rome' in Finley, *Aspects*, pp. 124–137.

Finley, M. I., *Studies in Ancient Society* (London, 1974).

Fitton, J. W., 'That was No Lady, That Was', *CQ* 64 (1970), 56–66.

Flemming, R., '*Quae corpora quaestum facit:* The Sexual Economy of Female Prostitution in the Roman Empire', *JRS* 89 (1999), 38–61.

Flemming, R., *Medicine and the Making of Roman Women* (Oxford 2000).

Flemming, R., 'Women, Writing and Medicine in the Classical World', *CQ* 57 (2007), 257–279.

Fogen, T., *Bodies and Boundaries in Graeco-Antiquity* (Amsterdam, 2009).

Foley, H. (ed.), *Reflections of Women in Antiquity* (London, 1981).

Foley, H., 'Women in Ancient Epic' in Foley, J. M. (ed.) *A Companion to Ancient Epic*, (Chichester, 2008) 105–118.

Forbes, C. A., 'The Education and Training of Slaves in Antiquity', *TAPhA* 86 (1955), 321–360.

Foster, J., 'Aeneidea: Two Ghost Scenes,' *PVS* 11 (1972), 77–79.

Frank, R. I., 'Augustus' Legislation on Marriage and Children', *CSCA* 8 (1975), 41–52.

Fraschetti, A. (ed.), *Roman Women* (Chicago, 2001).

Frederick, D. C., 'Beyond the Atrium to Ariadne: Erotic Painting and Visual Pleasure in the Roman House', *Cl. Ant* 14 (1995), 266–287.

Frederick, D. C., 'Reading Broken Skin: Violence in Roman Elegy' in Hallett, *Roman Sexualities* (1998), 172–193.

Freisenbruch. A., *The First Ladies of Rome* (London, 2010).

French, R. (ed.), *Science in the Early Roman Empire* (London, 1986).

French, V., 'Midwives and Maternity Care in the Roman World' in M. Skinner, *Rescuing Creusa* (1987), 69–84.

Friedlander, L., *Roman Life and Manners under the Early Empire Vols 1–4* (London, 1965).

Furst, L. R. (ed), *Women Physicians and Healers* (Lexington, 1997).

Gage, J., 'Matronalia', *Latomus* 60 (1963).

Gager, J., *Curse Tablets and Binding Spells from the Ancient World* (New York, 1992).

Galinsky, K., 'Augustus' Legislation on Morals and Marriage', *Philologus* 125 (1981), 126–144.

Gardner, J. F., *The Roman Household: A Sourcebook* (London, 1991).

Gardner, J. F., *Women in Roman Law and Society* (Bloomington, 1995).

Gardner, J. F., *Family and* Familia *in Roman Law and Life* (Oxford, 1998).

Garland, R., *The Eye of the Beholder: Deformity and Disability in the Graeco-Roman World* (Bristol, 2010).

Garlick, B. (ed.), *Stereotypes of Women in Power* (New York, 1992).

Gaughan, J. E., *Murder Was Not a Crime: Homicide and Power in the Roman Republic* (Austin, 2010).

George, M., (ed.), *The Roman Family in the Empire: Rome, Italy, and Beyond* (Oxford, 2005).

George, M., (ed.), 'Family Imagery and Family Values in Roman Italy' in George, *The Roman Family* 37–66.

Giacosa, G., *Women of the Caesars* (Milan, 1980).

Gill, C. (ed.), *Galen and the World of Knowledge* (Cambridge, 2009).

Gilman, S., *Hysteria Beyond Freud* (Berkeley, 1993).

Gold, B. K., 'The House I Live In Is Not My Own: Women's Bodies in Juvenal's Satires', *Arethusa* 31 (1998), 368–386.

Golden, M., 'Did the Ancients Care When their Children Died?' *G&R* 35 (1988), 152–163.

Golden, M., *Sex and Difference in Ancient Greece and Rome* (Edinburgh, 2008).

Gourevitch, D., 'Women Who Suffer from a Man's Disease' in Hawley, *Women* (1995), 149–165.

Graf, F., *Magic in the Ancient World* (Harvard, 1999).

Green, M. H., *Making Women's Medicine Masculine: The Rise of Male Authority in Pre-Modern Gynaecology* (Oxford, 2008).

Greene, E., *The Erotics of Domination: Male Desire and the Mistress in Latin Love Poetry* (Baltimore, 1998).

Griffin, J., 'Augustan Poetry and the Life of Luxury', *JRS* 66 (1976), 87–105.

Griffin, M. T., *Nero: The End of a Dynasty* (London, 2000).

Grimal, P., *Love in Ancient Rome* (Norman, OK, 1986).

Grmek, M., *Les Maladies a l'Aube de la Civilisation Occidentale* (Paris, 1983).

Grmek, M., *Diseases in the Ancient Greek World* (Baltimore, 1989).

Grubbs, J. E., *Women and the Law in the Roman Empire: A Sourcebook on Marriage, Divorce and Widowhood* (London, 2002).

Grubbs, J. E., 'Parent-Child Conflict in the Roman Family' in George, *The Roman Family* (2005) 93–128.

Gruen, E. S., 'M. Antonius and the Trial of the Vestal Virgins', *RhM* 111 (1968), 59–63.

Gusman, P., *Pompeii: The City, Its Life and Art* (London, 1910).

Gwynn, A., *Roman Education from Cicero to Quintilian* (Oxford, 1926).

Haase, F. (ed.), *Luci Annaei Senecae Operae quae Supersunt* (Leipzig, 1872–1874).

Hallet, J. P., 'The Role of Women in Roman Elegy: Cross-Cultural Feminism', *Arethusa* 6 (1973), 103–124.

Hallet, J. P., '*Perusinae Glandes* and the Changing Image of Augustus', *AJAH* 2 (1977), 151–171.

Hallet, J. P., *Fathers and Daughters in Roman Society: Women and the Elite Family* (Princeton, 1984).

Hallet, J. P., 'Martial's Sulpicia and Propertius' Cynthia', *CW* 86 (1992), 99–123.

Hallet, J. P. (ed), *Roman Sexualities* (Princeton, 1997).

Hallet, J. P., 'The Eleven Elegies of the Augustan Poet Sulpicia' in Churchill, *Women Writing* (2002), 45–65.

Hallet, J. P., 'Women Writing in Rome and Cornelia, Mother of the Gracchi' in Churchill (2002), 18–29.

Hallet, J. P., '*Feminae Furentes*: The Frenzy of Noble Women in Virgil's *Aeneid* and the Letter of Cornelia' in Anderson (2002), 159–167.

Hallet, J. P., 'Matriot Games? Cornelia and the Forging of Family-oriented Political Values' in McHardy, Women's *Influence* (2004) 26–39.

Hallet, J. P., 'Women in Augustan Rome' in James, *Companion* (2012), 372–384.

Hamanaka, T. (ed.), *Two Millenia of Psychiatry* (Tokyo, 2003).

Hamilton, G., 'Society Women Before Christ', *North American Review* 151 (1896).

Hands, A. R., *Charities and Social Aid in Greece and Rome* (London, 1968).

Hanson, A. E. 'The Eight Months' Child and the Etiquette of Birth: *obsit omen!*', *BHM* 61 (1987), 589–602.

Harkness, A. G., 'Age at Marriage and at Death in the Roman Empire', *TAPhA* 27 (1896), 35–72.

Harlow, M., 'Galla Placida: Conduit of Culture?' in McHardy, Women's *Influence* (2004) 138–150.

Harmon, A. M. (trans.), *Lucianus de Mercede Conductis, Lucan III* (Cambridge, Mass., 1969).

Harris, W. V., 'The Theoretical Possibility of Extensive Female Infanticide in the Graeco-Roman World', *CQ* 32 (1982), 114–116.

Harris, W. V., *Ancient Literacy* (Cambridge, Mass., 1989).

Hart, G. D., *Asclepius: the God of Medicine* (London, 2001).

Hawley, R. (ed.), *Women in Antiquity: New Assessments* (London, 1995).

Hejduk, J. D., *Clodia: A Sourcebook* (Norman, OK, 2008).

Helzle, M., 'Mr and Mrs Ovid', *G&R* 36 (1989), 183–193.

Hemelrijk, E., 'Women's Demonstrations in Republican Rome' in Blok, *Sexual Asymmetry*, 217–240.

Hemelrijk, E., Matrona Docta: *Educated Women in the Roman Elite from Cornelia to Julia Domna* (London 1999).

Hemelrijk, E., 'Public Roles for Women in the Cities of the Latin West' in James, *Companion* (2012), 478–490.

Hermann, C., 'Le Rôle Judicaire et Politique des Femmes sous la République Romain', *Latomus* 67 (1964).

Hersch, K. K., *The Roman Wedding*: Ritual and Meaning in Antiquity (Cambridge, 2010).

Hexter, R. (ed.), *Innovations in Antiquity* (London, 1992).

Heyob, S. K., *The Cult of Isis Amongst Women of the Graeco-Roman World* (Leiden, 1975).

Heyworth, S. J., *Cynthia: A Companion to the Text of Propertius* (Oxford, 2009).

Hill, T. B., Ambitiosa Mors: *Suicide and the Self in Roman Thought and Literature* (London, 1997).

Hillard, T., 'Republican Politics, Women and the Other Evidence', *Helios* 16 (1989), 165–182.

Hillard, T. (ed.), *Ancient History in a Modern University Vol 1*(Sydney, 1998).

Hinds, S., 'The Poetess and the Reader: Further Steps Towards Sulpicia', *Hermathena* 143 (1987), 29–46.

Hoffsten R., *Roman Women of Rank in the Early Empire As Portrayed by Dio, Paterculus, Suetonius and Tacitus* (Philadelphia, 1939).

Holland, L. L., 'Women and Roman Religion' in James, *Companion to Women* (2012), 204–214.

Holzberg, N., 'Four Poets and a Poetess or a Portrait of the Poet as a Young Man? Thoughts on Book 3 of the *Corpus Tibullianum*', *CJ* 94 (198), 169–191.

Hooper, R. W., *The Priapus Poems* (Urbana, Ill., 1999).

Hope, V. (ed.), *Death and Disease in the Ancient City* (London, 2000).

Hopkins, K., 'The Age of Roman Girls at Marriage', *Population Studies* 18 (1965), 309–327.

Hopkins, K., 'Contraception in the Roman Empire', *Comparative Studies in Society & History* 8 (1965), 124–151.

Hopkins, K., 'Elite Mobility in the Roman Empire' in Finley, *Ancient Society* (1974), 103–120.

Hopkins, K., *Conquerors and Slaves* (Cambridge, 1978).

Horsfall, N., 'Allia Potestas and Murdia: Two Roman Women', *Ancient Society* 12 (1982), 27–33.

Horsfall, N., 'Virgil and the Poetry of Explanations', *G&R* 38 (1991), 199–211.

Houghton, L. B. T., 'Tibullus' Elegiac Underworld', *CQ* 57 (2007), 153–165.

Hubbard, T. K. (ed.), *Homosexuality in Greece and Rome* (Berkeley, 2003).

Hubbard, T. K. 'The Invention of Sulpicia', *CJ* 100 (2004), 177–194.

Hus, A., '*Doctus* et les Adjectifs de Sens Voisin en Latin Classique', *RPh* 46 (1972), 238–245.

Hyde, H. M., *A History of Pornography* (London, 1969).

ICD: *International Classification of Diseases* (*10 version*, Geneva 2010) see WHO.

Ireland, S., *Terence: The Mother-in-Law* (Oxford, 1990).

Jackson, R., *Doctors and Diseases in the Roman Empire* (London, 1988),

James, E. L., *Fifty Shades of Grey* (London, 2012).

James, S. L., *Learned Girls and Male Persuasion: Gender and Reading in Roman Love Elegy* (Berkeley, 2003).

James, S. L., *Companion to Women in the Ancient World* (Chichester, 2012).

James, S. L., 'Virgil's Dido' in James, *Companion* (2012), 369–371.

Janan, M., *The Politics of Desire: Propertius IV* (Berkeley, 2001).

Janowitz, N., *Magic in the Roman World* (London, 2001).

Jenkinson, J. R., *Persius: The Satires* (Warminster, 1980).

Johns, C., *Sex or Symbol: Erotic Images of Greece and Rome* (London, 1981).

Johnson, M., *Sexuality in Greek and Roman Society and Literature: A Sourcebook* (London, 2005).

Johnson, W. A. (ed.), *Ancient Literacies: The Culture of Reading in Greece and Rome* (New York, 2007).

Johnson, W. H., 'The Sister-in-law of Cicero', *CJ* 1913, 160–165.

Jones, C. P., 'Stigma: Tattooing and Branding in Graeco-Roman Antiquity', *JRS* 77 (1987), 139–155.

Joshel, S. R., *Work, Identity and Legal Status at Rome: A Study of the Occupational Inscriptions* (Norman, 1992).

Joshel, S. R., 'The Body Female and the Body Politic: Livy's Lucretia and Verginia' in Richlin, *Pornography* (1992), 112–130.

Joshel, S. R., *Women and Slaves in Graeco-Roman Culture* (London 1998).

Kagan, D., *Problems in Ancient History Vol 2: The Roman World 2/e* (New York, 1975)

Kajanto, I., 'On Divorce among the Common People of Rome', *REL* 47 (1969), 97–113.

Kampen, N. (ed.), *Sexuality in Ancient Art: Near East, Egypt, Greece, and Italy*, (Cambridge, 1996).

Kampen, N., *Family Fictions in Roman Art* (Cambridge, 2009).

Kapparis, K. A., *Abortion in Antiquity* (London, 2002).

Keith, A., '*Corpus Eroticum*: Elegiac Poets and Elegiac *Puellae* in Ovid's *Amores*', *CW* 88 (1994), 27–40.

Keith, A., 'Tandem Venit Amor: "A Roman Woman Speaks of Love"' in Hallet, *Sexualities* (1997), 295–310.

Keith, A., *Engendering Rome: Women in Latin Epic* (Cambridge, 1999).

Keith, A., 'Critical Trends in Interpreting Sulpicia', *CW* 100 (2006), 3–10.

Keith, A., 'Women in Augustan Literature' in James, *Companion* (2012), 385–399.

Kent, J. P. C., *Roman Coins* (London, 1973).

Kenyon, F. G., *Books and Readers in Ancient Greece and Rome* (Oxford, 1932).

Kiefer, O., *Sexual Life in Ancient Rome* (London, 1934).

King, H., 'Once upon a Text: Hysteria from Hippocrates' in Gilman, S., *Hysteria Beyond Freud* (California, 1993), 3–90.

King, H., 'Self-help, Self-knowledge: in Search of the Patient in Hippocratic Gynaecology' in Hawley, *Women in Antiquity* (1995), 135–148.

King, H., *Hippocrates' Woman: Reading the Female Body in Ancient Greece* (London, 1998).

King, H., *Greek and Roman Medicine* (London, 2003).

King, H., *The Disease of Virgins: Green Sickness, Chlorosis and the Problems of Puberty* (New York, 2004).

King, H., 'Healthy, Wealthy and – Dead ?', *Ad Familiares* 33 (2007), 3–4.

King, J. E., 'Sophistication versus Chastity in Propertius' Latin Love Elegy', *Helios* 4 (1976), 69–76.

Kleiner, D., *I Claudia: Women in Ancient Rome* (New Haven, 1996).

Kleiner, D., *I Claudia II: Women in Roman Art and Society* (Austin, 2000).

Knapp, R. K., *Invisible Romans: Prostitutes, Outlaws, Slaves, Gladiators, Ordinary Men and Women … the Romans that History Forgot* (London, 2013).

Knight, R. P., *A Discourse on the Worship of Priapus* (London, 1786).

Kokkinos, N., *Antonia Augusta: Portrait of a Great Roman Lady* (London, 1992).

Koortbojian, M., '*In Commemorationem Mortuorum*: Text and Image Along the Street of Tombs' in Elsner 210–233.

Kraemer, R. S., *Women's Religions in the Greco-Roman World: A Sourcebook* (New York, 2004).

Krenkel, W. A., '*Fellatio* and *Irrumatio*', *W. Z. Rostock* 29 (1980), 77–88.

Krenkel, W. A., 'Tonguing', *W. Z. Rostock* 30 (1981), 37–54.

Kudlien, F., 'Medical Education in Classical Antiquity' in O'Malley, *The History of Medical Education* (1970), 3–37.

Laes, C., *Children in the Roman Empire: Outsiders Within* (Cambridge, 2009).

La Follette, L., 'The Costume of the Roman Bride' in Sebesta, 54–64.

Laidlaw, W. A., 'Otium', *G&R* 15 (1968), 42–52.

Langlands, R., 'A Woman's Influence on a Roman Text' in McHardy, *Women's Influence* (2004) 115–126.

Langlands, R., *Sexual Morality in Ancient Rome* (Cambridge, 2006).

Larson, J., *Greek and Roman Sexualities: A Sourcebook* (London, 2012).

Larsson, L. L. (ed.), *Aspects of Women in Antiquity* (1997).

Larsson, L. L., '*Lanam fecit*: Woolmaking and Female Virtue' in Larsson, *Aspects of Women in Antiquity* (1997), 85–95.

Laurence, R., *Roman Passions* (London, 2009).

Leen, A., '*Clodia Oppugnatrix*: The *Domus* Motif in Cicero's "*Pro Caelio*"', *CJ* 96 (2000) 142–160.

Lefkowitz, M. R., *Heroines and Hysterics* (London, 1981).

Lefkowitz, M. R., *Women's Life in Greece & Rome 3rd Ed.* (London, 2005).

Leigh, M., 'Funny Clones: "Greek" Comedies on the Roman Stage', *Omnibus* 54 (2007), 26–28.

Lewis, N. (ed.), *Roman Civilization Vol I Selected Readings The Republic 3rd Ed* (New York, 1990).

Lewis, N. (ed.), *Roman Civilization Vol II Selected Readings The Empire 3rd Ed* (New York 1990).

Liebs, D., *Summoned to the Roman Courts: Famous Trials from Antiquity* (Berkeley, 2012).

Lightman, M., *A to Z of Ancient Greek and Roman Women* (New York, 2008).

Lilja, S., *The Roman Elegists' Attitude to Women* (Helsinki, 1965).

Liveley, G., 'Who's that Girl? The Case of Ovid's Corinna', *Omnibus* 54 (2007), 1–3.

Lloyd, G. E. R. (ed.), *Hippocratic Writings* (Harmondsworth, 1978).

Lloyd, G. E. R., *Magic, Reason and Experience* (Cambridge, 1979).

Longrigg, J., *Greek Rational Medicine* (London, 1993).

Longrigg, J., *Greek Medicine: From the Heroic to the Hellenistic Age: A Source Book* (London, 1998).

Loven, L. L. (ed.), *The Family in the Imperial and Late Antique Roman World* (New York, 2011).

Lowe, J. E., *Magic in Greek and Latin Literature* (Oxford, 1929).

Luck, G., Arcana Mundi: *Magic and the Occult in the Greek and Roman Worlds* (Baltimore, 1985).

Luck, G., *Latin Love Elegy 2/e* (London 1969).

Lyne, R. O. A. M., *The Latin Love Poets from Catullus to Ovid* (Oxford, 1980).

Macmullen, R., 'Women in Public in the Roman Empire', *Historia* 29 (1980), 208–218.

Macmullen, R., 'Women's Power in the Principate', *Klio* 68 (1986), 434–443.

Maines, R. P., *The Technology of Orgasm: 'Hysteria', the Vibrator, and Women's Sexual Satisfaction* (Baltimore, 1998).

Maiuri, A., *Pompeii* (Rome, 1934).

Mander, J., *Portraits of Children on Roman Funerary Monuments* (Cambridge, 2012).

Manning, C. E., 'Canidia in the *Epodes* of Horace', *Mnemosyne* 23 (1970), 393–401.

Mantle, I., 'Violentissimae et Singulares Mortes', *CA News* 39 (2008), 1–2.

Mantle, I., 'Women of the Bardo', *Omnibus* 65, January 2013, 4–6.

Marshall, A. J., 'Roman Women and the Provinces', *Anc Soc* 6 (1975), 109–129.

Marshall, A. J., 'Tacitus and the Governor's Lady, A Note on *Annals* 3, 33–34', *G&R* 22 (1975), 11–18.

Marshall, A. J., 'Library Resources and Creative Writing at Rome', *Phoenix* 30 (1976), 252–264.

Marshall, A. J., 'Roman Ladies on Trial: The Case of Maesia of Sentinum', *Phoenix* 44 (1990), 46–59.

Martin, M., *Magie et Magiciens dans le Monde Gréco-romain* (Paris, 2005)

Martin, M., *Sois maudit!: Malédictions et Envoûtements dans l'Antiquité* (Paris, 2010)

Martin, M., *La Magie dans l'Antiquité* (Paris, 2012).

Martindale, C. (ed.), *Cambridge Companion to Virgil* (Cambridge, 2007).

Massey, M., *Women in Ancient Greece and Rome* (Cambridge, 1988).

Matthews, V. J., 'Some Puns on Roman *Cognomina*', *G&R* 20 (1973), 20–23.

Matz, D., *Voices of Ancient Greece and Rome: Contemporary Accounts of Daily Life* (New York, 2012).

McAuslan, I. (ed.), *Women in Antiquity* (Oxford, 1996).

McCarthy, K., '*Servitium Amoris: Amor Servitii*' in Joshel, *Women* (1998), 174–192.

McClure, L. K., *Sexuality and Gender in the Classical World: Readings and Documents* (Chichester, 2002).

McDermott, W. C., 'The Sisters of P. Clodius', *Phoenix* 24 (1970), 39–47.

McDonald, G., 'Mapping Madness: Two Medical Responses to Insanity in Later Antiquity' in Bosman (2009) 106–129.

McGinn, T. A., *Prostitution, Sexuality and the Law in Ancient Rome* (New York, 1998).

McGinn, T. A., *The Economy of Prostitution in the Roman World* (Ann Arbor, 2004).

McHardy, F.(ed.), *Women's Influence on Classical Civilisation* (London, 2004).

Miles, G. B., 'The First Roman Marriage and the Theft of the Sabine Women' in Hexter (1992), 161–196.

Miller, P. A., *Latin Erotic Elegy: An Anthology and Reader* (London, 2002).

Mohler, S. L., 'Feminism in the *CIL*', *CW* 25 (1932) 113–116.

Mohler, S. L., 'Slave Education in the Roman Empire', *TAPhA* 71 (1940), 262–280.

Moore, T. J., 'Morality, History and Livy's Wronged Women', *Eranos* 91 (1993), 38–46.

Moore, T. J., *The Theater of Plautus: Playing to the Audience* (Austin, 1998).

Moreau, P., Incestus et prohibitae nuptiae: *L'inceste à Rome* (Paris, 2002).

Morel, W., Fragmenta Poetarum Latinorum (Leipzig, 1927).

Morford, M. P. O., *The Poet Lucan: Studies in Rhetorical Epic* (London, 1996).

Morgan, T., *Literate Education in the Hellenistic and Roman Worlds* (Cambridge, 1998).

Motto, A. L., 'Seneca on Women's Liberation', *CW* 65 (1972), 155–157.

Mustakallio, K., *Hoping for Continuity: Childhood Education and Death in Antiquity* (Helsinki, 2005).

Myers, S., 'The Poet and the Procuress: the *lena* in Latin Love Elegy', *JRS* 86 (1996), 1–21.

Neils, J., *Women in the Ancient World* (London, 2011).

Nikolaidis, A. G., 'Plutarch on Women and Marriage', *WS* 110 (1997), 27–88.

Norman, A. F., 'Religion in Roman York' in Butler, *Soldier* (1971), 143–154 .

Noy, D., 'Wicked Stepmothers in Roman Society and Imagination', *Journal of Family History* 16 (1991), 345–361.

Nutton, V., 'Galen and Medical Autobiography', *PCPhS* 18 (1972), 50ff.

Nutton, V., 'The Drug Trade in Antiquity', *Journal of the Royal Society of Medicine* 78 (1985), 138–145.

Nutton, V., 'Murders and Miracles: Lay Attitudes to Medicine in Antiquity' in Porter, *Patients and Practitioners* (1985) 25–53

Nutton, V., *Ancient Medicine 2/e* (London, 2013).

Ogden, D., *Magic, Witchcraft and Ghosts in the Greek and Roman Worlds* (Oxford, 2002).

Ogden, D., *Greek and Roman Necromancy* (Princeton, 2004).

Ogden, D., *Night's Black Agents: Witches, Wizards and the Dead in the Ancient World* (London, 2008).

Ogden, D., *Polygamy, Prostitutes and Death: The Hellenistic Dynasties* (Swansea, 2010).

Ogilvie, R. M., *The Romans and their Gods in the Age of Augustus* (London, 1974).

Ogilvie, R. M., *Early Rome and the Etruscans* (Glasgow, 1976).

Ogilvie, R. M., *Roman Literature and Society* (Harmondsworth, 1980).

Oliensis, E., 'Canidia, Canicula and the Decorum of Horace's *Epodes*', *Arethusa* 24 (1991), 107–138.

Oliensis, E., 'Sons and Lovers: Sexuality and Gender in Virgil's Poetry' in Martindale (2007).

Olsen, K., *Dress and the Roman Woman: Self-Presentation and Society* (London, 2008).

O'Malley, C. D. (ed.), *The History of Medical Education* (Berkeley, 1970).

Orwell, G., *Coming Up for Air* (Harmondsworth 1962).

Pantel, P. S., *A History of Women from Ancient Goddesses to Christian Saints* (Cambridge, Mass., 1992).

Paoli, U. E., *Rome: Its People, Life and Customs* (Bristol, 1990).

Parke, H. W., *Sibylls and Sibylline Prophecy in Classical Antiquity* (London, 1998).

Parker, H. N., 'Love's Body Anatomized: The Ancient Erotic Handbooks and the Rhetoric of Sexuality' in Richlin, *Pornography* (1992).

Parker, H. N., 'Loyal Slaves and Loyal Wives' in Furst (ed.), *Women Physicians in Greece, Rome and the Byzantine Empire* (2004), 134-150.

Parker, H. N., 'Why Were the Vestal Virgins?' *AJP* 125 (2004), 563–601.

Parker, H. N., 'Women and Medicine' in James, *Companion* (2012), 107–124.

Parkin, T. G., *Old Age in the Roman World* (Baltimore, 2003).

Paul, G. M., 'Sallust's Sempronia: the Portrait of a Lady' in Cairns, *Papers* (1986), 9–22.

Peachin, M., 'Handbook of Social Relations in the Roman World' (Oxford, 2011).

Pearcy, L. T., 'Erasing Cerinthus: Sulpicia and Her Audience', *CW* 100 (2006), 31–36.

Pellison, N., *Women and Marriage During Roman Times* (New York, 2008).

Petrie, A., *Roman History, Literature and Antiquities* (London, 1926).

Petrocelli, C., 'Cornelia the Matron' in Fraschetti, *Roman Women* (1993), 34–65.

Phang, S. E., *The Marriage of Roman Soldiers (13 B.C. – A.D. 235): Law and Family in the Imperial Army* (Leiden, 2001).

Phillips, E. D., 'Doctor and Patient in Classical Greece', *G&R* (1953), 70–81.

Phillips, J. E., 'Roman Mothers and the Lives of their Adult Daughters', *Helios* 6 (1978), 69–80.

Pitcher, R. A., 'Martial and Roman Sexuality' in Hillard, *Ancient History* (1998) 309–315.

Plant, I. M., *Women Writers of Ancient Greece and Rome* (Norman, 2004).

Pollard, E. A., 'Witch-Crafting in Roman Literature and Art: New Thoughts on an Old Image', *Magic, Ritual, and Witchcraft* 3 (2008).

Pomeroy, S. B., 'Selected Bibliography on Women in Antiquity', *Arethusa* 6 (1973) 125–157.

Pomeroy, S. B., 'The Relationship of the Married Woman to Her Blood Relatives in Rome', *Ant. Soc.* 7 (1976), 215–227.

Pomeroy, S. B., 'Women in Roman Egypt: A Preliminary Study Based on Papyri' in Foley, pp. 301–322.

Pomeroy, S. B. (ed.), *Women's History and Ancient History* (Chapel Hill, 1991).

Pomeroy, S. B., *Goddesses, Whores, Wives and Slaves* (New York, 1995).

Pomeroy, S. B., *Spartan Women* (Oxford, 2002).

Porter, R. (ed.), *Patients and Practitioners* (Cambridge, 1985).

Potter, D. S., *Prophecy and History in the Crisis of the Roman Empire: A Historical Commentary on the Thirteenth Sibylline Oracle* (Oxford 1990).

Powell, A. (ed), *Roman Poetry and Propaganda in the Age of Augustus* (Bristol 1992).

Presshaus, J. D. M., 'Apollonius Rhodius and Virgil', *PVS*, 4 (1964), 1–17.

Purcell, N., 'Livia and the Motherhood at Rome', *PCPhS* 212 (1986), 78–105.

Puschmann, T. (ed.), *Alexander of Tralles, Twelve Books on Medicine* (1878).

Putnam, E. J., 'The Roman Lady', *Atlantic Monthly* 105 (1910).

Quinn, K., 'The Poet and His Audience in the Augustan Age', *ANRW* II 30 (1982), 75–180.

Radice, B. (ed.), *Terence: The Comedies* (Harmondsworth, 1976).

Raia, A., *Women's Roles in Plautine Comedy* (paper delivered October 1983) www.vroma.org/~araia/plautinewomen.

Raia, A. (ed), *Marriage, Divorce and Children in Ancient Rome* (Oxford, 1986).

Raia, A., 'Villains, Wives and Slaves in the Comedies of Plautus' in Joshel, *Women* (1998), 92–108.

Raia, A., *The Worlds of Roman Women: A Latin Reader* (Newburyport, Mass., 2001).

Rankin, H. D., 'Catullus and the Beauty of Lesbia', *Latomus* 35, 1 (1976).

Rankin, H. D., 'Catullus and Incest', *Eranos* 74 (1976), 113–121.

Rankin, H. D., 'Catullus and the Privacy of Love', *WS* 9 (1975).

Rankin, H. D., 'Clodia II', *AC* 38 (1969), 501–506.

Rapsaet-Charlier, M. -Th., 'Ordre Senatorial et Divorce sous le Haut Empire', *ACD* (1981) 17–18, 161–173.

Rawson, B., 'Family Life Among the Lower Classes at Rome in the First Two Centuries of the Empire', *CP* 61 (1966), 71–83.

Rawson, B., 'Roman Concubinage and Other de facto Marriages', *TAPhA* 104 (1974), 279–305.

Rawson, B., *Intellectual Life in the Late Roman Republic* (London, 1985).

Rawson, B., *Marriage, Divorce and Children in Ancient Rome* (Oxford, 1991).

Rawson, B., *Children and Childhood in Roman Italy* (Oxford, 2005).

Reinhold, M., 'The Generation Gap in Antiquity' in Bertman, pp. 15–54.

Ricci, J. V., *The Development of Gynaecological Surgery and Instruments* (Philadelphia, 1949).

Richlin, A., 'Sexuality in the Roman Empire' in D. S. Potter (ed.), *A Companion to the Roman Empire* (Oxford, 2006).

Richlin, A., 'Approaches to the Sources on Adultery at Rome' in Foley, *Reflections* (1981) 379–404.

Richlin, A., 'Invective Against Women in Roman Satire', *Arethusa* 17 (1984), 67–80.

Richlin, A., 'Carrying Water in a Sieve: Class and the Body in Roman

Women's Religion' in King, *Women and Goddess Traditions* (1997), 330–374.

Richlin, A., 'Sulpicia the Satirist', *CW* 86 (1992), 125–140.

Richlin, A., 'Julia's Jokes, Galla Placidia and the Romans Use of Women as Political Icons' in Garlick, *Stereotypes* (1992), 65–91.

Richlin, A., (ed.) *Pornography and Representation in Greece and Rome* (Oxford, 1992).

Richlin, A., *The Garden of Priapus: Sexuality and Aggression in Roman Humour* 2nd ed (Oxford, 1992).

Riess, W., '*Rari Exempla Femina*: Female Virtues on Roman Funerary Inscriptions' in James, *Companion* (2012), 491–501.

Rist, J. M., 'Hypatia', *Phoenix* 19 (1965), 214–225.

Roisman, H. M. 'Women in Senecan Tragedy', *Scholia* 14 (2005), 72–88.

Rose, M., 'Ashkelon's Dead Babies', *Archaeology* 50 (1997) www. archaeology.org/9703/newsbriefs/ashkelon.

Ross, D. O., *Style and Tradition in Catullus* (Cambridge, Mass., 1969).

Ross, D. O., *Backgrounds to Augustan Poetry: Gallus, Elegy and Rome* (Cambridge, 1975).

Rouselle, A., 'Body Politics in Ancient Rome' in Pantel (1992), 296–336.

Rouselle, A., *Porneia: On Desire and the Body In Antiquity* (Oxford, 1993).

Rowlandson, J., *Women and Society in Greek and Roman Egypt: A Sourcebook*, (Cambridge, 1998).

Rudd, N., 'Romantic Love in Classical Times?' *Ramus* 10 (1981), 140–158.

Rupke, J., Fasti Sacerdotum: *A Prosopography of Pagan, Jewish and Christian Religious Officials in the City of Rome 300 BC to AD 499* (Oxford, 2008).

Russell, D. A., 'Arts and Sciences in Ancient Education', *G&R* 36 (1989), 210–224.

Ryberg, I. S., 'Rites of the State Religion in Roman Art', *Memoirs of the American Academy in Rome* 22 (1955), 41.

Sallares, R., *Malaria and Rome: A History of Malaria in Ancient Italy* (Oxford, 2002).

Saller, R. P., '*Familia, Domus* and the Roman Conception of the Family', *Phoenix* 38 (1984), 336–355.

Saller, R. P., '*Patria Potestas* and the Stereotype of the Roman Family', *Continuity & Change* 1 (1986), 7–22.

Saller, R. P., 'Men's Age at Marriage and Its Consequences in the Roman Family', *CP* 82 (1987), 21–34.

Saller, R. P., *Patriarchy, Property and Death in the Roman Family* (Cambridge, 1994).

Saller, R. P., 'Symbols of Gender and Status Hierarchies in the Roman Household' in Joshel, *Women* (1998), 85–91.

Salway, B., 'What's in A Name ?' *JRS* 84 (1994), 124–145.

Santirocco, M. S., 'Sulpicia Reconsidered', *CJ* 74 (1979), 229–239.

Santoro L'Hoir, F. S., 'Tacitus and Women's Usurpation of Power', *CW* 88 (1994), 5–25.

Savunem, 'Women and Elections in Pompeii' in Hawley, *Women* (1995), 194–206.

Scafuro, A. (ed.), *Studies on Roman Women Part 2, Helios* 16 (1989).

Scafuro, A., 'Livy's Comic Narrative of the Bacchanalia' in Scafuro (1989), 119–142.

Scarborough, J., *Roman Medicine* (London, 1969).

Scarborough, J., 'Pharmacy in Pliny's Natural History: Some Observations on Substances and Sources' in French, *Science in the Early Roman Empire* (1986), 59–85.

Schaps, D. M., 'The Women Least Mentioned: Etiquette and Women's Names', *CQ* 27 (1977), 323–330.

Scheid, J., 'The Religious Roles of Roman Women' in Pantel (1992), 377–408.

Scheid, J., 'Claudia the Vestal Virgin' in Fraschetti, *Roman Women* (1993), 23–33

Scheidel, W., 'The Most Silent Women of Greece and Rome: Rural Labour and Women's Life', *G&R* 42 and 43 (1995–1996), 202–17, 1–10.

Scheidel, W., 'Libitina's Bitter Gains: Seasonal Mortality and Endemic Disease', *Ancient Society* 25 (1994), 151–175.

Scheidel, W., *The Cambridge Economic History of the Greco-Roman World* (Cambridge, 2007).

Scheidel, W., 'Demography' in Scheidel (ed.), *The Cambridge Economic History*

(2007), 38–86.

Schulz, C. E., *Women's Religious Activity in the Roman Republic* (Chapel Hill, NC, 2006).

Scobie, A., 'Slums, Sanitation and Mortality in the Roman World', *Klio* 68 (1986), 399–343.

Scurlock, J. A. 'Baby-snatching Demons, Restless Souls and the Dangers of Childbirth', *Incognita* 2 (1991), 135–183.

Seller, R., 'The Family and Society' in Bodel (2001), 95–117.

Sharrock, A. R., 'Womanufacture', *JRS* 81 (1991), 36–49.

Shaw, B. D., 'Age of Roman Girls at Marriage: Some Reconsiderations', *JRS* 77 (1987), 30–46.

Shelton, J-A., 'Pliny the Younger and the Ideal Wife', *C&M* 61 (1990), 163–186.

Shelton, J-A., *As the Romans Did 2nd Ed* (New York, 1998).

Shepherd, G., 'Women in Magna Graecia' in James, *Companion* (2012), 215–228.

Shepherd, G., (ed.), *Sexuality in Graeco-Roman Culture* (Oxford, 2005).

Shepherd, G., *Clodia Metelli: The Tribune's Sister* (New York, 2011).

Skinner, M. B. (ed.), 'Rescuing Creusa', *Helios* 13 (1987).

Slater, W. J. (ed.), *Dining in a Classical Context* (Ann Arbor, 1991).

Slater, W. J., *Roman Theatre and Society* (Ann Arbor, 1996).

Smith, P., 'Identification of Infanticide in Archaeological Sites', *Journal of Archaeological Science* 19 (1992), 667–675.

Smith, W. S. (ed.), *Satiric Advice on Women and Marriage: From Plautus to Chaucer* (Ann Arbor, 2005).

Snyder, J. M., 'Lucretius and the Status of Women', *CB* 53, (1976), 17–20.

Snyder, J. M., *The Woman and the Lyre: Women Writers in Classical Greece and Rome* (Carbondale, Ill., 1989).

Soren, D., 'What Killed the Babies of Lugnano?' *Archaeology* 48/5 (1995), 43–48.

Soren, D., *Excavations of a Roman Villa and a Late Roman Infant Cemetery Near Lugnano* (Rome, 1999).

Spaeth, B. S., *The Roman Goddess Ceres* (Austin, 1996).

Staden, H. von, 'Women, Dirt and Exotica in the *Hippocratic Corpus*', *Helios* 19 (1992), 7–30.

Stanton, D. C. (ed.), *Discourses of Sexuality: From Aristotle to Aids* (Ann Arbor, 1992).

Staples, A., *From Good Goddess to Vestal Virgins: Sex and Category in Roman Religion* (London, 1998).

Stehle, E., 'Venus, Cybele and the Sabine Women: The Roman Construction of Female Sexuality' in Scafuro, (1989), 43–64.

Stevenson, J., *Women Latin Poets: Language, Gender, and Authority from Antiquity to the Eighteenth Century* (Oxford, 2008).

Stirrup, B. E. 'Techniques of Rape: Variety and Art in Ovid's *Metamorphoses*', *G&R* 24 (1977), 170–184.

Stromberg, A., *The Family in the Graeco-Roman World* (New York, 2011).

Sullivan, J. P. 'Martial's Sexual Attitudes', *Philologus* 123 (1979), 288–302.

Summerton, N., *Medicine and Healthcare in Roman Britain* (Princes Risborough, 2007).

Syme, R., 'Princesses and Others in Tacitus', *G&R* 28 (1981), 40–52.

Tacaks, S., *Vestal Virgins, Sibyls, and Matrons* (Austin, 2008).

Temkin, O., *Soranus' Gynecology* (Baltimore, 1956).

Theodorakopoulos, T., 'Catullus 63, A Song of Attis for the Megalesia', *Omnibus* 61 (2011), 21–23.

Thomas, Y., 'The Division of the Sexes in Roman Law' in Pantel (1992), 83–138.

Thonemann, P., 'The Women of Akmoneia', *JRS* 100 (2010), 163–178.

Toner, J., *Popular Culture in Ancient Rome* (Cambridge, 2009).

Too, Y. L. (ed.), *Education in Greek and Roman Antiquity* (Leiden, 2002).

Totelin, L., 'Sex and Vegetables in the Hippocratic Gynecological Treatises', *SHPBBS* 38 (2007), 531–540.

Townend, G., *The Augustan Poets and the Permissive Society* (Abingdon, 1972).

Tracy, V. A., 'The Poet-Lover in Augustan Elegy', *Latomus* 35 (1976), 571–581.

Treggiari, S., 'Libertine Ladies', *CW* 64 (1971), 196–198.

Treggiari, S., 'Domestic Staff at Rome During the Julio-Claudian Period', *Histoire Sociale* 6 (1973), 241–255.

Treggiari, S., 'Concubinae', *Papers of the British School at Rome* 49 (1981), 59–81.

Treggiari, S., *Roman Marriage* (Oxford, 1991).

Treggiari, S., 'Putting the Family Across: Cicero on Natural Affection' in George, *The Roman Family* (2005), 9–36.

Treggiari, S., *Roman Social History* (London, 2002).

Treggiari, S., *Terentia, Tullia and Publilia: The Women of Cicero's Family* (New York, 2007).

Trimble, J., *Women and Visual Replication in Roman Imperial Art and Culture* (Cambridge, 2011).

Tuplin, C., 'Cantores Euphorionis' in Cairns, *Papers*, pp. 1–23.

Tuplin, C., 'Cantores Euphorionis Again' *CQ* 72 (1979), 358–360.

Versnal, H. S. 'The Festival for *Bona Dea* and the *Thesmophoria*' in McAuslan, *Women in Antiquity* (1996), 182–204.

Veyne, P. (ed.), *A History of Private Life Vol I* (Cambridge, Mass, 1987).

Viden, G., *Women in Roman Literature: Attitudes of Authors under the Early Empire* (Goteborg, 1993).

Villers, R., 'Le Statut de la Femme à Rome jusqu'à la Fin de la République', *Recueils de la Societe Jean Bodin II* (1958), 177–189.

Virlouvet, C., 'Fulvia the Woman of Passion' in Fraschetti, *Roman Women* (1993), 66–81.

Walters, H. B. *The Art of the Romans* (London, 1928).

Ward-Perkins, B., *The Fall of Rome and the End of Civilisation* (Oxford, 2005).

Watson, P. A., 'Ancient Stepmothers', *Mnemosyne* 143 (1995).

Watts, W. J., 'Ovid, the Law and Roman Society on Abortion', *AC* 16 (1973), 89–101.

Wenham, L. P., *The Roman-British Cemetery at Trentholne Drive York* (York, 1968).

Wheeler, A. L., 'Erotic Teaching in Roman Elegy and the Greek Sources Part II', *CP* 6 (1911), 56–77.

Wheeler, A. L., 'Erotic Teaching Part I', *CP* 5 (1910), 440–450.

Wheeler, A. L., 'Propertius as *Praeceptor Amoris*', *CP* 5 (1910), 28–40.

WHO *ICD, International Classification of Diseases* (*10 version*, Geneva, 2010).

Wildfang, R. I., *Divination and Portents in the Roman World* (Odense, 2000).

Wildfang, R. I., *Rome's Vestal Virgins* (London, 2006).

Wilkinson, B. M., 'Family Life among the Lower Classes in Rome in the First Two Centuries of the Empire', *CP* 61 (1966), 71–83.

Will, E. L., 'Women in Pompeii', *Archaeology* 32 (1979), 34–43.

Williams, G., 'Some Aspects of Roman Marriage Ceremonies and Ideals,' *JRS* 48 (1958), 16–29.

Wiseman, T. P., *Cinna the Poet* (Leicester, 1974).

Wiseman, T. P., 'Summoning Jupiter: Magic in the Roman Republic' in Wiseman, *Unwritten Rome.*

Wiseman, T. P., *Unwritten Rome* (Exeter, 2008).

Woodhull, M. L., 'Matronly Patrons in the Early Roman Empire: the Case of Salvia Postuma' in McHardy, *Women's Influence* (2004), 75–91.

Worsfold, T. C., *The History of the Vestal Virgins of Rome* (London, 1934).

Wyke, M., 'Written Women: Propertius' *scripta puella*', *JRS* 77 (1987), 47–61.

Wyke, M., 'The Elegiac Woman at Rome', *PCPhS* 213 (ns 330) (1987), 153–178.

Wyke, M., 'Mistress and Metaphor in Augustan Elegy', *Helios* 16 (1989), 25–47.

Wyke, M., 'Augustan Cleopatras: Female Power and Poetic Authority' in Powell, *Roman Poetry* (1992), 98–140.

Wyke, M., 'Women in the Mirror: The Rhetoric of Adornment in the Roman World' in Archer, *Women in Ancient Societies* (1994), 134–151.

Wyke, M., *Projecting the Past: Ancient Rome, Cinema and History* (London, 1997).

Wyke, M., *The Roman Mistress* (Oxford, 2002).

Yardley, J. H., 'The Symposium in Roman Elegy' in Slater, *Dining in a Classical Context*, 149–155.

Younger, J. G., *Sex in the Ancient World from A-Z* (London, 2005).

Ziebarth, E., *Neue Verfluchungstafeln aus Affika*, Boiotien und Euboia (1934).

INDEX